The Archipelago of Us

Reneé Pettitt-Schipp lived in the Indian Ocean Territories from 2011 until 2014. Her work with asylum seekers in detention on Christmas Island and the Cocos (Keeling) Islands inspired her first collection of poetry, *The Sky Runs Right Through Us* (UWA Publishing, 2018), and was shortlisted for the Dorothy Hewett manuscript prize and the CHASS Australia prize, and winner of the 2018 WA Premier's Literary Award for an Emerging Writer. Reneé's writing has been recognised through many literary awards, including the ACU literature prize, The Tom Collins Poetry Prize, the Ros Spencer Poetry Prize, the Grief Poetry Prize and the Trudy Graham Biennial Literary Award. Reneé currently lives and writes in Western Australia's Great Southern.

The Archipelago of Us

A search for our identity in Australia's most remote territories

Reneé Pettitt-Schipp

For Nek Su, for his courage and wisdom,
and with deep gratitude to Greta and Ashley Schipp,
who also made the Indian Ocean Territories their home.

Contents

Introduction: Approaching the Archipelago

This morning the world was still. One after the other booby birds flew past, a low white stream, running along island's edge and weaving around palm trees. At sunrise, I stepped out the door of the cottage, feeling like a girl stepping into a dream, into a scape of haze and humidity. To the west, light rested apricot, diffuse, over the glassed surface of sea. Just above, frigatebirds angled and twisted at speed, twin tail-feathers scissoring, steering their Jurassic bodies over the ocean. Other frigates reeled dark and high in the air, spectres coming in and out of cloud.

The sun is higher now and the day beginning to get hot, so I get into the small 4WD a friend has lent me, and drive slowly and wide-eyed into memory, into Silver City, where tired flats sit high on the hill in front of a glinting panorama of ocean. An old man in a worn cotton singlet leans out from an aluminium window, looking out as I look in. The streets are quiet. All along the turn-off, red crabs are rain-glazed and paint-bright. Behind them, the jungle rolls by, dense and layered: palms and pandanus, vine and banyan, tree ferns and elephant ears, a terrain of green reaching wide for light. But it is what I have forgotten that I am undone by, a scent rich and complex – the smell of journeys treading carefully over forest floor. It is the scent of life and death, rot and growth, and of those who stepped with me, stepping into me, their trace deep under my skin.

This is a story of return. Christmas Island is monolithic; a sole peak surrounded by endlessly shifting sea in Australia's most remote territory; an island a mere 350 kilometres from the southern shores of Indonesia, yet 1500 kilometres from the Australian mainland to which it belongs. In 2011, my family and I packed up our home near Perth and moved to this isolated semi-submarine mountain. My husband and I began teaching English to asylum-seeker children and young adults held in detention on the island as part of Australia's border protection policies under the Gillard Government. After a year, distressed and disheartened by the suffering we witnessed behind the wire, we made the decision to move to the Cocos (Keeling) Islands, 900 kilometres away. We lived on this tropical atoll approximately halfway between Australia and Sri Lanka for two years, before returning to the Australian mainland in 2014.

Though I chose to step away from its paradisaical shores, the troubled landscape of the Indian Ocean Territories never left me. This world of water lapped at my fringes night and day, bringing a relentless tide of questions, eroding beliefs about my country and who I thought I was. In particular, my experiences of Australia's detention system on both Christmas Island and the Cocos (Keeling) Islands refused to let me be. The story of the islands had become so irrevocably entangled in my own, that in 2016 I found myself boarding a plane back to the Indian Ocean Territories in order to make sense of my forever-changed life. What had I witnessed on the islands that I needed so strongly to make sense of? What was it, after five years, I was unable to accept and let go? Since childhood, I had understood my 'Fair Go' country as a place where everyone had an equal chance to work and thrive, and where each person's inherent worth as a human would be upheld. Did I still believe in my 'Fair Go' nation after all that I had seen?

These are the questions that found me standing back on the tarmac of this pristine and marginal world, that led me to be driving slowly into Silver City and all that lay beyond. This is the story of my gradual journey toward understanding – both an understanding of myself as someone completely undone and reinvented through my experiences of people and place, but also the tale of an intense reckoning with the mythology of my country, a tale told as 'history', but also revealed through silence. My journey is an invitation to other Australians who wish to face the history of their nation squarely: step with me between palm and pandanus, place your feet gently on the forest floor. Breathe the air of abundance and decay, take the hands of generations of people who have walked though this place, let our trace lie deep under your skin.

Christmas Island

It is not that you set out to oppose authority. In the act of writing you simply do. Your job, your reason for writing, is to uncover what the state and the conventions of your town normally hide. That's why you want to write – to tell what hasn't been told.

Grace Paley

1. Returning

The latent anxiety I feel about returning to Christmas Island is expressed by the way I have not finished packing two hours before my flight. It feels almost inconceivable this moment has arrived, that it is possible to return. My husband and I make it to the airport just an hour before my flight and, after checking in, it is a rushed goodbye, our lips meeting briefly, holding each other's eyes for a second before I dash through the entryway, winding my way quickly through empty Border Force lanes, passport stamped moments before the sign flashes 'GATE CLOSED'.

On the plane there are too many people. I look out the window at the bland tarmac, at the smear of cloud and drizzle of rain, and feel a huge sense of dissociation.

When the plane lifts off, it is as though a door closes behind me, I am being propelled forward toward something shimmering and wild in my memory, but I can't feel anything. I sit with my head resting against the window as Perth's cityscape disappears behind cloud. Time moves slowly. The woman next to me talks animatedly to her friend. I hope she does not talk to me.

After some time, the clouds begin to part and I can see the blue of the sea; we are still flying low. Soon the barely raised reef of what must be the Abrolhos Islands comes into view and something in me stirs, like a caterpillar in its twig case. Alongside the islands are the parallel forms of large ships, all pointing northward. The mottled shapes of low islands are abstract from this height, and the repetition of forms in the north-facing ships is beautiful, but

I do not get my camera out. I watch them – this scarce suggestion of land in a bold canvas of sea, framed by floating statements of state and industry. A low hum, a crackle and whir of synapses wake me like the click of fingers close to an ear, and I press against the window, feel my heart quicken, eyes alive.

I am watching now. I am watching the expansive plain of water, the way the clouds begin to grow vertical and become voluptuous, spill up and over themselves forming luminous kingdoms. The women next to me continue to chatter across the aisle. I soon begin to realise they are talking about familiar places and names, accommodation and tourist sites from the Cocos Islands. As they do, it dawns on me the plane's route has changed. Since the removal of large numbers of fly-in fly-out workers from Christmas Island as the detention centres' activities were scaled down, it is no longer imperative the flights serve Christmas Island first. Thursday's flight lands on Cocos, then goes on to Christmas Island. It suddenly dawns on me that I will land on the atoll before the monolith of Christmas Island and am taken aback – I feel unprepared, cheated. I thought I was doing this trip in chronological order, but now I am first being taken to a place I once called 'home', and meant it.

After two hours of flying above cloud, the pilot tells us we are about to descend. I lean to look out of my window, and there it is. A sensation akin to pain rises in my chest. Something I had lost is being gifted back to me, an exquisite offering lit by morning sun. The day is a brilliant blue, the water in the lagoon is clear as glass. I look down at the sand fanning around island's edge, its shapes of ocean, coral and carved blue holes, a painting patterned and brilliant. Over the deepest part of the lagoon, north toward Direction Island, the colour is steeped beyond comprehension.

A single dinghy parts the impossible blue with a clean V of white. The plane arcs sharply around the edge of the atoll, turns back, and begins to descend over roads I have known by foot and bike, pacing and pedalling under palm trees into headwind. We fly over beaches where I met hermit crabs, grey nurse sharks and egrets, over the large fig at Trannies Beach where a pilot handed me a small ball, the fluffy round form of a baby tern. It all streams past, salt plain and palms, friends' homes and the one road where the local bus is heading out to the ferry at Rumah Baru. As we fly along the length of West Island, images, memories and faces flash up as the plane's wheels come down. Soon we bounce onto the tarmac, braking heavily. And this – this was the view from my home: airstrip, palm trees and azure lagoon, night herons stalking insects in grass.

The plane reaches the edge of the runway and turns, crawls slowly back the way it came. The aircraft's window now looks out the other side of West Island, framing a view of the sea, the reef, the homes along the runway, my blue home facing the runway. They have cut down the palm trees. The aircraft comes to a halt, a gangplank is attached and a forklift drives noisily in. The cabin door opens to the familiar scent of dry grass and salt, sun and trade winds. We are asked to disembark.

Some familiar Cocos Malay faces greet me as I walk down the metal stairs to the tarmac, past two girls, faces framed in colourful *tudungs*, whom I recognise as my former students. I don't stop, walking past the rope and people in their Border Force uniforms, out down the beige 1970s hall and into sunlight, out into a crowd of faces, so many faces of people I thought I would never see again. I am hugged briefly but warmly, then through the crowd comes a slim, short woman with dreadlocks.

'Trish!' She puts her arms around me, and we hold each other long and close.

'Quick, come and see the boys!' She takes me by the hand into the brick building of the Club where her two youngest sons share a large lounge chair, eating bread. Trish's youngest boy, who had slept on my deck as a newborn, is now sitting tall and straight like any child. It is too much to take in.

'Do you want to take some bread with you to Christmas Island?' Trish offers, and Tony, Trish's husband (and part-time baker), comes over with a wide grin.

'Well, well – look who the plane brought in!' We hug, and I stand dazed and overwhelmed.

'No, no, Trish,' I say, 'my bag is packed full with veggies, but thank you.'

'Are you sure? Do you want a smoothie? Tony is doing banana smoothies too now!'

'No,' I laugh, remembering Trish's eternal generosity, 'I better get back on, but I will be back, I will see you guys in a week.'

'Are you sure?' Trish says. 'You probably have another five minutes before they make the call.'

'You know me, Trish, I'm a Virgo, don't want to miss my plane.'

The truth is, it is all too much and I need to retreat. We hug again and I step through the gate, between familiar faces in Border Force uniforms who insist on patting me down and doing a bag check. Then I am seated back by my window on the plane.

The plane arcs once again and I turn back and look over the outer reef where the waves break, forming a bright white fringe at the end of cobalt sea, spreading forever and uninterrupted to the horizon. Where the reef ends and the atoll starts, the lines become painterly, like great brushstrokes made from above, a paintbrush moving in continuous smooth strokes around each small island. On each islet I am implicated: a camping place here, a sailing trip there, here paddling over the wide back of an ancient turtle feeding on seagrass. At this height, the detail is unknowable but incredibly beautiful, an artwork in turquoise, blues and greens. I crane my neck but the atoll's horseshoe shape grows smaller, barely visible, then disappears. I sit animated, alert. Now it is nine hundred kilometres to that very different place of brutal beauty, to a semi-submarine mountain imbued with a dark history, where life pushes up, shouting and glimmering, fringed by a delicate crochet of sea foam in light.

Nearing Christmas Island, the plane descends through dense vapour, so at first the scene is hidden, then abruptly the thick clouds part and the island's image is revealed – a place fit for pirates and Crusoes, castaways and children with conch shells. The rainforest is so lush it spills over the sides of cliffs, and its abundant canopy catches the sun and folds its secrets into shadow. Overhead, golden bosun birds shimmer, trailing bright plumes over green. A glimpse, then the plane hits the tarmac and the brakes groan, working hard to pull up quickly on the island's alarmingly short runway. Out of nowhere, as the plane comes to a halt, a large black drone appears by my window, moves sideways and up, jerky and erratic. I am thrown, shocked, but my attention is turned toward the plane's interior as passengers start to disembark. When I turn my gaze back to the window, the drone has gone, leaving me to wonder if I ever saw it at all.

As those of us on board step onto the tarmac and its hot-bath humidity, my lungs remember, breathe deep. Inside the airport – that looks more like a shed by a paddock than a place to board a plane – we queue briefly, then collect our luggage. My bags bulging with stores of fresh vegetables are glanced at, then I am ushered through by Border Force officers. I push my trolley out into the sunlight to see my friend Jo waving as she stands by the rail.

'Hi.' She hugs me like we saw each other last week. 'I hope you don't mind but I am also picking up Pete. He was on your flight.' As she speaks, Pete steps through the doorway and waves. Pete is a friend of my husband, and the Mandarin teacher at the local high school. He is also one of the interviewees I teed up while I was on the mainland. He turns to me and we embrace, then pile our things in the back of Jo's small 4WD, our bags and veggies spilling over onto the seat at the back.

Jo and Pete chat in the front of the car as Jo drives. I stay quiet, extracting myself from the conversation to take in the terrain in front of me. To return. I have returned. A sensation like heat courses through my body, I hold it in my chest, will it to wait. Jo drops me at my accommodation and I am grateful to be left alone. I place food along the bench, my books in piles beside the bed, then step out on the deck. Several metres in front of me the ocean jostles, is edgy in a way I have seen nowhere else. Watching its uneasy aspect, I picture the ocean floor, its inconceivable depths – no wonder the water cannot break or resolve.

Grabbing my swimming gear, I jump on the bike left leaning out the back of the cottage. Its tyres are flat. Undeterred I set off, pushing hard against the resistance of rubber, past frangipani trees leaning against mildewed walls, out into heat and light, past the supermarket, under the enormous industrial arm of the phosphate chute to where the island's cliffs rise like a sudden foreign country and trees layer their lives up impossible slopes, leaf against leaf, tree against tree, an exultation of life over which scores of birds circle, reel, glide or come to rest.

In the cove, I lean my bike against the pergola and slip out of my clothes. I am grateful for sun on my body, on my bathers, the memory of heat. Water like a child's bath. Stepping in. Afraid of sharks, I stick close to the shallow reef, laugh out loud through my snorkel as blue-green parrot fish crunch audibly, their small mouths working at the coral, the suspended clouds of white as they excrete out sand. Whatever was left sleeping in me is now wide-eyed, nerves quick to know: *Oh this, you are here, you have returned!*

2. Trees Honour the Company They Keep

I wake sweating into the rising heat of the day. Feet kicking off sheet, slowly my eyes begin to register the profusion of light pouring in through the windows. Walking out to the balcony I am silent, stunned, still unable to grasp I am back. After making a coffee, I wander over the grass, out to the edge of the low cliffs in front of the cottage. Watching the movement of the ocean, I am turning something over in my mind. As the water rises and falls, surges and retreats, I am searching for a pattern, moving memories around like pieces of a puzzle. There is something bigger at stake in my return to this place, something that spans more than the Indian Ocean Territories, a question arising largely, but not only, from the three years I spent out here on the islands.

I cast my mind back, try to trace the first fine fractures in what has become a widening crack in my world. In 2009, two years before I came to Christmas Island, I found myself sitting in the back of a troopy in the Kimberley region of Western Australia, heading out into a haze of heat and red dirt, boabs and spinifex flickering by. My excitement and slight trepidation grew the further we headed into the heart of this country. Through the small windows in the back of the 4WD, I could see the wide blue sky spreading out to the horizon in every direction. As we came into Fitzroy Crossing, a flock of brown kites heralded our arrival, circling slow, languid and watchful in the heat.

Twenty minutes on the other side of town, we bounced down a dirt road until the community came into view. Despite the distinctively flat plain, all the buildings were perched high above the ground on impressive steel stilts. The roof of the school, my principal and driver told me, was designed to double as a helipad in case the river broke its banks in the wet. In the evening, voluptuous clouds threw their billowing brilliance into the blue canvas of sky above plains of dry grasses. Egrets and jabirus, edgy and elegant, gathered by small pools of briny water in the dry riverbed. Summoning courage, I walked along the riverbank with a hefty stick to ward off the dogs that I could hear howling in packs nearby, watched Brahman bulls arrive in clouds of dust, navigating down the bank to the water.

My trip to the Kimberley has come with its warnings – the struggles of the communities here are no secret. Incarceration rates for Aboriginal children in Western Australia are fifty-two times higher than for non-Aboriginal children, one of the highest rates in the world. Both Fitzroy Crossing and Halls Creek are largely cordoned off in the minds of West Australians. When visible at all, our country's media casts them as dangerous and unpredictable spaces, wild and untameable. However, it is precisely this wildness that has drawn me.

Like Christmas Island, the Kimberley was first colonised in the late 1870s for guano mining. Initially, the occupation of the Kimberley was largely peaceful, with a majority of the white population coexisting with the Indigenous population. However, as colonists from New South Wales and Queensland drove their stock over the Red Centre, they brought with them the violent logic of the border that was playing out in devastating ways in the regions from where they came. The profound influence of these new arrivals led to Indigenous people in the Kimberley (including children) being chained by the neck, hanged, shot, poisoned and burned until in less than two decades the twenty-seven different tribal groups, representing between ten thousand to thirty thousand people (a quarter of the total number of Aboriginal people in Western Australia) were reduced to 'approximately' five thousand.

At the time that I arrived in the Kimberley, I knew none of this history. Somewhat naively, I packed my bag with stickers and shiny pens, happy to bribe my way through my three weeks of relief teaching work before heading back to Perth again. What could possibly happen in three weeks? But as I was shown my classroom and left to my own devices, it was not the stickers or pens the students wanted, they wanted my sunflower seeds, salty plums and almonds. They were hungry. I was shocked, but happy to be among these playful and spirited children, happy to share. In the first week all my snacks were claimed and my packets of pens and stickers remained unopened. What rattled me out there was not the children's behaviour, it was their hunger.

The principal told me that the community was in mourning. The Aboriginal community there had very recently lost an important local artist and Elder, and a young man had committed suicide by hanging himself with the inner tube of a tyre. Several days after this revelation, the students and I made paper together. I hung their new rectangles of pulp to dry on the verandah in the afternoon sun. While on duty at lunchtime, I discovered the children gathered around the makeshift washing line. The children laughed, making gagging sounds as they formed nooses around their necks with the rope. I packed the line away and hung the wet paper from the steel railing. The principal told me to watch out for the dead boy's twin – he was on suicide watch. Two days ago, they'd had to coax him down from the helipad, she said. So I did, I looked out for him as he struggled. The boy and I played Uno on the mat while the class waited. He settled down. There appeared to be no support for him, the dead boy's mother or anyone else in this tiny town. For several nights, the football oval was flooded with light; I pulled the covers over my ears, my eyes. I had been told what it meant, but did not understand what I was supposed to do, when the evil spirits were in town.

It is a long way from the desert to this isolated island closer to Indonesia than Australia, but there is something that happened in the Kimberley that speaks to what I witnessed here, something that deeply unsettled what I believed about my country and, in turn, how I see my place within it. I was raised with a strong sense of my own good fortune. I was brought up with the proud knowledge I was seventh-generation West Australian, and could trace my heritage through the landscape – the Wheatbelt, Swan Valley and South West – back to the arrival of the ship *Caroline* on Garden Island in the 1800s. I was born in the 'Lucky Country', belonged in the land of the 'Fair Go'. But I no longer seem to be able to make sense of the nation where I live or what that means for who I am.

After my brief time teaching in the Kimberley in 2009, I returned to Fremantle, teaching English to migrant and refugee children whose families had been granted humanitarian or working visas by the Australian Government. These children arrived by plane from countries all over the world, including Bhutan, Syria, Benin, Uganda, Cambodia and India. I loved my job, and the children I taught brought me so much joy. But as I watched asylum seekers arriving in increasing numbers at the margins of the nation on the nightly news, and heard the polarising language with which the media and politicians were increasingly demonising the people who had turned to Australia for safety, I wished so much I could do more. The following year, I saw an advertisement for a teaching position on Christmas Island. I submitted an application, and less than two years after my trip to Fitzroy Crossing, my husband, daughter and I found ourselves boarding a plane, and our new lives in the Indian Ocean Territories began.

On the day after I arrive, driving back through my old suburb of Silver City, the excitement of first arriving in 2011 in this strange and exotic place comes back to me. The singular peak of Christmas Island thrusts 360 metres above the Indian Ocean, its distinct aspect bending the skyline. When I first arrived, the horizon appeared to me to be like a curve of an enormous glass marble glinting in sun, causing my new home to feel continually surreal. Beyond this vista, only 360 kilometres away, Java sits on the other side of the sea. Christmas Island consists of an area of only 165 square kilometres, so from the air it is easy to take in the island's form in its entirety – its distinct three-pronged shape, formed by North West Point and Egeria Point to the west, as well as the aptly named South Point and North East Point. From the car window, however, I can only see as far as Smith Point at the end of the cove, the water dazzling, a shifting sheet of light between drab buildings.

Reaching the turn-off at Poon Saan, rather than heading back to the cottage, I take a right turn and drive out of town to Margaret's Knoll on the east side of the island. Near the airport, I pass giant robber crabs at the edge of the asphalt, then hit the wide dirt road of North-South Baseline Road. It is a short trip through the rainforest to the turn-off. I turn from the main road and into jungle, where the track is littered with puddles from recent rains. Red crabs scatter as the car bounces into the carpark. No-one else is here.

Walking along the short boardwalk under bright strata of foliage, I step up onto a small platform perched at the edge of a high cliff. Thick clouds have gathered and the island-scape has become monochrome, darkness and light. The wind is cool, the ocean glints silver, sky curtained by cloud, the rainforest plummeting dramatically down the cliffs below. A brown booby circles, both beautiful and comical with her large webbed feet dangling from her perfectly silhouetted form as she attempts to land. I watch her circle and reel, circle and reel against the play of light until a fine drizzle of rain forces me back into the shelter of the forest.

In the hush of undergrowth, white-eyes call and hop, given away by the flurry of their small feathered wings. A red crab slowly lifts a branch of pale lichen to its mouth. Broad brown rainbow fungi hold pools of water and fallen rotting leaves. In all this green, the world is luminous once again. Taking out my new lens, I attach it to my camera and begin to photograph pandanus that stand like strange tall creatures, roots rendered as thin clusters of legs, hair spiking into the canopy above. I zoom in on the blue–pink forms of young robber crabs, photograph the red crab eating lichen until the crowd of mosquitos on my legs becomes unbearable and I retreat back to the car.

Finding no repellent in the car, I leave the forest, driving past the airport once again, where the robber crabs have retreated from the day's heat into the cool shade of the jungle. When I turn right into Poon Saan, the suburb's buildings below glint in sun as they cascade toward a view of the sea. I continue down the long winding road cut into the island's cliff face to where Settlement perches on the ocean's edge and pull into the driveway of my cottage. The cottage's owner walks over as I drive in. Chris is a short lean man in his thirties with an island tan. He seems both laid-back and full of nervous energy as he chats to me on the cottage verandah, his face calm, open, body twitching with minor movements. He asks if I have everything I need. I say I do, except for the flat tyres on the bike. We start talking about the wear and tear of salt and humidity, and end up sitting on the deck drinking tea, watching a goshawk riding low over grass and layers of sprawling pink-flowering vine. Glad to have someone to talk to, I ask Chris about the bathroom where, by the sink, the faded black characters of Japanese script painted on a muddy yellow backdrop have been carefully left, the clean pale blue of more recent paintwork framing and contrasting their stark forms.

'Yes, they're great, aren't they?' he replies. 'I asked someone once, I think they literally mean "rice" or "grain store", something like that. Nothing too profound. This place was built in the nineteen thirties, probably a servant's quarters I am thinking, but when the Japanese invaded during the war, they took it over and used it as a storeroom.'

Since the comparatively late beginning of this territory's known human history, Japan has never been a stranger to Christmas Island. Between 1918 and 1945, Japan purchased seventy-five to eighty per cent of Christmas Island's phosphate. It is little wonder, then, that during World War II, the Japanese considered Christmas Island an asset worth acquiring. During the month of February 1942, Japan attacked Christmas Island in an air raid that killed three men. Bombings continued throughout the month of March, destroying military equipment and communications. On 7 May 1942, troops began to arrive and the Japanese formally took control of the island.

The Japanese continued to occupy Christmas Island, using the islanders to make small amounts of phosphate, until their sudden and unexplained evacuation during December 1943. With exception of the lethal rape of a bedridden woman when troops first landed, it appears the reputed brutality of the Japanese soldiers did not hold true on Christmas Island. Perhaps the soldiers felt their vulnerability too in this strange and isolated world. The evacuation of the Japanese troops continued until June

1945, with the exception of fifteen soldiers who finally departed on 24 August, curiously leaving the islanders with a year's supply of opium but little food.

As Chris and I look out over the water, he tells me about other traces of Japanese occupation on the island: bottles, wash basins, lookouts and bomb stores, and as he does, I notice the cloud has begun to clear. I take our cups and tell him I am going to get moving while there is a window in the weather, as I am planning to head out to the Chinese cemetery.

'Good idea,' Chris says. 'In fact, it's a shame you weren't here last week. It was the twenty-fifth anniversary of Gordon Bennett's death – you know the big union guy?'

'Yes.'

'Well, they had a huge service and celebration last week, it was massive. He is still so important to the Chinese here – he basically saved them. That would have been an interesting thing to write about. Anyway, you will see all the offerings and flowers and everything on his grave when you get there.'

Chris returns to his house next door and I head inside and grab my backpack. There is dark cloud to the east, but I take the risk anyway. I soon recall how exercise always felt more laborious in the island's thick humidity. As I lived in Silver City near the top of Christmas Island, most of the friendships I formed ended up being from that part of the island, so I had only ever driven through this end of Settlement. Today, walking at a slower pace allows me to take in the old colonial architecture, see the way the island is always trying to return its structures to the earth, covering walls in black mould, filling gutters with fernery. I wonder how old the thick-trunked frangipanis are, whether they started as new cuttings on a long boat trip from Asia, to find the island's rich soil in the 1930s. The old trees' canopies are covered with pale pink or white-and-yellow flowers, their petalled forms leaving a floral shower over yards of grass. As I reach the end of Settlement, in the distance a small low-walled area sign-posted 'European Graveyard' becomes visible. I had never noticed this separate graveyard so close to Settlement before.

The sun has started to come out, lighting up the banyan trees on the road reserve and upping the humidity. The sea flashes bright on my left between trees. I stop and dig around in my bag for some protection, but remember I have not brought any suncream, only a hat, as it seemed the threat of rain was more likely. As I come around a curve in the road, on my right, the terrain opens up where the jungle has been cleared, and the concrete plinths and headstones of graves become visible. I cross the road and begin to look at the headstones, most of which I can't read as they are written in Chinese script, but find pleasure in the red and black shapes of the Chinese characters, and I am intrigued by the sight of fruit, incense, Scotch Finger biscuits, cans of soft drink and small cartons of juice left at different sites.

Christmas Island's population has been diverse from the outset, and its rich cultural makeup continues to be one of the community's defining features. In the 2016 census, of the population of around one thousand eight hundred people, more than forty-three per cent of Christmas Islanders are recorded as having both parents born outside of Australia, originating predominantly from Malaysia and China. More than fifty per cent of households speak a language other than English at home. The main language groups are Malay and Mandarin, but they also include Cantonese, Min Nan (part of the Sino-Tibetan language family group, commonly referred to as Hokkien) and Tagalog (a Malayo-Polynesian language predominantly spoken in the Philippines). I savour the visual expression of this richness as I walk between headstones adorned with artful script, gradually making my way to the back of the graveyard to where the island's cliff begins to rise and booby birds fly pale-bodied and black-winged along the ridge. I am drawn to where a headstone is nestled beneath the canopy of a wide banyan tree. Here, the gravesite is almost an artwork, the concrete of the headstone the same colour as the tree's labyrinth of roots, both surfaces mottled and loved by lichen and mould. Both tree and monument reach north across the Java Trench to Asia; it seems roots reach back differently here.

After walking a little further along the road, I arrive at the site of two enormous white columns holding up a red setting sun backdropped by an ancient frangipani with a wide canopy of flowers. Two stairs lead up to a large concrete platform, something more like a small courtyard than a grave. Inside this courtyard are two marble steps that lead up to a headstone covered in black Chinese characters. On the uppermost step, three jars hold large stubs of burned incense sticks, while on the first step, a packet of Arnott's Orange Slice biscuits and three oranges are placed on separate plastic plates, and three small cartons of juice with their straws inserted are placed behind. I am standing at the site of the Coolies Memorial.

In June 1899 (nine years after Christmas Island was annexed to the British Empire), a small ship was seen anchored off Christmas Island. The ship held, among other people, a group of 120 Chinese men. The men were employed for pitifully low wages to do the back-breaking work of removing the island's rich phosphate stores by hand under an intense tropical sun. Many were to die of beri-beri, a disease discovered later to be the result of vitamin B1 deficiencies in the food supplied by their employers. Settlement cemetery was originally built in response to the large number of deaths of Chinese labourers at the old hospital, when the beri-beri epidemic reached rampant proportions by 1901.

This original group of 120 was followed in time by many like them, men from poor villages in the provinces of Kwangtung (Guangdong), Kwangsi (Guangxi) and Fukien (Fujian), as well as Hainan. The workers would never see their homelands again. Of those who did not die from disease, many were beaten to death or killed by accidents on the mine. The indentured labourers who did survive were so poorly paid they were never able to afford the fare to return to their families or to be buried alongside their ancestors. The Coolies Memorial, erected by the Chinese Literary Association with the assistance of the Christmas Island Phosphate Commission in 1971, seeks to acknowledge the hardship endured by the Chinese indentured labourers and counter the erasure of their lives from the landscape. 'This memorial,' the headstone reads, 'honours our Chinese ancestors and late friends, and commemorates their story of endurance and courage, written with their blood, sweat and tears. Lest we forget.'

Perhaps it is the ancient frangipani radiant with blossom speaking to the abundance of white marble, or perhaps it is the evocation of hope in the rising sun held high on its columns, but despite the incredible suffering the site represents, the space feels peaceful and light. I linger a moment longer, taking in the memorial's impressive design, then continue weaving my way through the cemetery grounds.

Some headstones are small and old, marked only by a simple plinth of concrete or the strategic placement of a red brick. Others are grand, containing glossy enamelled photographs, guarded by ornate statues or decorated tiles. I cross the street, back toward the ocean, feeling the sun beginning to beat on my winter-pale skin, hot on my shoulders. Soon I come across a thin strip of sloping ground between road and ocean, containing a stand of seemingly younger frangipanis. Here lies a series of what I recognise, from my time on the Cocos Islands, to be Islamic graves erected by the Malay community. The graves are a rectangular border of concrete laid at the foot of the trees, without script of any kind. Instead they consist of two stone markers, one at the head and one at the feet of where the deceased lies. Over the graves, the trees have scattered handful upon handful of blossoms, so it seems that the trees bless the deceased, honouring the company that they keep.

The site of Gordon Bennett's grave is unmistakable. Even from a distance, the large green octagonal roof is easily visible. Decorated with botanical sculptures, the structure is held up by eight red-tiled pillars to form an expansive pagoda. Two steps lead up to a red concrete floor where, off to the side, two ornate concrete tables are surrounded by similarly decorated concrete stools. At the centre of the pagoda is a high marble plinth at the base of which have been set bunches of flowers in two ceramic jars as well as a large terracotta pot filled with sand. Inserted in the sand are scores of incense sticks and skewered burned cigarettes. Surrounding the pots and vases are bottles of water and rice crackers scattered on a plate and in containers on the floor. On the first level of the marble plinth is a can of beer, what looks like juice or spirits in a paper cup, as well as cups of what appears to be water. On the second level, a lotus-shaped candle sits in a green glass saucer. Next to this is a lighter, a plastic dish piled with an assortment of lollipops, an orange and an apple. On top of the marble grave is the headstone that reads in both English and Chinese, as well as an embedded framed photo of Bennett – the image of an open-faced and attractive man, bright-eyed, with well-defined features. Playfulness exudes from a half-formed smile, forming two dimples either side of his face.

Gordon Bennett, or Tai Ko Seng (Big Brother Who Delivers) as he is known to the Chinese population on Christmas Island, has an almost godlike status on the island. Watching archival footage of Bennett's interactions with the Chinese population, and more recent footage from the ongoing memorials of the anniversaries of his death during July each year, it is hard not to be moved by the affection and dedication between this idiosyncratic and somewhat unlikely leader and the Chinese community.

Born in 1944, Bennett was a hard-drinking, chain-smoking Englishman who dropped out of school at the age of fifteen. Bennett's father was a coal miner and union general secretary in the UK, and I wonder if that early influence was what led Bennett to take up his position in Australia as general secretary of Western Australia's Water Workers Union after his arrival in 1971. It was this position that led directly to his appointment as secretary of the Union of Christmas Island Workers (UCIW), a newly formed collective born from uprisings over poor work and living conditions, as well as the excessive powers of the British Phosphate Commission (BPC). Self-assured, witty and charismatic, with a genuine interest in the rich culture of the Chinese, Bennett quickly won over the members of the union as well as the larger Chinese community. With the support of local workers, Bennett took on the formidable role of challenging the seemingly untouchable phosphate company.

The BPC began running the Christmas Island phosphate mine after George Clunies-Ross and Sir John Murray, the original leaseholders, sold the company to Australia and New Zealand after World War II. Before the rise of the union movement on Christmas Island, the BPC was responsible for what were described as third-world conditions for mine workers on the island. On top of the poor living conditions, the BPC was responsible for forced repatriation, withholding of wages and barring re-entry as punitive measures used against men employed on the mine, while paying workers around one quarter of the wages of Australian employees on the mainland. A plaque at the site of the UCIW's original office records Bennett's legacy as the 'Elimination of colonialism, elimination of racism, wage parity with mainland Australia, Migration Act (Australian citizenship), permanent residence status for Christmas Island, mine re-opening in 1990 and fair housing allocation'.

Bennet was also responsible for helping to form the Phosphate Resources Limited (PRL), a mining company formed by the Chinese community when, after the union's successful (and sometimes aggressive) negotiations of wages and conditions with the Australian Government, the Labor Party controversially shut down the mine in the 1980s. Bennett became shire president and PRL chairman, but ultimately the weight of his responsibilities, as well as his heavy drinking and smoking, contributed to a massive heart attack on 30 July 1991, a year after the battle to reopen the mine was won. Bennet was forty-seven when he died.

Ancestor worship and offerings imbued with symbolism are not unusual on Christmas Island, but this expansive pagoda is an enormous and heartfelt tribute to an equally big personality, a man not only loved but remembered in ritual acts of worship by many on the island. At the bottom of the marble headstone that stands at the centre of the pagoda are a wreath and bunches of flowers, bougainvillea and palm, crisp after days of sun. 'You lived life to the fullest, my love,' the headstone reads, 'and changed the lives of so many people through your staunch belief in justice, equality and truth and your complete unselfishness.' A laminated poster among the flowers reads, 'Twenty-five years on, and forever in our hearts.' I can almost see the large gathering of Chinese Christmas Islanders filling this space, spilling out over the grass, faces lit by the glow of candlelight. Among tendrils of incense ghosting the gathering crowd, I can imagine a couple of men leaning down, placing the skewered cigarettes I can see in the sand, burning Bennett a few Winfield Blues.

The monument is raised on the edges of a small slope, where an ocean breeze catches my hair as I make my way back down the steps, the sea a restless luminous canvas glimpsed through thick greenery on the other side of the road. Walking among the last of the headstones, I consider the elements of feng shui with which the Chinese community designed the memorial space. As many of the Chinese labourers did not have the means to have their bodies expatriated back to their home country, features of the cemetery site were designed to perform a symbolic role, metaphorically bridging the deceased through movements of birds and invitation of water back to their homeland. Birds reel, move incessantly, leaving and returning, as the ocean extends sapphire and shimmering toward the horizon. I watch, my mind stepping up and out, feeling this pull, an almost tactile thread, this layered and dynamic path across the sea.

I continue walking past the graveyard, wondering how far it is to The Grotto, one of the island's dramatic sea caves. Ominous clouds begin to form, coming in from the south. They move toward me, low and foreboding, rendered striking by the sky's high backdrop of blue. To my left, obscuring the ocean, is a tall stand of pandanus. The repeated shapes of the plants' stark lines seem sculptural against the sky's brilliant hue. I stop and get out my camera as brown boobies and Christmas Island frigatebirds glide into the scene.

Christmas Island frigatebirds are endemic to the island and are the rarest species of frigatebirds in the world. This is one of only three nesting sites on the island, and with a population of only 1200 breeding pairs, the species is vulnerable to extinction. I try to capture these unique creatures as they come over the sculpted foliage, set against the layered cloudscape, but can't quite get the shot I want. The sky becomes increasingly dark as a wide front eats all traces of blue. Within minutes, the place where I am standing is utterly transformed.

Dense clouds erase the light, and the island's cliffs to my right become silhouetted, the layers of foliage at their feet obscured by shadow. First ten, then fifty, then what appears to be hundreds of frigatebirds begin to soar along the ridge like dark spirits gathering, colluding, haunting the land. The birds soar up, up, high into the wind and almost disappear, circling and wheeling, their strange arrowed shapes stark against grey. Then, just when I think they have gone, behind me first a few birds, then ten, twenty, thirty, fifty birds flow along the ridge line once again, silent and foreboding, once more climbing up, up into the troubled sky.

I put my raincoat on and stand in fine drizzle at the side of the road, staring up at the island's cliffs. The bird's movements feel ritualised, an enactment of an ancient dance shared between birds, cliff and cloud, instigated by a shift in wind. I feel completely irrelevant, yet not excluded. Despite the road and signposts, the place feels wild and untamed, loaded with latent power. As I stand damp and unmoving, hair pasted in wet stripes across my cheeks and forehead, I am completely exhilarated – a lone witness to this incredible unfolding scene.

The birds begin to dwindle and I become aware of my sodden hair and shoes. It is time to keep moving. Realising I have been walking for over an hour, I start to feel each step on the long narrow stretch, walking south along the island. Soon sounds from the golf course come over the canopy and I know it can't be far.

Finally the sign for The Grotto appears, faded and tucked behind foliage, and I hear the welcome hiss of that breathy dragon that, in stories still told, swam from China to live above this cave half claimed by sea.

Along the path, red crabs scuttle sideways over a yellow-brown carpet of wet fallen leaves. The smell of jungle rises up, greets me like a rush of joy, and I step smiling toward the open mouth of sibilating rock. The sight is even more beautiful than I remember – before me a luminous, liquid, aquamarine jewel is set into the floor of this small limestone cave. There is a sense of menace as the trapped air is forced out with each surge of tide in a breathy rush. The pale blue light that reflects up from the white sand at the bottom of the cave illuminates the fat stalactites suspended from The Grotto's rocky roof. A parrot fish scopes the cave floor for food, soaked in light. Yet the cave's beauty is shockingly undermined by a grimy rim of rubbish that has been forced up and onto the rocks at The Grotto's entrance with the surge of tide. Twenty or thirty faded thongs lie scattered over the rocky entryway, interspersed with plastic water bottles and broken pieces of foam. One large piece of white foam lies trapped in the water of the cave, moving up and rushing back beside the parrot fish with each rush of tide.

Here beauty and ugliness are starkly juxtaposed. Despite the three years I spent coming and going from Christmas Island, I have never seen The Grotto littered like this and, after watching the fish move through the jewelled light for several moments, I leave. The rain has brought out many more red crabs, the numbers so large they cover the forest floor as they feed on wet leaves. I bend to watch one crab, with a particularly bright leaf, lift small yellow sections to her mouth. She goes to scurry away, but when I stop, so does she, and she lets me watch her deliberate movements – cut of claw, bright detritus raised, red pincer to slit of mouth. Time has slowed, there is no hurry, and I am tired from the long walk. I become aware of a low soft soundscape, scuttle and snip, lift of leaf to a crowd of mouths. I stay like that for a while, crouching low, watching this glistening array of creatures eat through their day. And they watch me until they grow bored and return their attention to their tasks.

I am reluctant to leave the crabs, sad to leave the bright layering of red lives among the yellow and brown scattered foliage, but I am starting to get hungry too. Soon I am moving back among the graves, the world wet, sun again beating hard against my skin. Back in the Chinese cemetery, I glimpse a stark marble headstone engraved and painted with bold red characters. Against this, two enormous yellow grasshoppers mate. It strikes me as something of a portrait of this place, how the island seems to hold you hard up against it, life and death, virility and decay, brazen with colour, filled with creatures from many countries, all of us finding ourselves washed up here one way or another.

3. Our Tenuous Place

Back at the cottage, the silver bosun birds tumble, sending out a screechy repartee as they roll in improbable backward somersaults, head always upright but bodies spinning back and around like small ferris wheels, trailing their one long plume elegantly behind them. Inside, I strip back to my underwear and flop onto the double bed, turning on the air-con for a break from the humidity. The small cabin cools quickly, and I lean over to the bookshelf embedded in the cottage's wall and flick though a series of books about the island's history.

Black-and-white photos show stiff portraits of white men in pith helmets, children buttoned into sailor suits and grim images of coolies working the exposed phosphate mines. When I lived here in 2011, with the exception of a handful of staff at the school where I worked, I barely got to know any members of the island's largely Chinese population. However, I was consistently amazed by the generosity of the Chinese community, by the street festivals, dragon dances and cultural celebrations they regularly organised. It was their warm invitations to these events, their willingness to feed the entire island, even filling large eskies with soft drink and beer, that brought together the diverse groups of people living here, linking the largely transient white population with the more enduring members of the community.

The energy of the Chinese festivals routinely brought to life the otherwise quiet streets, with drumming and cymbals, ritual and singing, and the bright hypnotic dances of the dazzling red dragons, often brought over especially from China. In particular, my first experience of Chinese New Year celebrations comes back to me. A recent arrival, I was in awe of my new home, its complexity and beauty, its peace and rugged geography, every day unearthing some new layer. Four weeks after we landed, we were invited up to a large feast near the top of the island, at the old suburb of Drumsite. As we joined the crowd it took me a while to believe we could help ourselves to whatever we liked – rice dishes and satays, pork crackers and noodles. The sense of abundance on an island where a lettuce alone could cost twelve or thirteen dollars, was striking.

After dinner we stepped out onto the street where a long dragon twisted and convulsed as muscled young men drummed and cymbals clashed in high pitches. All along the street were the crumpled shapes of enormous paper lanterns. People formed small groups, together holding up each lantern's form, crouching to light the candle at its base. The lanterns lit up with an orange glow that spread its warm light onto the crowd's faces. Then, as gas was created by the candle's heat, the lanterns began to slowly lift like floating golden wishes. Gently they rocked, lifting high, high into the endless black of night, until the space above our heads was filled with soft strata of light.

I close the book, too tired to take in more than photos. Being back on the island has filled me with an enormous sense of peace and exhilaration. I doze, drifting in and out of sleep, washed with memories, filled with happiness. When I wake, the day is getting late, and I move to the window, where the silver bosun birds continue to throw up their strange ceaseless sounds, rolling in tight circles of flight. Heading to the bathroom for a shower, I glance again the faded Japanese script above the sink.

It is when I start to take off my top, and the scrape of strap sends a searing pain across the surface of my skin, that I realise I am seriously burnt. Coming straight from the end of a long Perth winter, my skin is pale, has not developed any form of resistance to the emphatic tropical sun. Getting into the shower, I turn up the cold so my limbs do not ring with pain. Afterwards I slather myself in moisturiser, feeling sheepish that at forty-something I have managed to do so much damage to my body. It is my shoulders that are the worst, both a deep shade of red, and I wince at the sensation of cold cream on my radiant skin.

I turn in front of a small mirror on the back of the bathroom door to assess the damage on one shoulder and then turn to examine the other. It is then that I see it and, with a jolt, turn my shoulder back in the mirror's frame again. Two moles on the edge of my shoulder are not only completely burnt, but somehow over the winter months, I had not seen that the small dots have changed and grown, so that what was once two separate brown marks, has completely morphed into one dark and irregularly shaped mass. I feel a sick sensation in my stomach.

Turning away from the mirror I am a little dazed. I finish getting dressed, then turn the same shoulder back to the mirror, hoping to reassure myself that it is not that bad. But it is, everything tells me the marks on my shoulder looks very, very wrong, and it is all I can do to stop the rising sense of panic in my chest. In a flash, all the wonder of my adventure leaves and I feel frightened and alone. After making myself dinner, I sit out on the deck as the sun sets. The silver bosuns have gone, and I am left with a pale smear of sunset over sea. I eat mechanically, then do the dishes, rifle through the tourist information looking for the number for the hospital. Finding it, I put it aside to ring to see a doctor in the morning. I call my partner but don't want to say a thing about my shoulder, only tell Ash about my walk through the graveyard and the wheeling silver bosuns. After hanging up, again I examine the marks in the mirror, fears unrelieved. Once in bed, I cannot sleep, toss and turn until dawn's light creeps in through the timber blinds.

In the morning I ring the hospital as early as possible. They cannot fit me in until four-thirty the next day. My heart sinks; it is such an unbearably long time before I can put my mind at ease. Deciding to walk off my fears, I head south along the island's edge. The morning is hazy, there is no glow of wonder for me today. I feel a rush of resentment and anger, cannot muster the will or energy to push the sensation down. *What is wrong with this place*? I think. *Why does it seem to want to force people hard up against suffering and mortality, against the tenuous fact of our lives?* Five years ago, when I lived here, I arrived in a community struggling to come to terms with the drownings from the Christmas Island boat tragedy, Australia's worst peacetime maritime disaster in more than a century. Several months later, my father was diagnosed with terminal cancer. He visited me here, his body a hollow shell, his masculinity eroded, his confidence shattered. I begin to cry. I am desperately trying not to leap to conclusions but cannot force my feelings of fear and dismay away. Here on this island I am abuzz with ideas, with so much unfinished work left to do. My daughter has already lost two grandfathers and an uncle. I don't want her to suffer anymore. I want to continue to share life with her, I want to live.

The tears are coming heavy; I cannot find courage or perspective, feeling small and scared, unable to overcome what the strange shape on my shoulder seems to be suggesting. Reaching the grassed area past the police station, I continue toward the cove, walking along the edge of the water by small sea cliffs. The sea jostles restlessly against the jagged rock. In the waters of Flying Fish Cove, light rain falls over a huge, blue ship tethered to the anchor buoys. Suddenly, from the drizzle, a rainbow emerges, arcing over the cove from one side of the bay to other. A choked cry rises up from my chest. I am filled with a strong sense of peace and acceptance at the sign of the bow's curved colour, luminous and enormous, rising over the cove's sheer cliffs.

4. Suspension

That afternoon, my friend Yvonne arrives. I am very grateful for a familiar face after my rough night's sleep, and even happier that she is willing to go for a dive. Yvonne is slightly younger than me, in her late thirties, with a tumble of golden-blonde curls that fall to her shoulders. During my time on Christmas Island, Yvonne worked as an assistant with the asylum-seeker students in the family detention centres at Phosphate Hill. She consistently embraced the students with her warmth and generosity, as well as her thick Afrikaans accent. As I get into her car, I feel there is a gentleness, a sense of compassion, in the way that she relates to me, an unspoken understanding about why I am here, why I need to return. Though the reasons for the need to come back to this island mountain remains a question, I know it has something to do with the unsettling impact of what we both witnessed in detention, as well as the traces and memories of the young people whose lives briefly came into our own.

At Flying Fish Cove we put on our snorkelling gear quickly because Yvonne has two small children and a limited window of time. Our conversation is cut short as we both bite on our snorkels and slip into the deliciously warm sea. As we set off, I can see that the coral has died back on the shallow reef, and the soft corals that used to sway luxuriously from the small limestone burrs are gone. Without warning, a whitetip reef shark appears in the metre of water in which we are moving along at the reef's edge. The grey creature is large for a reef shark, looks at us briefly with her black circle of eye, then, with a quick whip of her tail, moves past us in a spurt, disappearing into blue.

Yvonne waits for me and checks I am okay, knowing I am scared of sharks, but her confidence gives me courage and together we swim on, moving into deeper water, where the wide aquarium I remember opens to me and a wellspring of happiness rises in my chest. All around me is the inconceivable vibrance of shifting colour – sapphire-blue water that only becomes more striking as I look out away from the shore. Below this, large plate corals stretch their thin structures, metres wide, beneath which the head of a moray eel rises like a bobbing periscope. Leatherjackets are suspended near the surface, fragmenting the sun's rays, the blue canopy of water rendering them more flock than school. A giant trevally flashes silver from the reef behind us. We swim out deeper, floating over a dream-scape, a wide undulating terrain of layered corals, world hushed by the water in our ears.

All at once the reef falls away, and there is a sheer drop into blue, the wall of rock disappearing into watery darkness. This cliff here is three kilometres straight down to the ocean floor. I float, suspended, over this seemingly never-ending edge, briefly washed with vertigo and an irrational sense that I could fall. Clouds of bright neon fish flash at the reef's edge, ornate corals offer their colours to the light. Another whitetip reef shark comes along the edge of the drop-off, moving from the water's shadows into light. It is only a small shark, slim and shorter than my own body, so I will myself to be resilient as she begins arcing her sleek streamlined form, circling something on the reef directly below me. Next to the shark, a neon-yellow coral half the size of the shark is lit by the lowering sun. Around the coral, tiny fishes swarm, glinting and disappearing as their bodies turn. In all this colour and light, the smooth movements of the shark are not ominous but instead gift me a lens through which to witness her exquisite grace. Mesmerised, I watch her strong body turning in contracting circles, stage-lit, until her interest wanes and she begins to glide low over the reef, disappearing into the shadow of the headland.

When I arrive at the hospital the next afternoon, I am relieved there is no-one I recognise in the foyer. A young couple sit holding their son, the woman's olive face framed by her patterned headscarf, the man in a t-shirt and sarong. The child climbs their legs, wriggles around and then slides back down the line of their limbs. An old man with a goatee and a thin, high-cheekboned face sits by the window. When my name is called, I get up and follow the tall young doctor who is already making his way back down the hall. He shows me into a bright clean room and asks how he can help. I explain about the changes in the marks on my shoulder and he takes out a kind of magnifying glass and asks if he can have a look.

Turning my shoulder toward him, I pull back on my tank top and he looks at my skin in silence.

'Well it ticks all the boxes,' he says. 'I think the best thing we can do is to take a biopsy now. We can send the sample out on the next flight, when is that, Tuesday? Oh, today. We won't make today's flight; I think we can send the sample off on Saturday.'

'How long will it take to find out?' I ask, containing the sinking feeling that this man is not going to abate my fears.

'Say it goes out Saturday, then a few days to get there, a few days in the lab – how long are you on the island?'

'Until next Tuesday, then I am heading to Cocos for a week.'

Why don't you get the nurses on Cocos to give us a ring once you are there? I imagine we will know by then.'

I am taken through to a surgery room where I am asked to remove my top. I wince, realising I am wearing a beige bra, instantly feeling much older than this pale, bearded young doctor. A male assistant comes in; they shine a lamp on my body, give me a needle and remove a small part of my shoulder. The doctor stitches the hole together with what looks like fishing wire.

'No swimming for three to four days,' the doctor says cheerily, 'then come back on Saturday and a nurse will take the stitches out.' The nurse dresses the wound with a large adhesive bandage and I am ushered toward the door. Before I even make the waiting room, the doctor is asking the nurse where a good place to go swimming is on the island, and the men stand beneath the foyer's map pointing at different bays.

'Goodbye,' I say, but they barely glance over their shoulders.

I only have seven days left on this stunning tropical island, and the doctor has told me for four of those I cannot swim. I drive back down the island's slopes feeling flat, trying not to be angry, craving the people I love three thousand kilometres away.

5. Remembering

Waking the next day, I make up my mind to try to rise above my flatness and fears. I drive out to the cove and decide to walk up the steep road to Tai Jin House to look at the memorials and sit out at the fuel buoys. At the west end of the cove is a miniature bay with a beautiful outlook over several small rocky islands that rise up from the reef. The rocks are shaped like angular oblongs placed lengthwise on the water, their small peaks occasionally decorated with one or two bonsai-like trees, making me think of sea temples in Indonesia or Japan. An Abbott's booby has chosen the nearest island as a nesting site, and her bright white baby, as big as a hen and fluffy as child's toy, rises comically and blue-faced as I near the water.

Christmas Island's topography is consistently dramatic, and often feels harsh, even violent, but at this bay there is a gentle sigh of sea, and the rainforest tumbles in lush abundance down cliffs toward the water. Last time I sat here, I was with a large group of asylum seeker boys and young men. I remember one boy in particular who had arrived on his own, only fourteen years of age, from Iran. This student was loved by everyone who met him, he was so open and warm, so alive in his young skin, that the older boys happily befriended him, the staff took him under their wing. I drove the students up to the lookout at Territory Day Park, where the young men looked down in silence at the jetty where they had first arrived on Christmas Island, escorted from their old wooden boats by the Navy. It is here the students must have begun to realise they had survived their dangerous journeys, finally making that first footfall onto land.

From the lookout, the students, teachers and I had then gone out to The Grotto and watched the water dance in the limestone cave, then came back to this beach to eat our lunch. Some of the teenage boys sat with their arms around each other's necks, most were quiet, others had lost their ability to smile. They ate their lunch in the shade, looking as ordinary as any bunch of boys, and I found myself completely confronted by their sheer humanity, seeing them out of the detention centre, realising I was the one who had to put them back into what, despite the euphemisms, for all intents and purposes was a prison.

When they finished their meals, the boys asked if I would take their photos, and they posed on the edge of reef, in front of the angular shapes of islands, playful now, sunglasses pressed against their faces, scarves flicked with a flourish around necks. I have a photo of two best friends, young men framed in a portrait, faces soft, eyes full of tenderness. Afterwards, one of the young men came to me and placed a small gift of coral in my hand. I no longer recall his name, don't know where he went, but the sculpted fragment of coral sits on my dressing table, each morning urging me not to forget.

I begin my ascent up the thin asphalt road that climbs the steep slope up to Tai Jin House and beyond that to Smith Point. As the canopy closes over me, the smell of damp leaves rises up all around. The creaking calls of booby birds rise in the distance, and sea glints in blue through a fine dark filigree of leaves. At the side of the road, large boulders protrude, around the base of which run small rivulets of water in which red crabs gather.

I have begun to sweat already, but all this huff and puff gets me out of my head and back into my senses, nerve endings alive to the living world. Reaching the top, I step out into the light, where Tai Jin House, an expansive two-storey colonial residence framed by white pillars and wide verandahs, sits like a forgotten world. Meaning 'big boss' in Hokkien, Tai Jin House was originally built for Christmas Island's resident magistrate, and later the British administrator, whose role was to do whatever was required to retain order in this remote outpost.

In a single day, the British-appointed district officer might be called upon to play the role of health officer, judge, post agent or port official. The officer also helped settle disputes between different cliques and factions on the island, as well as handling the unlikely duty of selling opium. Tai Jin House presently houses a fascinating museum that documents Christmas Island's history and is used for special occasions, such as the island's annual ball, as well as the occasional class of Tai Chi.

From the top of the hill, near where the island's limestone cliff drops dramatically away to views of the sea, the asylum seeker memorials become visible, tucked into a strip of grass between the road and cliff. I am not ready to look at them yet, so I keep moving past Tai Jin House, past the World War II guns mounted at the top of the hill. Rounding the point, I walk beneath the cool shade of banyan trees hanging their fibrous threads luxuriously over the road. After about fifteen minutes the gate to the water treatment plant becomes visible and I take the limestone track surrounded by thick green clouds of fleshy beach cabbage down to the cliff looking over the fuel buoys.

On this small singular island, it was at this cliff, hanging somewhat perilously over the surging water, that I could almost always find a way to be alone. The water here is implausibly blue. On its surface floats a single yellow leaf, the scene Photoshop-bright. Suspended over the water runs a rusted chain as thick as my thigh that disappears into the blue, running out to secure the fuel buoys. The light is incredible. The buoys are lit bright, sun painting them like giant coloured toy drums, yellow and red, patterned by salt and seams of rust. The grey forms of common noddies are dotted along the yellow surface of gently rocking buoys. The birds land, sway with the buoys, looking slightly non-plussed, then take off, fly in circles and land again. Along the rusted chain, a string of noddies also rest and preen, tucking their light-grey heads into the darker downy pillow of their bodies.

Crouching down, I shuffle out as close to the edge of the cliff as I dare. In the brilliant colour of the water, a lone red fish is washed in and out as it tries to feed on coral while the water surges and rushes around the rocks. Booby birds fly in and out, watching their nests. From here I can follow the shape of the next bay around to West White Beach, trace a line with my eyes back up the steep slope, know behind that ridge, hidden by jungle, is the notorious Christmas Island Immigration Detention Centre, commonly known as the North West Point detention centre. I remember looking out over this same ridge from my home the day of the detention centre riots, alerted by the city-sound of sirens, to see the crest of the hill ablaze.

It is so quiet here today. I am wearing my bikini, so I remove my t-shirt as a relief from the humidity, feeling the sun and the gentle breeze on my skin. The noddies on the chain and I watch each other, both sitting with our different reasons for staying, while the water rushes in and out of rock. I watch the red fish sway and feed in the surge, the yellow leaf on its blue bed, the noddies dozing peacefully in the sun. Suddenly, silently, from behind the point, comes the dark angular shape of a Border Force vessel. It jolts me as it glides into view without a sound. I feel exposed, on display, sitting out on the cliff. Hastily I dress, pushing back my anger and begin to pack my things, turn back for one more glimpse at the buoy, its form painterly and beautiful in light, then move quickly back up the track and away from the possibility of watching eyes.

It is drizzling a little now, and the banyan trees create a welcome canopy as I make my way back toward Tai Jin House. The jungle leaning over the road becomes blurred, its world of greenery grey and muted. Soon I step out of shade and into pale light. The rain eases, but Flying Fish Cove remains obscured and dull beneath thick grey sky. Walking toward the point, I first arrive at the memorial of the lost sailor, Leading Seaman Cameron Troy Curr. The details of his death in 2002 are laid out in bronze and set into a plinth of rock in front of the commanding building of Tai Jin House, beside a flagpole where island state ceremonies take place, surrounded by a memorial wall erected by the 2nd Combat Engineer Regiment. In the rock below his plaque is the photo of an almost childlike young man with pale skin, looking directly at the camera in his sailor's uniform and hat. I look at the war memorabilia – a large steel anchor, the end of a grey painted canon or enormous gun. Out on the water, the Border Force ship is turning back out to sea.

Walking along the edge of the cliff heading back toward Flying Fish Cove, I come across a space where the lawn becomes a thin strip between the road and the cliff's edge, interspersed with trees and signage. It is here I find a crude concrete slab in the rectangular shape of a grave, in which is set a badly damaged rudder. The front of the slab has been softened with a smatter of smooth coral rocks, over which couch grass sends out runners to brown in the tropical sun. Set among the pebbles is a small bronze plaque that reads:

SIEV 221
15 December 2010
We will reflect on this day with sadness.
The loss of each person's life diminishes our own
because we are part of humankind.
AS YOU READ THIS PLEASE REMEMBER ALL ASYLUM SEEKERS
WHO HAVE ATTEMPTED THIS TREACHEROUS JOURNEY

The first time I saw this monument, despite the touching epigraph, it struck me as incredibly odd, and I feel this unease once again. I recall contacting the Department of the Prime Minister and Cabinet to find out if any asylum seekers had been consulted about the form of the memorial. No-one responded to my calls or emails. I find it hard to imagine the families of the deceased sitting comfortably with a memorial that falls short of plainly stating that anyone had died, let alone its striking failure to the mention the number of men, women and children whose lives were lost, as well as the events that had led to their terrible deaths. The sinking of the SIEV 221 on 15 December 2010 saw the violent drowning of fifty people, including fifteen children, as their struggling fishing boat was smashed against the island's jagged cliffs. It was a disaster that sent shockwaves across the world, yet the tragedy's vague memorial is placed by a kerb next to a road alongside street signage. The site of the SIEV 221 memorial is so obscure that even tourists looking for the memorial (having heard about it only through word of mouth) have been unable to find it, a site more like a traffic island than a place for grieving and reflection.

Though SIEV 221 is the name used most often to identify the fated vessel, the acronym and number used on the memorial were given to the fishing boat by Australian Government authorities.

SIEV (Suspected Illegal Entry Vessel), is a loaded title as it incriminates those on board through the implication they were acting illegally. This is despite the fact that seeking asylum is legal in Australia, as the country is a signatory to the 1951 Refugee Convention that acknowledges the right to flee to safety as a human right. Those aboard the boat would have referred to the vessel as the *Janga*, yet the memorial imposes an abbreviation that entails stigma juxtaposed with a number instead of a name, dehumanising those the memorial is purporting to humanise.

I compare the ambiguity and invisibility of the *Janga* (SIEV 221) memorial with that of Leading Seaman Cameron Troy Curr. The site of the young man's monument is in context, set among its various military signifiers in a place designated for ceremony and memorialisation with its flagpole, sweeping views out to sea on one side, backdropped by the historically significant and architecturally grand Tai Jin House on the other. I consider what we learn about Cameron Troy Curr through his memorial – what he looks like, his dates of birth and death (1981–2002), his position in the Navy, the ship he was on, where he went missing, the search for his body, the loss to his family and a little about his character. Yet at this site commemorating the deaths of so many Iraqi and Iranian people, the details remain hidden, obscured, the monument shockingly functional and bland.

A week before my flight to the islands, I met Christmas Island Shire President and General Secretary of the Union of Christmas Island Workers, Gordon Thompson, while he was in Perth for a conference. A big man with an even bigger personality, Gordon is held in somewhat polarised regard on Christmas Island, but I have a huge amount of respect for his courage and outspoken stance, advocating for the rights of asylum seekers on and off the island. Though it was winter, we sat outside at a riverside café as he lit his cigarette in the non-smoking courtyard and told me about the books he was reading, his background, and the history of unionism in the Indian Ocean Territories. After some time, I began to ask him about his experience of asylum seekers on Christmas Island. I asked if it was true that locals threatened to burn down the memorial of the *Janga* were it to be built at the site of the tragedy, a place of low sea cliffs in the middle of Settlement, outside the Golden Bosun bar.

'That's correct,' Gordon told me, 'so we ended up with that propeller, that bent propeller, in a concrete plinth in an isolated place by Tai Jin House, where no-one can ever move or destroy it.'

I move on to the small monument that has drawn me here – the SIEV X memorial. The SIEV X tragedy occurred on 19 October 2001 when 353 men, women and children drowned in international waters on their way from Indonesia to Christmas Island. In this case, the boat is not known to have another name. On mainland Australia there are incredibly moving stories that attest to the good in 'us'; where many Australians have actively stepped up, publicly resisting the extreme dehumanisation witnessed elsewhere. In Canberra, Australian author, activist and psychologist Steve Biddulph was instrumental in initiating a striking, affecting memorial to those aboard the SIEV X who drowned in 2001. The memorial, initiated in 2002, is located in Weston Park, Yarralumla, poignantly close to the location of the Australian Government itself. Three hundred secondary schools were invited to take part in the construction of a monument designed specifically to show the impact and scale of loss of life when the SIEV X sank. Three hundred and fifty-three poles (one pole for each life lost) were placed in an organic formation designed by a

Brisbane student, to reflect the outline of the boat using the actual dimensions of the sunken vessel. The memorial overtly states that those who chose to commemorate the loss of asylum seekers' lives refuse to 'be defined by fear or greed'.

Interestingly, while the ACT Government was supportive of the memorial, the National Capital Authority was placed in an awkward position when the Howard Government opposed the memorial's installation, and permission to erect the memorial was withheld for a year. In an act of defiance, two thousand Canberrans, three hundred artists, as well as church and school groups, joined together in a special ceremony in which the memorial was held up by hand for five minutes. The act of protest was covered by national and international news networks, its powerful statement broadcast in the middle of the Howard era of politicising and demonising refugees' lives. A year later, the memorial poles were physically installed and have remained in place ever since. A friend recently chanced upon this memorial when walking around Lake Burley Griffin: 'It was so unexpected; I didn't know anything about the sinking, and there it was among the trees, I just stumbled upon it. It was amazing to see the sheer scale, to really understand the number of lives lost. I walked up to one pole and it had the name and age of the child who drowned. I realised the child was the same age as my son – I was deeply moved.'

By contrast, the SIEV X memorial on Christmas Island is a simple affair, initiated and lovingly constructed by local Christmas Islanders. Somewhat troublingly, despite the moving and personal way in which the massive loss of life is commemorated, the SIEV X memorial is located even further toward the bushes at the side of the road, situated by a traffic light, behind which the cliff face rises up, plants spilling down its surface, and the jungle begins to take over the space once again. But before I even reach the monument's base, I can see something is terribly wrong. Instead of the scene I remember, with hundreds of rocks inscribed with the names of those who drowned, the concrete base of the monument lies exposed, with a scattering of pebbles lying on the surface interspersed with rotten fallen leaves. A sick feeling rises in my stomach. Where have the rocks gone? How do scores of weighty coral pebbles simply up and disappear?

Yet the plinth with plaque at the centre remains. It reads:

SIEV X

19TH OCTOBER, 2001

In memory of the 146 children,
142 women and 65 men who drowned on
their way to Christmas Island in search
of freedom and a better life.

AS YOU READ THIS PLEASE REMEMBER ALL ASYLUM SEEKERS
WHO HAVE ATTEMPTED THIS TREACHEROUS JOURNEY

I realise for the first time that the two asylum seeker monuments speak to each other: the epitaph of the *Janga* (SIEV 221) memorial has been made to echo that of the SIEV X. At least this hidden plaque gives us some information. But the absence of rocks disturbs me. I look around, hoping they were simply scattered by a whipper snipper and perhaps lie by the fence or along the road, but the inscribed pebbles are nowhere to be seen. I begin to remove the rotten leaves and twigs between the remaining rocks. In that moment I feel watched, look around, but there is no-one there. Walking to the garden at the back of Tai Jin House, I pick bright blooms of bougainvillea and leaves of red and yellow croton plants and take them back, tuck them under the remaining stones. I walk back down the hill feeling heavy, beneath a colourless sky. The ocean no longer winks between the trees.

6. Pete Parts the Wild Horse's Mane

When Jo picked me up from the airport earlier that week, Pete and Jo had chatted about the Tai Chi classes that Pete runs on Wednesday nights at the Community Hall in Poon Saan. After my day visiting the memorial sites, I decide this could be precisely what I need.

At around six in the evening I get in the little car Pete has lent me and drive up the steep slope into the heart of the island's Asian community to join his class. The setting sun casts the Poon Saan flats as an enormous rectangular silhouette. The satellite dishes – by day inconspicuous – are now sharply defined, a black crowd of futuristic creatures perched silently on the apartment's form.

In the hall, the walls are awash with light, saturated by a radiant orange hue, as the sun drops like a rounded ember into a curve of darkening sea. Once inside, the directional light makes the stark hall seem cinematic, its open doors framing a spectacular view over Poon Saan and the ocean beyond.

'Reneé!' Pete says. 'How are you going? I have been meaning to call but it has been busy since I have been back on the island. I am sure you remember what it's like when you've been away ...'

'I do!' I say, imagining Pete having to scrub the mould that seems to make itself at home on the walls of peoples' houses the moment they step onto the plane. I tell Pete my work is going well, about my trips to the cemetery and memorials, and we tee up a time for me to interview him the next day.

'I am a bit nervous,' he laughs. 'What if I don't say anything important?'

'You don't have to,' I reply, 'you're an islander, you've lived here for a long time. Don't forget, Pete, most teachers only stay two or three years, so your perspective can't help but be unique!'

Pete raises an eyebrow playfully, then asks about the dressing on my shoulder. I dismiss it as something minor and avoid this point of conversation in such a public context; my desire to confide in someone is too pressing, my need for reassurance too great.

'Well, we may as well get started,' Pete says to the small gathering of diverse locals, including the local pharmacist, the island's Director of Infrastructure, a mechanic and the woman from behind the counter at the only newsagency. 'We are all at different levels so I will go fairly slowly. Don't worry about getting each position perfectly, just try and follow along.' People take their positions and Pete stands at the front of the room. He talks us through the first couple of steps and we copy. I notice the local mechanic, tall and lean from his labour, moves effortlessly, with certainty, knowing each position by heart.

Once we have the hang of the first few moves, Pete breaks down the rest of the initial series into several parts, explaining the name and meaning of each move and why it is important. The names of the actions are beautiful, poetic – part the wild horse's mane, white crane spreads its wings, carry tiger to mountain – and as he names each one, I have the bizarre realisation that my friend really is Chinese. This thought strikes me simultaneously as both profound and ridiculous. Of course Pete is Chinese, he has been the Mandarin language teacher at the local district high school for years, and I have always been aware of something of Pete's background through our conversations about travel and our shared interest in languages. I had asked to interview Pete with his cultural knowledge in mind. Yet it seems to me now that I had never really considered how Pete's Asian origins affected his identity. With his broad Australian accent, habitual board shorts and surf t-shirts, I had generalised that despite our ostensible differences – my blue eyes and freckled face, and Pete's olive skin and brown eyes set distinctively closer than mine – our experiences of life were reasonably the same.

Pete asks us to follow his actions, joining all the positions together in one continuous movement. I cannot take my eyes off him. A man in many ways like my own father, wry, self-depreciating and emotionally reserved, Pete has unexpectedly transformed into a dancer, graceful, open, confident and lithe. The light catches his high cheekbones, his grey goatee and his lean limbs. Each finger is poised, angled artfully, his wrists turn, his arms gesture out toward the sea. On this occasion, Pete is dressed in a white singlet and plain cotton shorts, and in this cinematic light, someone I have known for years is rendered a stranger, an archetype, timeless, a Chinese man in an island village moving with restrained beauty, aligned with a history I am only beginning to understand.

7. At the Bottom of Our History Is Race

In the morning, I drive up the island's slopes, through Poon Saan heading south to the suburb of Drumsite to interview Peter Wei Cheon Ch'ng. Here, near the top of the island, the landscape flattens out and the road runs parallel to a dusty covered conveyer belt transporting phosphate to the cove for export. Beyond this, the ocean is a thin line glistening in the distance.

Turning off the main road, I drive into the new housing development the government has built for teaching staff. I pull into Pete's driveway, climb the garden stairs and knock on the glass sliding door. No-one answers. While I wait, with a small sense of irony I notice the Education Department has given Pete a ground-floor flat that looks over a small Chinese temple. Out of the corner of my eye, I see someone move. I wave and Pete comes to the front door, which I see now is slightly to the left.

'Sorry, have you been there long?' he asks. 'I didn't hear the doorbell.'

'Sorry, I didn't see there was one, it's all a bit fancy in these new apartments...'

'I know,' Pete agrees, 'but they've done a pretty good job for the Department, don't you think?'

'Yes,' I say, looking around at the bright rooms and open-plan kitchen, quite different to the run-down aluminium home my family shared, full of missing louvres and mould-stained doors.

'I thought I would cook us some lunch,' Pete says, walking back to his gleaming new breakfast bar. 'Do you eat omelette?'

I say I do, that he shouldn't have, but he is already mid-mission, the exhaust fan goes on and he turns to the fridge for eggs.

'So ...' Pete says in between looking for frypans, 'it's good you're doing this, writing about the island, I mean, about asylum seekers and the history here – these stories really need to be told. Because it's the remoteness and isolation that allows things to happen here, still does. Did you hear they had a "Protector of the Chinese"?' Pete raises one eyebrow as he looks at me, then turns his attention to the stove. 'So we need these things out in the open, so people understand. But it's not only the people on this island, it's the people on the *main* island, Australia, who are divorced from what's going on, that are being given false information, or you could say "propaganda", so they don't know and they don't want to know, it's very sinister.'

As Pete talks, I feel moved he has made the effort to cook me lunch so soon after his return. Though we saw each other every day at work when I was on the island, it was my husband and Pete who became friends, through their shared love of playing music. Pete and I have never really spent much time together before, so it is strange to be together like this; strange, but good.

I tell Pete about being out at the fuel buoys and the Border Force vessel's slow slide into my day's frame. As he cuts up onions, I mention I find it interesting he has used the word 'sinister' to talk about what plays out in the Indian Ocean Territories, how it hits the nail on the head for me about something disturbing and unspoken, an unseen, largely unfelt toxicity behind all the beauty and richness of the place.

'And the two aspects were never reconciled,' I say. 'What was incredible and what was beautiful simply sat alongside what was evil and dark, and both things remained true but couldn't quite speak to each other.'

'Well, even more so now there is the terminology "Border Force", and they've all got black uniforms, it is very much like a Nazi uniform. I happened to meet the head of Border Protection a couple of years ago at a dinner when they were still called "Customs" – he was a really nice guy. He said, "Oh yeah, I've got to pack a gun now."'

I feel my body tense at Pete's casual reference to the presence of the Border Force on the island. The Australian Government established the Australian Border Force in July 2015, an agency which resumed control for immigration, customs and border protection, modelled on the UK. The Border Force was established as part of a legislative act that introduced new secrecy provisions preventing those who worked in Australia's detention system from speaking about what they witnessed. During the time of my return to the islands, it was unclear whether the law could be applied retrospectively – for example, whether I could legally share what I witnessed in Australia's detention system from 2011 to 2014. I had received conflicting legal advice from universities and publishers, but reassured myself that the Australian Government was unlikely to imprison a white middle-class woman for sharing her stories – the government simply could not afford the bad press. However, the penalty for revealing 'protected information' was a two-year jail term should my judgement turn out to be wrong, so the latent stress remained.

Suddenly the smoke alarm goes off and Pete swivels around. From the frypan a cloud of thin smoke is rising, beginning to fill the room.

'Oh no, I forgot I was heating the oil!' Pete removes the frypan and turns off the stove and fetches a broom to turn off the smoke alarm.

'Sorry, Pete,' I say, 'I should let you cook.' I shake off my fears and walk over to the couch and start to unpack my recorder and notebook to give Pete some space. When Pete has the kitchen back under control he comes and joins me, sitting across from me, my small recorder resting on the glass table between us. He begins telling me about when he first arrived on the island in 1979, how he had shared a plane with Gordon Bennett. I check my batteries, turn on my device and press 'record'.

'When I arrived, Gordon Bennett was also on the plane, flying in to take up his post. After they registered the union with the Federation of Unions, the Christmas Island Workers Union became official and we had three of the most amazing years. Within the first few weeks there was a strike and they stopped work, it was very exciting and very emotionally powerful. Of course, I loved the drama, they had a hunger strike and a tent city like the Aboriginal people outside Parliament House. There is an amazing amount of history, politics ...'

Thinking back to the polarising effects on the community that the detention of asylum seekers had when I lived there, I ask Pete if he felt that the union movement divided the island at the time.

'Oh, definitely,' Pete replies, 'the government of course supported the private company, the BPC. You have to remember it was a monopoly, so that's why the company could do virtually anything they wanted here because they subsidised Australian farmers for generations – cheap phosphate. Isolation means ignorance, misinformation, you don't know what is happening.'

I ask Pete if he felt particularly passionate about the conditions for Chinese labourers because of his own heritage. He agrees emphatically and begins to tell me about his own encounters with the British Phosphate Commission.

'Initially I was the only Chinese person allowed to live in Silver City,' Pete tells me. 'At the welcome to all of the teachers, I felt a bit uneasy about this, so I went up to talk to the manager of the BPC. They were all English, predominantly. I went up to him and I asked "So, tell me, why am I allowed to live in Silver City?" I was just being cheeky, playing with the fact that I was not white. He replied, "Because you are an honorary white." I was fuming and upset at his response, so I nearly resigned and left. But I had met Gordon Bennett by then and so I thought, no, these are interesting times. I won't leave.'

As he speaks, Pete has become animated, leaning toward me, his eyes lit, body alive. His experiences of racism in what he thought to be a progressive country in such recent times as the late 1970s have evidently had a lasting impact. He makes eye contact, is present with me, yet from time to time his gaze focuses on a point beside me, like he is seeing the people and places he has encountered on the island all over again.

'The teachers were immediately members of the Christmas Island Club,' Pete continues, 'which was *the* white place, and I remember going to movie nights. There were about four or five Asian supervisors at this time who were allowed to be members and a couple of them were also allowed to live in Silver City because of their standing. When we went to the club on movie nights, all the Asians would sit to one side and the whites on the other, so this is really apartheid in modern Australia in nineteen seventy-nine. Such a shock. The other islanders, including the teachers, were told not to get involved.'

'Someone told me once there were even separate swimming pools, Pete – is that true?'

'Yes, there was a swimming pool down by the post office and no Asians were allowed because Asians had a separate swimming pool. The Asians' pool was a cooling pool for the big machines, so the water would gradually get hotter and hotter and dirtier and dirtier over the course of the day. So one night, I smuggled some Asian friends into the CI Club to swim there. The next day I got a call from the same English guy.'

Pete holds up a make-believe phone, extending his thumb to his ear and his pinkie finger toward his mouth, as he impersonates the austere voice of the British Phosphate Commission's manager, "Peter, I believe you had some *non-members* at the pool?"' Pete starts to chuckle, then shakes his head. 'I said, "Do you mean Asians?" I told him he could stick his membership and stopped going there from that point. Christmas Island was an amazing place then, it was an amazing time.'

Pete tells me that there were, in effect, two communities in the late 1970s on the island: the Asian community and the white community. The white community lived predominantly in the colonial buildings overlooking the ocean in Settlement (where I have hired my accommodation for this trip), as well as in Silver City where the government workers were accommodated, while the Asian community lived further up the slopes in Poon Saan. Pete tells me that if, as an Asian person, you were found walking through Settlement, the white community would ring the police and you would be physically removed.

'It was crazy,' Pete tells me. 'Apartheid.'

In those days, Silver City housed a lot of teachers, with several teachers also housed at Drumsite, where he currently lives. The Malay population lived in the Kampong down at Flying Fish Cove. All the big houses belonged to the British Phosphate Commission.

'So it was really sharply defined,' Pete says, and I consider the ways in which the community continues to be structured in much the same way, though presumably now by choice, as members of the Christmas Island population tend to be drawn to live alongside people with common heritage.

'Were the Malay people allowed to come to the CI Club?'

'Oh no, no Malays at all. There were only a few Chinese, you know. So again, I think this is how distance and living on an island protects a lifestyle and a worldview. Even the schooling system was separated. The fact is that people had rarely even heard of the islands, and this excluded us from the mainland consciousness, there was a kind of monopoly over people's lives. It was the same with the cheap phosphate, no-one recognised what was happening to the workers here, the whole thing was bordering on unethical, almost criminal, I think. If a company did that today ...' Pete looks over at the pile of chopped onions on the bench in the kitchen. 'Anyway, enough of that, I will shut up for a while and cook!'

After we have eaten, Pete tells me that despite all of the challenges of island life, what keeps him on Christmas Island is the way it pares things back, returns him to the question of what life is about. He tells me that he has shed a lot of baggage here, particularly the baggage that comes with the need for material possessions. The island has become a place that has helped him live simply, move slowly. I remember when I left the Indian Ocean Territories, I promised myself that I would take this experience of simplicity back with me, a life largely offline, where there was enough time, where you could be present, do one thing in each moment and stay with it until it was done. A life of reduced options, having no family and limited friends, meant I experienced, for the first time in my adult life, there being enough time for everyone and everything.

Yet once back on the mainland, the happiness afforded by this way of being slipped away. It did not seem possible to translate the island pace to the stimulation and richness of city life. Now, sitting here with Pete, I remember what I have lost. Christmas

Island, with its layered human history, has been troubled from the start, but for those allowed their freedom on this semi-submarine mountain, what it gifts you is in many ways a rare simplicity, what feels like a step back into another time.

As we continue talking, I am intrigued to learn Pete was born in Singapore, not China as I had assumed, and moved to Australia when he was only thirteen. He left a violent father, but was ready for a new adventure, moving in with his adoptive family in Sydney. His new family were kind, but life was hard, and it was only once Pete left Asia that he remembers experiencing racism for the first time.

'When I was growing up it was the White Australia policy, the Yellow Peril, whereas these days it is mainly prejudice against Muslims. When I went to boarding school, I was called a "boong" because they didn't have any other names. We had kids from New Guinea and they called them "boongs", so I was a "boong". And then there were Italians who were "wogs", so I was a "wog" ... So I was called "boong", "wog", and the Vietnamese were called "slopes", so you'd get bundled up in all of that. And I can laugh about it now, for the most part. Once I became a teacher, I think I had the respect I wouldn't otherwise have had. That is why I was so determined to speak English better than Australians and I wanted to do a degree in English. I was also born in a British colony, so by accident I have been very fortunate in my working life, but I never thought I was going to be standing in front of a class of people who would call me a "wog" and help them realise I was simply another human being.'

While I had a vague sense of the White Australia policy as a racist piece of legislation severely limiting non-white migration and employment in Australia's colonial past, it is not up until this point in my conversation with Pete that I comprehend that this policy continued to exist in Australia's constitution well into recent history. The *Immigration Restriction Act 1901* marked the formal beginning of the White Australia policy. It was one of the founding pieces of legislation introduced to the newly formed parliament on 23 December 1901. The White Australia policy remained within our constitution until its dismantling in the mid-1960s, and was not officially eradicated until the Whitlam Government introduced policies such as the *Racial Discrimination Act 1975*. Ironically, it is actually within the White Australia policy that we see the first notions of our 'Fair Go' nation articulated. White Australia saw itself as a 'new' country, establishing its identity as a progressive 'working man's paradise' that rallied for equal rights and opportunities for its citizens. However, these rights and opportunities were sanctioned for 'desirable' Australians only. Those cast as inferior and therefore receiving lower wages became a threat to this ideal – that is, non-whites, Aboriginal and Torres Strait Islander Australians and even women. The legislative response was made to directly limit non-white migration to Australia, but the hostility in the nation was most overtly directed toward people of Asian descent, who were seen as intellectually and morally deficient. Our 'Fair Go' nation was born out of negation.

This sanctioned hostility toward Asian culture contributed to the racism that Pete had to endure after his arrival in Sydney as a thirteen-year-old. Pete tells me his way of navigating this prejudice and learning to cope with racism in his adult life was by acquiring a persona that enabled him to throw himself into his white world, essentially by playing the clown.

'Good morning, I am your Engwish teacher,' Pete would say to his new class of year seven students, straight-faced, deadpan, waiting for their response, and from this sense of play, connection and respect between him and his students was formed. 'So really, that was fun, then. I was very lucky. But I had to become this clown to overcome my stuff.'

Hearing Pete's last statement – the idea that his experience of racism was 'his stuff' – I feel a dull sense of sadness, a small amount of shame. When I was on Christmas Island in 2011, Chinese Christmas Islanders made up sixty per cent of the population. Yet apart from the interactions with members of the community through my workplace and the rich festivals organised by the Chinese community, the extent of my interactions with the island's dominant culture was largely limited to ordering sweet-and-sour fish on a Friday night at Lucky Ho.

I wonder at this, and think back to my own upbringing, to my formative ideas about Asia. I remember watching a group of Chinese tourists walking with friends and family at Cottesloe Beach, my mother's quiet aside about the 'Asian Invasion'. I can hear the spite in my father's tone talking about 'the Japs', and his tirade of quiet curses directed at 'Asian drivers'. I am left with the sense of a group of people hardly visible in my middle-class suburb in the hills of Perth, and barely tolerated. The silence and anger around Asian culture in my home, especially from my father, cause me to wonder what my father had learned from his own father, who returned from World War II hard and troubled, violent and schizophrenic.

To be fair, I recognise the main reason I did not actively form relationships with members of the Chinese community, or any community members apart from work colleagues and asylum seekers, was due to my own experience of being overwhelmed by what I witnessed working within Australia's detention system. Yet I begin to wonder if there was a vague and unacknowledged influence from the mundane racism that I encountered during childhood. Perhaps that is one reason I am here, perhaps that is why I feel the need to listen carefully, deeply. I want Pete to whittle away at that latent part of me that unknowingly continues to gives prejudice a home.

As the interview draws to a close, Pete and I begin to talk about the sea and the link it forms between him and Asia. Pete tells me he was born on an island, and this distinct geographical orientation affects his experience of place.

'I think I always liked that idea of being almost surrounded by a force, an element, and it comes up with the Tai Chi approaches I was talking about, the energy. I love it.' Pete tells me about *dantian*, or the 'sea of qi', the 'sea of energy' within us all, and the fluidity of water, literally and metaphorically connecting him with his own history, with Singapore, China and Hong Kong.

'I didn't realise you lived in Hong Kong as well!' I say, feeling my notions of Pete's identity becoming unravelled, teasing out to be something far more intricate than I first considered.

'When I lived in Hong Kong, I thought I would stay there for ever,' Pete says, 'because the Asian part of me sometimes wells up and I think *I don't really belong here*. I can be sitting with a group of people and having a great time, there is nothing wrong – it is almost schizophrenic sometimes. I think, *Oh, today I just want to be Asian*, or something. So I go and see an Asian friend. It's weird. When I moved to Christmas Island it was like, not coming home, like coming home to Singapore, but coming home to myself, I think. That's what it was. My impressions of Christmas Island were very positive; it was exciting with the politics of it as well. I am very privileged, I feel, to be here. The ocean comes and goes, it is good, it is transient, it suits my nature. I have this kind of love affair with this island and that has everything to do with the ocean.'

We start to wrap up because Pete needs to get to the post office before it closes at three. As I pack up my things, he tells me that while he feels ashamed of many aspects of Australian culture, he holds hope for change.

'Australia as an island is so isolated, but we are changing. Two of my three kids are already married to non-Asians, my grandkids will all be Eurasian, so the integration between cultures will happen. For that reason, I think Australia can still be a great country if it wants to be, or we can choose to be a mediocre country that stumbles along. But I think at the bottom of our history is race, starting with Aboriginal Australians. If we don't face that one...' and here he trails off. I pick up my bag and recorder. We hug goodbye briefly and then Pete hurries to grab his keys.

After my conversation with Pete, I am shocked to find we have talked for three hours, and I laugh wondering how long this conversation will take to transcribe once I am home. Then I become conscious of the fact I don't actually mind. The stories Pete has told me feel incredibly important to my own understanding of the country where I live and the nuances of identity that to take time with the recordings feels good, feels right. To trace the residues of racism in my own life is both confronting and freeing: confronting that, despite my best efforts, I have not entirely removed prejudice from my mind; freeing that Pete's stories can help me see it, each story giving me a chance to set some rigidity in me free. It is as though in the act of honouring the weight of Pete's words, we both came out the other side a little lighter, his stories helping me to step more gently on the earth.

8. A Door in My Ribs

Driving away from Pete's home in Drumsite, I sit with all that he has shared, and understand that his honesty – the sharing of some of his most difficult experiences with me – is a privilege, a gift freely given. Returning to my little cottage in Settlement, I lie once again under the air-conditioner, bathed in sunlight. Outside, an ancient frangipani holds deeply coloured blossoms against the sky. Later that afternoon, feeling refreshed, I make my way down to Flying Fish Cove. I cannot swim due to the incision in my shoulder, but at least I can cool my feet in the water, watching the sun lower itself into the sea.

Driving past the Chinese Literary Association, I glimpse a small temple, then the community chalkboards, where all the island's notices are written in bright colours, come into view. 'In Loving memory of Mr Gordon Bennett, Saturday 30th of July @ 2.30pm, Resting Place, Chinese Cemetery', one panel reads; 'Special Screening, *The Big Brother of Christmas Island, The Legend of Tai Ko Seng*', reads another, and I am sorry to have just missed such an important occasion for Christmas Islanders. 'Plastic-free July' reads another, but I miss the rest as I turn left off the roundabout, pass the Kampong and drive down toward the water.

At the cove, the day is bright; it will be a little while yet before the sun sets. The phosphate ship has finished being loaded – a plume of thin brown dust hovers around the vessel like a dull aura. The enormous blue ship I noticed earlier sits further out to sea, past the drop off. *OCEAN SHIELD, SYDNEY* bold script reads along its prow. Bright life rafts glow orange, embedded high in the body of ship's stern. A large crane sits at the vessel's centre.

Coral pebbles clonk under my feet as I near the shore. By the water's edge I hunt for shells, lift coloured shards of sea-worn glass to the light. I pick up one coral rock and turn it over, observing it is around the same size as those used to form the SIEV X memorial. Picking up another, then another, somewhat guiltily, I glance over my shoulder, hoping no-one sees what I am about to do. It is not my monument, I was not here when more than three hundred people drowned out beyond the horizon in this same sea, yet I do not feel I can leave the memorial so diminished. I feel torn, wonder if there is someone I should contact, someone I should ask. Still, I feel so strongly the need to resist the forces of forgetting, the ache of silence surrounding each lost life.

Going back and forward between the pebbled beach and my belongings, I pile around twenty coral stones by my towel. None of the people scattered along the bay seem to notice. I return and rest my feet in the gently lapping water. The sun is low on the horizon now, clouds layer themselves, some white, thin and wispy, high against the blue; others gather low and grey, yet not foreboding. I head out along the jetty where the shapes of fish are visible in the water below. At the end a man is fishing from the lower platform. I take the steps down to the grey plastic mesh that hovers above the water's surface and ask him if he is having any luck.

'Not yet,' he replies, 'it's just an excuse to be here, really.'

He introduces himself as Tom. Tom is tall, broad-shouldered and fair-haired, with an open face, wearing his hi-vis work clothes. He asks why I am here and we talk about island life, its cliques and challenges, the beautiful simplicity, the pared-back slowness of it all. I talk about my own frustration with the ins and outs of small-group politics, especially with the loaded job of teaching asylum-seeker children during my time on Christmas Island, and share my disbelief about a time when a teacher (who had been there at the scene on the day of the Christmas Island boat tragedy) later suggested labelling a new cocktail for work drinks as 'Refos on the Rocks'.

'Yeah, but sometimes you've got to laugh at the darkest things,' he says, 'or you go mad. I don't have a problem with that.' Then he adds, 'I was there too, actually, on that day.'

We both look out to horizon where Tai Jin House has begun to become grander than usual, a stark silhouette surrounded by sharply defined palms, their bold shapes striking against the glowing sky.

'At first I thought it sounded like people at the footy,' Tom says, 'you know, the rise and fall of voices.'

It was about six am when Tom stood on the verandah of his home near Rocky Point, trying to make sense of the sound. He grabbed his camera, thinking something historic might be happening, and ran out toward the sea, toward the Golden Boson pub.

'There was a boat at the edge of the island,' Tom continues, 'all the people on board. One guy said, "I wonder if we could throw rocks at them from here." I said, "Come off it, mate, there are little kids in there."'

I flinch, look toward him, but Tom does not seem to see.

'The backflow from the cliffs was keeping the boat away from the rocks. At one point, the prow dipped and a man stepped off the boat and onto the rocks. I said, "Shit! Look, there's man standing right there!" As the boat came further around the point, it became windier and there was no longer the backflow to push it away from the rocks. It began to take on water.'

Now that Tom has begun to tell me his story, it seems hard for him to stop, the words welling out, as if from a capped spring, a river wanting to find its way to the sea. The handful of swimmers have left the bay as the day comes to an end; there is no longer anyone else around. In front of us, the water glints in the last rays. I look up to the edge of the cove, past the infrastructure of the small port, to where Rocky Point sits out of sight. I imagine the boat metres off the edge of the island, the powerful swell of the wet season surging and foaming against the cliffs. So different to the stillness of the dry season, these days of blue skies and wide horizons, of glassy paradisiac waters.

Tom tells me the boat had begun to smash against the cliffs. The islanders on shore ran to get life jackets to throw into the water, trying to urge the asylum seekers to swim away.

'There were dead babies floating in the water,' Tom says without emotion. 'The islanders had a rope and they tried to form a chain, while at the same time holding up their arms to avoid the debris from the broken boat the swell was throwing in the air. Everyone was getting covered in diesel and water. People in the water reached for the rope, but then a wave would come, draw back, and the asylum seekers would be gone. I knew there were caves under the water beneath the cliff. I saw a little girl with blonde hair, maybe five or six years old. She was between the sinking boat and the cliff. A man was standing there looking pretty stunned on the broken boat. The people had their clothes ripped off by the surge. All the people drowning had lost their clothes. There were so many people, it was too much to take in, so I just focused on the little girl.'

Tom looks at me now as he speaks, but his eyes are full of memories, vivid and raw. He tells me the girl had a life jacket on, that he signalled to the man on the boat to reach out and grab the little girl.

'He lifted her up by her life jacket, up and out the water like a ragdoll,' Tom tells me, 'but she was still breathing and moving her head. Then a wave came and slammed the boat against the cliff. People and debris were strewn everywhere. We knew the Navy was around the corner at Ethel Beach. We thought they must be coming at any moment. Another Navy vessel was further out to sea. No-one came. Until the boat was in pieces and spread across the coast, nobody from the Navy arrived. When the Navy finally turned up at the scene, there was pieces of broken boat and bodies scattered everywhere. We were signalling from the cliff to the officers in the Zodiacs where people were still alive.'

Tom looks down at the water. 'Nobody talks about it. They had some kind of memorial service or something, but I didn't go, it was people not directly involved who wanted to be in on the action, wanting to be seen to be there.'

I don't move, don't make a sound, just try to hold, to contain the weight of what he has just told me. I do not tell Tom I was one of those at the memorial service. Instead I look out at a dramatic black headland obscuring the sun, a yacht picturesque on the water's glass, the sky burning, blazing with orange light.

When I return to my cottage, there is no longer any question. Tom's story, though about the *Janga*, has galvanised my will to redress the undoing of the SIEV X memorial. I log on to my computer and start to search for the SIEV X online commemoration sites. I take the rough, round coral pebbles I have collected and a black marker from my computer bag, and begin to inscribe the names listed on the screen – 'Zahara, 9 years', 'Miya, 4 years', 'Diya Alsadi' (no age listed), 'Raged Alsadi' (no age listed), 'Amir, 61' and, heartbreakingly, simply the word 'Baby'. I can no longer wait for my actions to be sanctioned, for permission, to care whether others judge my decision as right or wrong. Each act of inscription becomes an honouring, each name a will to see and grieve, a pushback to those in authority, as well as those living on this island, who insist on other people's erasure. These lives meant something, each person brimming with hope for their future, each person wishing to live the fullness of their one human life.

I line the coral pebbles along the arms of the lounge chairs and when it is done, and there are no more pebbles on which to write, I stop crying, wipe my eyes. For each act has felt like a door in my ribs pushed out against a harsh wind, opening me wide, inviting the whole beautiful, troubled world in.

9. Hand Held to the Flow

On Saturday morning I drive up the slope from Settlement through Poon Saan then turn left, heading to the top of the island up the steep slope of Phosphate Hill. Here the hospital sits high on the ridge, looking out over the sporadic building sites of a small new housing development designed to take advantage of the site's wide vista looking over the sea. Once inside, I do not have to wait long before a nurse steps into the waiting room and calls my name. Stepping into the small consulting room, I am surprised and delighted to see that the nurse is Jeannette, a Cocos Islander who married into, and has become a part of, the Cocos Malay community. Jeannette's blue-green *tudung* frames her pale face, spilling out in folds over her shoulders and nursing uniform.

'I wondered if it was you when I saw the name on the form,' says Jeannette, putting down my file, and we embrace, then get talking about Cocos life, about my time on Christmas Island and about my interviews, as she and Nek Su are on my Cocos list.

'I am here doing some shiftwork for a few weeks,' Jeannette tells me. 'We head back to Cocos on Saturday, I think Nek Su would be happy to go tomorrow, he is already missing his fishing!'

I am grateful to have Jeannette, rather than a stranger, remove my stitches when I feel so vulnerable. Jeannette commiserates that it is a horrible feeling, she has had several biopsies too, but reassures me, though more cautiously than I would like, saying, 'I am sure it is probably okay, I think you might find it will all work out fine,' but her brow furrows as she takes out the plastic thread from my shoulder, and after the last section is removed, she does not look me in the eye.

When she has cleaned up, we return to talking excitedly about Cocos, about the colour of the water, people and places we know, about the joy of being surrounded by beauty, the peace of floating on the lagoon when the world is still. Soon I realise I should go as Jeannette has other patients to attend to, so we hug one more time and I step out of the hospital, out of the air-conditioning and back into the shock of the day's humidity.

I head back down Phosphate Hill Road, where the ocean is riding improbably high on the horizon, turn left onto Murray Road and drive straight out of town. Leaving the asphalt and turning into a wide powdery limestone track, I feel a new freedom, moving out in widening circles to places and memories I hold dear. A phosphate truck passes me, its wall of metal throwing up a plume of white dust, then I am alone, swerving around potholes driving into the deep embrace of the rainforest.

Even though I am hesitant about taking Pete's car on such a rough track, I can imagine the Dales glistening in the morning light. I am keen to get another taste of the island's wild heart. In my pack there is water, snacks and plenty of repellent, as well as my fully charged phone, though it is unlikely there will be any reception if I get stranded out there.

The Dales are a unique, Ramsar-listed wetland boasting seven near-pristine watercourses. As well as being incredibly beautiful, this ecosystem also provides the habitat for wetland-dependent, nationally threatened species, including the Abbott's booby bird and Christmas Island frigatebird. Christmas Island supports the greatest diversity of land crabs on an oceanic island anywhere in the world, and the Dales are a striking visual reminder of this, with all twenty species found on the site. Most notable is the red crab (which number tens of millions on the island, and whose spawn in turn provides the habitat and feeding ground for whale sharks in the surrounding waters), endemic blue crabs and the large, forbidding forms of robber crabs. Hughs Dale (where I am heading today) is particularly loved and frequented by islanders and tourists alike, as it is one of the rare places on the island where the permanent and perennial streams that course the island actually come to the surface.

Having believed I would never see this lush and magical world again, I am filled with joy and much anticipation, bumping my way along the road lined by tall, profusely flowering yellow bushes. At the sight of the workshop shed, I turn off Murray Road onto North West Point Road, and it is here I remember I will have to drive past the turn-off to the highly secretive North West Point detention centre. Even the thought fills me with rage, and I thump the steering wheel, feel my shoulders tense.

Soon the enormous green sign comes into view, with a curved line indicating the road to the Dales on the left and another short line that extends to the right, at the end of which are the letters IDC. The initials further incense me. In 2011 the detention centre was one of the largest employers on the island, yet it hides behind the ambiguity of three letters, the sign's abbreviation obscuring its dark economy: Immigration Detention Centre – a site of twelve attempted suicides or incidences of self-harm *every day*. The large infrastructure of the centre does not even rate a dot point on the tourist map beside me.

Pulling over on the verge across from the sign, I walk into the luminous rainforest on the path that leads down toward West White Beach, picking up a branch to clear the webs across the way made by large striped orb spiders. Here the frigates call and click their long beaks, others carrying large twigs and branches to nests high in the canopy. Booby birds groan like dissatisfied old men, or croak conversationally from treetops. The familiar, surprisingly sweet smell of rotting leaves and guano rises up, air thick with water and humming with green. As the track starts to become steeper, I stop and turn back. The forest will soon give way to limestone cliffs, meaning walkers have to scale the small face using an anchored length of rope. Being here on my own and not having told anyone where I am going, I am reluctant to take the risk.

Sweating into the humidity, I walk back up the path and out into the clearing, stopping at the detention centre gate. It is open and no-one is in the small, purpose-built guard's office. During the time of the riots, the boom here was down and guards stood edgily, twitching with tension in their black uniforms, talking into radios, one guard even following me part of the way as I took the path down to the beach.

Here on the road heading into the centre, I stand on my toes, try to see at least a little way in to the detention area, but the secrecy of the site is well planned and effective, foliage and a small rise in the hill screening off almost all of the view in. Only the slightest flash of roof and a glimpse of the centre's ominous high foyer are visible, the rest is obscured and unknowable. From my previous visits I know that the incarceration area is littered with CCTV cameras and I don't want to draw attention to myself, so I get back in the car and close the door behind me. Back onto North West Point Road, I take the first turn left, heading west, driving under long arms of orange hibiscus, down into rainforest and the watery world that is the Dales.

Pulling into the first carpark, I stop, get out and look down at the 4WD track below. The road is steep, chiselled and uneven from the action of runoff carving small canyons in its surface. I walk the rest of the way down and at once am pleased with my decision, as all around me layers of life, impossible to witness from a car window, open up to me. Fungi layer themselves up textured trunks, supple cups catching rain. Lichen and mosses paint brown trunks in a palette of greens, darkest khaki to an iridescence that is almost white. Strange plants splay like rubber fans from rotting logs, while other plants form sculptures that speak to me of the sea: coral shapes so layered and textured they are almost their own landscape, variegated colours looking calcified yet soft to touch.

I climb over logs toward the sound of water. One of the streams has come to the soil's surface, and I discover a scene so perfect it almost feels contrived. An incredibly clear tributary rendered almost invisible by its lack of sediment weaves its way through a small gully lined with tree ferns. Wide roots curl out and catch the water with their curved shapes, and in the small pools formed by their brown cups, light-blue crabs stand with their claws in the gently flowing water, pincers raised at my arrival like a salute.

Taking off my shoes, I immerse my feet in the cool water, follow the flow further downstream, where it cascades over a tumble of limestone. Over the limestone, a thick white layer has formed like a wide smooth stalactite, resembling what could easily be an artisan's water feature in an elaborate garden. Within the flow of the water, the rocks' grooves have trapped leaves of the brightest red – angled and stationary, lit and glistening, they are small installations in a world of greens and browns.

My experience of environments rich in biodiversity on Christmas Island and the Cocos (Keeling) Islands taught me daily that a deep joy resides where we see life thrive. I feel it here, where the triumph of life is resounding, light exultant in leaves, abundance pushing up rich and strong. I laugh out loud with joy, stand there drinking the beauty in, looking, breathing, watching.

Only reluctantly do I leave and make my way back to the road. Once back at the dirt track, I continue down the slope, where banyan trees drape their elaborate shapes across the path, forming living archways, and I feel heralded, as if I am stepping through an ancient threshold. Reaching the bottom carpark, I am surprised to see no other cars there, then recall it is the time of the Festival of the Hungry Ghost, so many Chinese Christmas Islanders will not venture into the jungle for fear of troubled spirits at this time.

This idea of troubled spirits does not worry me; in fact, I am pleased to be alone in my return to such a special place. Past the signage, I step onto the boardwalk, and memories seep their way into me. I feel a choking sensation in my chest but keep moving, letting it wash through me, holding the burning gift of being able to return. Past the boardwalk, another clear stream spreads wide across the forest floor, and twenty or thirty red crabs glisten in its shallow waters. Walking through mud, I am reminded of my first experience of robber crabs madly waving their massive claws, like alien trolls guarding this entrance as my family stepped hesitantly between their bodies. It is drier here today and the path is clear. While it makes the thoroughfare easier to navigate, I miss their heralding, their strange blue-and-orange armour, large antennae breathing in an olfactory picture of each intruder.

At the stairs, I begin to ascend the hill up through what has to be one of the most incredible sights on earth. Hughs Dale is a place of beauty expressed in the extreme, like walking into Avalon, sunlight glistening in a world hushed with foliage. Here, Tahitian chestnuts form a wide grove, ancient and enormous. Beneath their repeated forms, buttress roots curl in a sheen of water ten or twenty metres wide. In its flow, red crabs and robber crabs sit like strange creatures from another planet, lacquered by light resting on their water-bright shells. The air is filled with the sounds of birds whooping and calling, percussion of water falling, wind-song whispering in the leaves.

I walk slowly, drinking in every leaf, every creature, climbing the steps until I reach the end of the path. And there it is, the waterfall, its storeys of liquid light, cascading over its own mineral formation, ferns and mosses, lichen and limestone. And at the base of its flow, so vividly, I can see him, trousers rolled up to his shins, his face troubled but alive – Massom, with his hand held out to the flow. In that image is all the beauty and heartbreak I have held for five years; in that memory, I began to comprehend the reasons why I have returned.

10. Behind the Wire

I first met Massom through a woman called Michelle, whose family lived on Christmas Island. Michelle was an education assistant at the school where I was working, writing her PhD about Australia's detention system. She had actively built relationships with many asylum seekers, both in the family detention centres at Phosphate Hill and out at North West Point, the latter purpose-built for adult male asylum seekers. Michelle knew I was interested in working with asylum seekers and was struggling to support the number of people with whom she had formed relationships, so she offered to take me out to North West Point to meet a friend.

I don't remember the drive through the rainforest, nor do I remember what we talked about, but I do recall the strange feeling of driving into a zone that was cordoned off from the life and eyes of the public, like a large blank space on a collective map. As we drove in, razor wire shone in large luminous curls, an endless glistening swell in the muted light that made its way between clouds. At the corners of buildings, over doorways and along walkways, the repeated forms of metal boxes – CCTV cameras – cast their gaze over every angle and surface. I can no longer visualise the details as we passed through security, though Michelle must have spoken through the intercom for us to be let into the foyer, then there would have been paperwork, signing in and our bags passing through the X-ray machine, then stepping through the metal detectors as if they were a portal to another world.

What stays with me is the series of steel reinforced doors, thick as the span of my hand, that we had to wait for the guard to unlock in order to pass through, as though we were in a place surrounded by violent rapists, treading among serial killers. It felt incongruous, that vulnerable people fleeing this very kind of violence would find themselves locked up as though they themselves had committed their nations' crimes.

We walked down a dull tunnel, through more locked steel doors. While we waited for the doors to be opened, the architecture became oppressive. Here I was diminished, found myself losing my desire to speak. We came out of the corridor and into a room where someone watched us from behind a desk through a window. First, we met a young Iranian man who had some English. Michelle and the man chatted, but I couldn't focus, struggled to think. The young man talked about the extreme boredom in detention for him and his friends. Michelle encouraged him to keep going to the gym, to keep active. The man told us he could not always go to the gym because the camp was currently so crowded, but he reassured Michelle he would go when he could. Michelle gave him some biscuits and a guard took him away.

The room continued bearing down on me, fluorescent light casting a cold light on the stark and featureless small spaces, claustrophobic in the extreme. There was no colour, there were no pictures, no windows except those between rooms that left me with a sense of being continually watched. I felt my mind starting to detach from my body, everything in me saying, *Run! Run!*

I was struck by the sensation of feeling ridiculous, helpless, like I was a voyeur or a scientist witnessing some kind of gruesome experiment. *What happens to young men if we do this, and then this, and what about that …* Michelle turned to me and I smiled, trying to look appreciative of her efforts to include me. A year later when I moved to Cocos, I would revisit this memory, watching news footage of long-term detainees in this same detention centre on TV. The men on the screen, having committed no crime and being offered no future, dug their own graves in the courtyard, lay down and asked to die. But in 2011 at North West Point with Michelle, I had no concept of what would play out in years to come for detainees held on this island and elsewhere. We waited as the guard brought in another young man. We were introduced to Massom, who had come with a friend. Massom was a lean Afghan man in his early twenties, with high cheekbones and olive skin. He wore a silver ring set with a large turquoise stone. Massom only spoke Dari, so he was accompanied by a friend who had offered to translate.

Massom's friend Reza was also Afghan. He was short, chatty and affable, although he did not smile. By contrast, everything in Massom's body language started to ring alarm bells in me. Though he looked fit, Massom stood stooped, almost curling into himself. His eyes had a glazed and haunted look, as if everything in him would like to disappear. I felt a sense of panic rising in me. For a moment I was no longer in the room. I sped away to the mainland, where I stood as a child, ten years old. A security guard wearing a blank face pressed a button inside glazed double doors. With my mother and two siblings, I walked through one door into a tiny foyer that felt even smaller as the first door closed behind us. We stood quiet and suspended in this strange sealed place, neither inside nor outside. Then a second door opened to a sullen woman at a checkpoint in the high-security psychiatric unit, who pointed us to a yard surrounded by barbed wire. Here I found the stooped form of my highly medicated father. With his elbows on his knees on a rough wooden bench, he lifted his head only slightly, said hello, voice strange, body racked with shame and defeat.

Michelle began to introduce us, and I was brought back to the present. I waved hello and tried to look into Massom's eyes, but he kept his brow low. I thought of the elephants at Perth Zoo, cordoned in concrete too long. There was great excitement as the new enclosure was built, a lush and generous expanse filled with gardens, ponds and vines. When the elephants were finally moved, they walked in the same figure of eight, didn't touch the grasses, didn't roll in dust. Round and round their footsteps went, pacing their mind's perimeters, forever inscribed with the size and shape of their former cage.

My mind whirred, my heart beat so hard I could feel its hurried rhythm in my chest. Massom's voice did not sound right, like his tongue was thick, like he had no air. He fidgeted, distracted, body wilting before us. My mind repeated over and over what I immediately and deeply knew: *if this man is forced to stay much longer in this place, he will not survive.*

Michelle gave the men biscuits and chocolate, and Reza began talking about what had been happening in the detention centre since Michelle's last visit. Michelle asked Massom if he had heard anything more about his visa. As Reza translated, Massom's face wore an expression like he was in pain. He became more agitated, even animated, talking in small bursts, his brow furrowed, his hand with the blue stone rising and falling as he spoke.

Reza interpreted, telling us that Massom had been through his second round of interviews. Massom could not sleep, he was worried. The Department of Immigration had been using Iranian interpreters, and Massom believed that the Iranian interpreters were racist toward Afghan people. He was upset because he feared the interpreters were downplaying his case – he worried that they would not pass on information vital to gaining his refugee status.

Michelle asked Massom about his inability to sleep, and Reza interpreted that Massom tossed and turned all night, that he could not stop thinking about what had happened to him, he went over and over all he had been through in Afghanistan. He had been waiting for his visa for months, just waiting with nothing to do except worry about the interpreters and sit around.

'He is scared he is going to go crazy,' Reza told us. 'He said he is worried he is going to be sent back to Afghanistan and things will be even worse than before, because not only will he be back with all the problems in his country, but he will also be crazy. He says he can't wait anymore, he is very scared he is going to go crazy.'

Michelle encouraged Massom to hang in there, assured him that his visa was being progressed and that she would keep coming to check on him. Reza excused himself and left for his appointment. Michelle tried to continue to the conversation with small phrases of Dari, checking in with Massom on her pronunciation, but real conversation became virtually impossible. Eventually we said goodbye and Massom bowed slightly with his hands pressed together.

'Thank you,' he whispered in English, then the guard came and we were taken away, back through locked and steel-bolted doors, under surveillance cameras, through X-ray machines and back outside, the fence wire glinting brightly in midday sun.

Michelle must have been used to this, she was chatty, seemed almost cheery, but I could barely speak. I asked her how to apply to take people out of the centre, vowed to myself I would get this man out from behind the wire, that I would help him hold on to life until the day he was handed his visa.

11. A Person Like Any Other

It took me several calls and a large amount of legal paperwork, but the day finally came around when my husband, Ash, and I were able to take Massom out of the detention centre and show him a little bit of the island where he lived. I organised to take another asylum seeker, Ehsan, who acted as a volunteer interpreter in my classroom, so Massom was able to communicate with Ash and me. Ehsan was an Iranian student around seventeen years old, slim, intelligent and pale-skinned with immaculate nails. He had a strong command of English though his first language was Farsi. Farsi and Dari are similar languages, so it made some communication with Massom possible.

We picked Ehsan up first from the Phosphate Hill family compound, signing him out at the security checkpoint where the overweight, bleach-blonde Serco guard sternly warned us he was due back at three p.m. 'and no later'. We then headed back out into the national park, bumping our way over the white dirt road toward North West Point. Arriving at North West Point for the second time, though the site remained confronting, I felt almost breathless, hardly believing that, despite all the signs signalling a site of punishment and deprivation, Massom would be allowed to step through the door's portal and into our lives. And after more form signing and an even sterner warning, he did. The air became light. We walked out to the car in sunshine, and there he was with us. Massom became a person like any other, sitting in the back seat of our car.

We drove up the small hill and out of the detention centre. Heading back toward town, a cloud of frigatebirds wove their dark paths over a conglomeration of old sheds. Massom pointed and Ehsan asked what they were called. We talked about the frigates, driving along like it is the most ordinary thing in the world.

As we bumped over the wide limestone road, I turned to Ehsan in the back seat. Ehsan and I had been working together for some months, and I knew he was self-assured and open to robust discussion, so I felt I could ask him questions that I would not ask of other detainees.

'Ehsan,' I ventured, 'I am not meaning to be disrespectful, but I would like to learn more about your story. It is just a bit confusing trying to work it all out. I guess for most people it would be easy to see why Massom is seeking asylum as there is a war in Afghanistan, but there is not a war in Iran, though clearly people have needed to leave. I guess I have wondered: why it is people need to flee?'

'Ah, well,' said Ehsan, sitting up, leaning forward in his seat (I was relieved to see I had not caused offence), 'at the moment with a new government, Iran is very oppressive, you cannot speak freely and the president wants to force a particular form of Islam on the people, but it is not really Islam, it is something far more extreme. He wants to use Islam as an excuse to control the people. But it was not always like this. Historically, Iran has been one of the world's great powers. Iran was a leader in the arts and education, a centre of philosophy, literature and debate of new ideas. Many people do not understand that women were free to wear what they liked, even miniskirts, into the late nineteen seventies. In fact it is quite ironic, you see, because at that time you could actually go to jail for wearing a hijab! But when the new government came to power, everything changed. My father and I were both at university. I don't know really what to say, how to explain, except to say to you what it is like when you are at a protest and you hear the shots fired and you have to run. You run and you run until you cannot run anymore, but you hear the guns firing behind you, and even though your legs are burning, all your muscles aching, you have to find it in yourself to just keep going.'

I dropped my eyes, a little ashamed that he had to spell this out to me, that Ehsan had to relive such a terrible ordeal.

'Thank you, Ehsan,' I replied quietly, and he settled back in his seat. I turned to the front of the car and looked out of my window in silence.

We drove along Murray Road and back through town, heading out to The Grotto, so we could show the men where the ocean hisses through the gap in the rock and how the pool of water at the base of the cave glows like an apatite gem. The contrived nature of our outing together gave the moment all the strangeness of a first date. We then drove out to the cove, where Ash and I sat and chatted to Ehsan under the shade of a wide tree, while Massom walked out over the coral beach toward the water. I thought he was glad to be out of detention, but he did not look happy, and I felt my disappointment, realised I should have known it would take much more than this. Massom walked back toward us, wanted to give me something. In my hand he placed the gift of a small white shell.

Before we headed back to the detention centres, Ash and I drove Massom and Ehsan to Territory Day Park. There, from a lookout at the edge of a sheer cliff, you could watch the golden bosun and brown booby birds gliding above the forest canopy and look over the aerial-like view of Flying Fish Cove. We gazed down at the birds and saw the shape of the reef below them – the small submerged islands of coral, bright flippers of divers pushing through the surface. Beyond that was the vast curved horizon over which both men had come, the jetty their first landfall after their dangerous journeys at sea. Massom was quiet, he looked at the view below and out toward the horizon for a long time, like he was reading something in the water, then we all turned around and got back in the car.

I felt like I had let Massom down, like there was something more I could have done, though I didn't know what. As we got out of the car at North West Point, he paused before he undid his seatbelt and said something, his eyes searing, intense.

'He says thank you and wants to ask if you will come again, please. He is very grateful, but he wants to make sure he will see you again,' Ehsan interpreted.

'Yes, Massom,' I replied. 'I promise you, every month I will be here until you get your visa.' Ehsan interpreted what I had said and then Massom responded quickly, looking back at me.

'He says thank you,' Ehsan said. 'He says thank you very much, but please, he just asks you – don't forget.'

The woman from the Department of Immigration I had been liaising with had been consistently warm and appreciative of our efforts to help. However, the third time I went to apply to take Massom and Ehsan out, the immigration liaison officer had changed. They had never heard of me or Massom, said they didn't know if this arrangement was possible. I reassured the official that it was very possible, in light of the fact we had already taken Massom out several times. I gave the name of the last officer I arranged the trips with, Massom's identity number and the previous forms we had signed. Eventually, the officer relented and, realising he was unaware of what had happened in the past, I applied for a longer period of time with the young men. To my surprise, it was approved. We got five hours.

Each successive time I took Massom out, he seemed to unfurl

like a slowly opening flower. He stood taller, his eyes became animated, responding more and more to the world around him. I was heartened. It was breathtaking to watch, a confronting power to own. For just a moment, I was able to gift another human being their freedom.

On this day we had decided to head out to the Dales. As the car passed under the elaborate draped limbs of banyan trees, I had never seen Massom look so alive and was moved that something so simple could bring so much pleasure to another human being. He stared out of the window to where the clear stream ran parallel to the road, the water offering us glimpses as it came in and out of gullies and between tall stands of ferns. I watched Massom watching the blue crabs, half in and half out of the water.

We pulled into the bottom carpark, covered ourselves with insect repellent and had a large swig from our water bottles so we didn't have to carry them. Ash, Massom, Ehsan and I walked toward the boardwalk, at the start of which several signs had been placed.

'Wow', Ehsan said. 'Ramsar, I know this, this is amazing.'

'Yes,' I say, 'the Dales are a Ramsar-listed wetland, it is a very special place. So great to be able to get that international recognition, especially in such a remote part of the world.'

'Yes, but do you know that Ramsar is a place in my country? The Ramsar Convention was named after a city in Iran where it was first signed, I think in the seventies. It is so amazing to see it here, here!' Ehsan exclaims, gesturing to the rainforest around us.

'That is amazing!' I replied. 'I had no idea.'

But Massom was not interested in the sign. He had stepped onto the boardwalk and began to walk beneath the towering Tahitian chestnuts, where the frigatebirds were beginning to call with a long, low *whooooop*, *whooooop*, *whooooop*. Massom pointed to the canopy above his head.

'Monk?' he began to ask.

'Monkeys? No, they are birds,' I laughed, and flapped my arms to show what I meant. Massom turned in a circle where he was standing, he raised his arms, raised them high and wide, turning and turning, laughing and looking at us in disbelief. He was exhilarated, standing in the jungle, with the wild sounds of the world all around him. I watched him, knowing something incredible and important was happening, a shift I had started to believe was not possible. He turned and whooped, beaming with joy, and all I wanted to do was watch, to be filled with the wonder of that moment, watching everything in Massom spark and glow.

Soon we arrived at a juncture, where we turned left and began the ascent up the gentle slopes of the hill alongside the clear, wide stream making its unhurried way to the sea. The climb became steeper, the air filling with the acrid smell of moisture and leaves. Sweating into the tropical heat of the day, we finally reached the last platform, and as we did, I took my final step up and then desperately tried to stop myself bursting into laughter. For there at the pinnacle was not only the thunderous wall of water cascading between lush ferns and netting the light, but at its base sat a beautiful young woman with long blonde hair in a bright pink bikini.

I couldn't help but glance briefly at Massom and Ehsan. They both looked completely stunned but seemed to be trying not to stare, so I busied myself with my bag and gave them a moment. I wondered how far this scene must have felt to the men from the concrete and steel of their respective detention centres. Soon the girl and her older friend dressed and left, and we all went and stood with our feet in the flow, reaching out to cup the water, feeling the spray from the fall form a thick fog around our faces.

We explored upstream, where the water pooled wide and clear beneath tall trees, and where yet more blue crabs and red crabs hid among elaborate roots. Years later, writing from Melbourne, Massom will tell me this was one of the best moments in his life.

12. The Wild Air

When I organised a trip to The Blowholes, I did not know this would be the last time I would see Massom. When we signed him out of North West Point, he looked distracted, did not meet my eye. When we finally got through the paperwork, received the usual sullen warning to get him back on time, and made it out to the carpark, Massom turned to Ehsan, indicating he would like him to interpret. Massom talked to Ehsan and then Ehsan turned to us.

'He says he wants to thank you so much for coming. He says, though, that he has been a bit worried, it has been a long time, he was very worried that you would not come.' I tried to push away the guilt that Massom had to wait almost two months between visits.

'Ehsan, can you tell Massom,' I said, looking at Ehsan and then directly into Massom's eyes, trying to show I understood and was sorry for his stress. 'Can you tell Massom that the liaison officer changed again. It was very hard to get to see you both this time, they would not return my calls and I had to email lots of times. Please tell him I am very sorry, that I did not forget him, but there was nothing I could do.' Ehsan interpreted and Massom, though his brow was furrowed, nodded in understanding. The men talked.

'He says he understands, he is sorry to ask, but he was worried.'

'Sorry,' I said directly to Massom, and he nodded once more, bowing his head and looking away, seeming to try to contain his emotion. We got in the car. I did not tell Massom that though the repeated change in liaison officers had been a huge challenge, each time the newly appointed officials becoming more and more obstructive, the delay had been somewhat of a reprieve for me. My father had been diagnosed with stomach cancer and, though it was treatable, my sense of responsibility to him as well as my young students – many of whom are beginning to struggle psychologically with the conditions of long-term detention – was starting to feel overwhelming. I barely had a life outside of my work with asylum seekers, and my advocacy for the people I worked with increasingly alienated me from other islanders. The asylum seekers were starting to become one of my only sources of friendship, yet the government exerted such a huge amount of control over asylum seekers' lives that I could only see my 'friends' when the government allowed. We all lived with the constant uncertainty that any of the detainees could be transferred at a moment's notice, and no-one would be told where.

On this day I had decided to drive away from the North West Point detention centre and the Dales beyond, to the other end of the island. We headed out on North-South Baseline Road, and through the window I stared into the dense canopy: the wide, green leaves of elephant ear plants; the bird's nest ferns layering life within the forks of trees; vines and ferns; bright fungi and trunks wearing coats of lichen and moss, all held beneath the high roof of a lush canopy. Here life pushed up, urgent and potent, and something in me was resounding like a well-cast bell.

'Miss Reneé?' Ehsan seemed to like calling me this, as though it was my real name, not a title given to me in the classroom. I didn't mind; in fact I had come to love my new name, the term now filled with so many positive associations, even preferring the mistaken title 'Miss My-name', given to me by some of the younger children.

'Yes, Ehsan,' I turned in my seat as Ash drove, greenery whizzing past the windows.

'I wanted to ask – if you don't mind – do you or Ashley believe in ghosts?'

'Well, I am not sure, Ehsan,' I responded, 'I have never seen one, but I don't think that necessarily means other people's experiences of ghosts are untrue. Why?'

'It's just there is a very strange thing. You see, I don't really believe it, but in the detention centre there are many people who do, it is mainly the Afghan people. And the Afghan people are saying that there is a ghost by the toilets, that she is a little girl and she is crying. And though I don't believe in ghosts myself, they are so upset, you can see it in their faces, like it is real. It is a very strange thing.'

I recall thinking at the time that this was odd, that there were no workers' children at the time of Chinese indentured labour at Phosphate Hill, wondering who such a small ghost could possibly be. Years later, reading back over Zainal Madjid's speech given at the *Janga* memorial service and listening to Tom's incredibly moving recount of the boat tragedy, I will think back on Ehsan's story, putting together pieces, traces that suggested a reason for the appearance of such a young and grief-ridden ghost.

We reached the turn-off, and as we turned into the cool canopy of trees, the way became littered with red crabs. I showed Ehsan how to take a branch and gently sweep and scare the crabs to the side as the car crawled along the track at walking speed. Finally, we made it to the carpark and again coated ourselves with mosquito repellent and suncream before making our way between sharp pandanus toward the small sea cliff.

The Blowholes have a striking mythical feel to them. On the boardwalk, visitors can walk out into jagged rock, witness a scene that seems actively hostile to life: thin slices of limestone thrust up, a sea of calcified knife-edges. Between the sharp ridges of rock, a perennial mist hovers as the ocean, breathy, restless, hisses up between holes in the outcrop, sending out a fine spray of mist. The mist settles, forming a series of small salty rock pools, and the water surges up once again, slowly eroding and smoothing the spaces between. In that strange light, these dips read like an exaggerated moonscape, rock becomes the repeated form of crater upon crater. Somewhat impossibly, brown grapsus crabs cling to the side of the serrated rock, their variegated forms edgy and erratic as people walk between them on the boardwalk. In the distance, the ocean is blue beyond belief, a glinting cerulean plain. The signage tells us that here, too, the sea cliff plunges kilometres straight down to the ocean floor.

On this day the ocean felt more alive than ever as Massom and Ehsan turned their heads to its hiss and growl. Small towers of water pushed up, making us jump, we caught our breath at its sudden liquid columns of light. We wandered between the rocks, not really talking, eye contact and gesture a conversation that included us all. Then, without warning, a lump of blue swell rushed under the lip of rock and into the network of underground caverns. The air shouted its way out of the rock, pushing up a dazzling fountain of seawater high over the young men's heads. They began to run, but the water outdid them, throwing bright white balls over their bodies. They stood shocked for a moment, then with a look of relief, realising they were safe, began to laugh. They looked down at their wet clothes, at each other's glistening faces. Animated, breathless, they laughed hysterically, exhilarated, animated, wild air whipping at their bodies.

We went to a café for lunch and here again I felt the disjuncture. Ehsan was happy, ordering a hamburger and chips, but I could see the distress written across Massom's face. In that moment

I realised: bacon and eggs, hamburger, ham and cheese croissant, what was meant to be a treat was a minefield for a Muslim man trying to order something that was halal on the menu. I kicked myself for my oversight, bringing back the furrowed brow on Massom's face as he picked through his tomato-and-cheese toastie, where I am sure the fat of a pig would have found its way. I apologised to Ehsan for not considering a halal menu when I chose the café, but he smiled and said, 'There is Muslim, like this, very strict,' showing one hand, 'and Muslim like this,' unfolding his other immaculate pale hand. 'It's not a very big deal.' He bit happily into his burger, sipped on his vanilla milkshake.

'Don't worry too much, he will be okay,' Ehsan said, indicating, but not looking at, Massom. Ehsan was getting tired of translating, did not pass on everything Massom said, and I started to see the world of detainees brought with it the challenges and tensions played out in their respective nations.

As we laboured through our meals, all at once Massom sat up and began to point excitedly, saying something.

'What is he saying, Ehsan?' I asked.

'Oh, something about that lady with the blonde hair over there, I think she is his case worker at the detention centre.'

I turned and saw a slim young woman directly behind us in a brown-collared Department of Immigration shirt. Massom was pointing right at her, smiling, but she pretended not to see him, turning her head away from him and leaning in closer to focus on her friend. Massom seemed to find this hilarious, watched her, his eyes lit up and animated, like it was the funniest thing in the world that they should be at a café together. I stared at her, wondering why she would not acknowledge him, but he didn't seem to mind.

As we finished our meals and were about to head off, Massom said something in earnest to me. I looked to Ehsan, and Ehsan stated without expression, 'He is saying thank you, thank you so much to you both. He is very happy that you came to get him, he was waiting every night for you to come. He says you are like a mother to him.'

I burst into laughter, wondering how old Massom thought I was, and Ash and Ehsan laughed with me. I looked up to see Massom, wearing a face both confused and hurt.

'Oh no, please tell Massom I am sorry. Please say thank you, he is special to me too, being like his mum just made me feel old.'

Ehsan said something, but Massom still looked confused, and I worried I had offended him, worried that Ehsan has enjoyed distinguishing himself from Massom through his ability to make sense of the joke, while Massom could not, and I was left with not knowing how to bridge the apparent gap.

It was late afternoon as the four of us drove down to Waterfall Bay, a small cove tucked away immediately beyond the island's defunct resort. Cliffs wrapped around this small beach filled with thin forms of coconut palms. Waves surged over the reef but the tide was low, leaving piles of flotsam, rubbish and coconuts along the shoreline. Ash had brought his machete and I asked Ehsan if he knew the best way to open coconuts. He looked at me, surprised.

'I wouldn't have a clue,' he said, seeming somewhat repulsed at the idea. He saw I was taken aback, and then patiently explained, 'There are no coconut trees in Tehran.' My face reddened slightly, finding my overgeneralising of asylum seekers' lives exposed. Of course, Ehsan was urban through and through: he lived in Tehran, the most populous city in Western Asia. When you are surrounded by close to nine million people, the chances are you don't have many occasions to crack open coconuts.

I turned to Massom, and he took the coconut and machete. Given the efforts at security, I considered this was probably not the kind of activity immigration had in mind for detainees. But

Massom was so natural with the blade, opening the coconut in seconds, breaking the white flesh into pieces and handing them to me. We sat down on a large log that had washed up and ate the coconut. I showed Massom how the robber crabs had emerged at the smell, throwing them a piece. He watched the enormous crustaceans lift the fleshy fragments to their mouths.

Tenderly, Massom knelt down and fed small sections of coconut to each one, handing me fresh pieces so I could do the same. Eventually I indicated I had had enough, and Massom became silent, staring out to the horizon, his mouth a small line on his poker face. We were all quiet now, slow, and I wondered whether this, too, was tiring for them – being with me, with Ash, whether they reached a point where they were ready to make their way back to their strange homes.

The sun had become low in the sky, and I was worried the men would miss their evening meals, so we walked back to the car. The sun was setting as we dropped Ehsan back to the family compound, and I watched Massom looking at Construction Camp, its faded dongas surrounded by low green pool fencing, the islanders' playground and community cricket field visible beyond. I wondered how this clear disparity must feel.

When we got back to North West Point, it was dark. I handed Massom some photos from our trip to the Dales months before and a copy of a surfing magazine. I indicated he needed to put the photos in the magazine. Volunteers and teachers were not allowed to give photos to detainees of the asylum seekers on excursion, or on Christmas Island at all, but Massom had asked for a copy as we had dropped him off on our last trip. I printed the photos for him in full knowledge that these images of beauty and of him being somewhere other than detention were exactly the kinds of things that could see him through.

We waited at the glass door under the CCTV camera and someone pressed a button so we could go in. I stood in the foyer and tried to catch someone's eye, but no-one would look our way.

'Excuse me,' I said to the woman in a blue Serco shirt at the counter. She looked at me with clear distaste.

'Look, we are busy at the moment, you will have to come back in the morning.'

I looked around at the empty foyer.

'Oh,' I said, very tempted to take Massom away, 'you don't want your client back then?' The woman looked shocked, raised her head to see that the man standing next to Ash was in fact a detainee.

'Well, you should have said!' she replied angrily, and she pushed a sign-in sheet toward us. A man came around the counter and asked Massom to put his water bottle and magazine on the conveyer to go through the X-ray. Massom put them down, and the guard picked up the magazine and flicked through the pages. My heart went into my chest. Massom looked sideways at me, and we stood there silent and waiting. But the guard did not seem to notice, put the magazine back on the conveyer belt, and the water bottle and hidden photos passed to the other side. Massom watched them, then stepped through the metal detector and did not look back.

One month later, Michelle told me that Massom had been given his refugee status. I was thrilled, Massom was on his way, any moment his visa would come, he had made it. I told myself Massom did not need me to take him out now. My father's diagnosis had changed: the treatment of the tumour on his stomach was successful, but in the meantime the cancer had spread to his liver. I was finding it hard to get information – my father seemed confused, making it difficult to grasp what this new diagnosis meant.

Finally I called the oncologist, leaving my mobile number with the secretary. When the oncologist called me back, I was in the car. The line was full of static, we ended up shouting in order to make ourselves heard. But between the crackles of the line and the car's diesel engine the words finally made it through – my father's cancer will be fatal – he had eight weeks to live.

It was a Wednesday afternoon when I saw Michelle chatting to some teachers outside my classroom. I grabbed my things, locked my door and joined them on the concrete path. The day was humid and sweat gathered in the creases at my elbows and knees. The teachers were talking about a TV program I didn't watch, but I stayed a while, listening to their conversation, needing the company.

'When do you head off, Michelle?' I asked.

'Tomorrow,' she replied, 'I think it's time to get back to Perth, start to knock this thesis on the head. My supervisors are starting to get a bit narky! Oh, Reneé, did you hear about Massom?'

'No,' I replied, 'I haven't seen him for a while.'

'It is very sad. He tried to kill himself, I hear he has been medivaced off the island.'

I did not believe it. 'But he had his refugee status,' I said.

'I know, I know, just makes it all the sadder. I heard he swallowed razor blades and bleach, but he survived.'

'Where is he now?'

'In Melbourne somewhere, apparently.'

'Oh, okay.' My mind went blank. People began to chat about food in Melbourne. I picked up my bag and said goodbye to the group. Walking away, I felt nothing. I did not feel a thing.

13. Leaving Space

The pressure to remain silent about asylum seekers and the cruelty of the detention system was so pervasive during my time on the island it seemed to suck the oxygen from the atmosphere. Yet silence is never total and erasure never complete. All around me small cracks occurred in this culture of amnesia, and light and air leaked into the shuttered room of our conversations, sometimes from the most unlikely places: a compassionate Serco officer here, an outspoken nurse there, a surprising story of connection or compassion from a tradie consigned to work on the detention sites, even if some invariably lapsed back into old prejudices.

One of these moments of light and breath on Christmas Island occurred the first time I heard Zainal Majid speak. Zainal was President of the Islamic Council in 2011 and was asked to talk at the memorial service of the boat tragedy on behalf of the SOS volunteers present on that day. Before Zainal had spoken, I had begun to give up hope that the absolute horror experienced by the asylum seekers aboard the *Janga* would ever be openly acknowledged, the service acting as some kind of bland sanitisation of the extreme suffering that took place on the island's shores. But after the address by the island's imam on behalf of the Islamic community, Zainal had stepped up to the microphone, quivering with raw emotion, his words imbued with the authenticity of a human inhabiting his vulnerability. Exposing his brokenness to the large audience of locals, officials and politicians, Zainal sobbed his way through his recount of what took place on that fateful day.

Zainal's courage had engendered the enormous amount of respect I have for this local Malay man. I had hoped for a chance to speak with Zainal in particular during my visit, not only about his experiences of the tragedy, but also to get a sense of how he saw his island home. I felt this was a person I could trust, who would be honest with me, and whose lens might very different from my own, both as a Malay Christmas Islander and as a man deeply connected to the Muslim population on Christmas Island. However, I felt intimidated by Zainal's title, President of the Islamic Council – a position he had held for five years – and I had no real inroad into the heart of the Islamic community through my own contacts. I resigned myself to the fact that this interview would probably never happen.

However, while warming up for Pete's Tai Chi class in Poon Saan, the local mechanic and I had got talking about my research. The mechanic turned out to be a friend of Zainal's and happily gave me his mobile number, and Zainal, though somewhat surprised by my phonecall and request, kindly agreed to meet with me at the Kampong. So on the day after my walk through the Dales, I once again clamber into Pete's little white car and bounce along the island's foreshore to interview Zainal. As I drive, I glance at the CLA Club restaurant, its long rectangular form raised on stilts, visualise the large deck on the other side that allows for magnificent views over the water. It must have been somewhere along here that the cooling pool for the mine's engines was once located (the same one where the Asian community was permitted to swim), since washed away by violent storms that swept the foreshore in the 1980s. I continue through the roundabout and its chalkboards, past the post office where the 'whites only' pool had so recently enforced its strange apartheid. Beyond the post office, gently putting on the car's brakes, I drive down a small steep slope where, nestled in the cliffs, the blue form of concrete flats rise above a screen of banana trees, giving shape to the Malay Kampong that looks over the port and Flying Fish Cove.

I love the old photographs of the residences at Flying Fish Cove – the stilted homes among the palm trees lining the curve of the bay. I did not understand until recently, reading accounts of the Flying Fish Cove landslides, that in the 1930s Flying Fish Cove also contained European homes. Known as the 'Edinburgh' settlement, these expansive colonial pieces of architecture occupied the eastern end of the bay while the Malay community inhabited the westernmost end. This juxtaposition surprised me, and I went on to read how the side-by-sideness of the cultures living here led to moments of integration among the island's inhabitants, especially evident in the children as they played together on the cove's foreshore, the white children learning Malay from their amahs. In fact, Malay became the most commonly spoken language for basic communication at this time, most likely due to the simplicity of the Malay's grammatical structure, born as a result of its roots as an ancient trading language used in the ports of South-East Asia. I am continually kept on my toes out here in the Indian Ocean Territories – in this unique world, race relations are never as simple as they first seem.

With a few exceptions, the Kampong is now almost exclusively Malay. I pull into the carpark by the water under the *Barringtonia,* where these box fruit trees have scattered their enormous pink-and-white pom-pom flowers along the bay. From here the beautiful shape of the mosque's minaret is visible, a small tower with a golden curved roof, its shape mirrored in the pointed silver decorations installed above the mosque's windows. Behind, the hillside pushes up steeply, turning into a high cliff, a layered wall of intricate greenery.

Walking up the stairs to the Malay Club restaurant, I can feel the tension in my body. I am outside my comfort zone, both in my unfamiliarity with the space – the Kampong was a place I rarely visited on the island (the restaurant was closed during the time I had lived here) – but also because I am interviewing a senior religious figure in the community. As I step onto the deck, Malay music plays loudly from inside the club, where several women in pale and patterned *tudungs* are preparing food, the delicious smells of *makan* filling the air. I am washed in a wave of language for me far more suggestive of the Cocos Islands than Christmas Island, yet the familiarity of the Malay dialect helps me feel a little more at ease. By the sliding door that leads into the restaurant, an older man and his female companion lean against the glass, chuckling quietly and chatting in what sounds like Cantonese.

I attempt to look comfortable, sitting on my own at the back of the restaurant, while all around me people joke and talk. The smells of kretek cigarettes and cleaning products waft toward me in alternate dissonant waves. A waiter comes out and delivers milkshake glasses full of sweet cold tea to a group of people. I look out toward a nearby apartment block painted a shade of pale pink, where a woman hangs out her washing on the small verandah of her flat. To my left, children happily play in the mosque's shade.

I made sure I dressed appropriately for the meeting, clothing covering my shoulders and knees, and now I wonder if there are any other protocols I may need to consider. I draw on my experiences of relating to Elders of the Islamic community on the atoll, and can still visualise the horror in one *nenek*'s face on Home Island when I went to hug her husband as we were leaving Cocos to move back to the mainland, her reluctance to let me even shake her husband's hand. I decide it is probably appropriate that, as a woman, I do not touch Zainal. *I will avoid shaking his hand,*

I think to myself, to make it easier for us both. I keep looking up over the grass, past the mosque, to see if I can see a man in a white *thobe* and prayer cap, as I nervously ensure I have enough pens and check the battery level on my recorder.

'Ah, you are already working before we even start the interview!' I hear a voice say.

Much to my surprise, I look up to see Zainal coming around the corner, wearing steel-capped boots, navy Hard Yakka work pants and a collared shirt with yellow hi-vis panels. It dawns on me that Zainal must work on the mines, the island's main employer, and that he must be meeting me during his lunchbreak. Zainal shakes my hand warmly, which throws me even more, and I quickly try to adjust my preconceptions of my interviewee as we walk across the grass to a picnic table beside the mosque on the other side of the lawn. I like Zainal's choice of location, away from the noise and music of the restaurant, but where we can catch glimpses of ocean between the apartment buildings. Despite the wind interfering with my recordings (which I counter with a bag placed on the windward side), I can see people physically relax when they are interviewed outside, and both the interviewee and I can look up and out at the island or the ocean, and be reminded of exactly where, and what, we are talking about.

Zainal must be in his late forties, perhaps early fifties, though it is hard to tell as the Malay population on Christmas Island, with their olive and often unfurrowed skin, can appear younger than their chronological age. Zainal is lean, and sports a head of thick, wavy black hair. His face is as open and unassuming as I recall, but in this much less harrowing context his mouth breaks easily into a smile. His movements are fluid, almost laconic, his body language depicting a man down-to-earth, relaxed and at ease with himself. As I set up my microphone, he buys us each a small carton of juice.

When he returns, I ask him to sign the interview permissions and paperwork, which he does, seeming somewhat bemused, politely asking me for a second time how I got his number.

Once I have set my bag up to divert the wind, I start my recorder, and we both laugh, self-conscious at the seeming formality of the moment.

'Well, let's start at the beginning,' I say, asking Zainal how he came to be on the island. Zainal tells me that he was born on Christmas Island – his father came from Malaysia to work on the mines, while his mother came from Indonesia. Zainal's wife, Farida, came to Christmas Island as a nurse from Singapore. Farida was the Malay teacher when I was living on Christmas Island, a self-assured and intelligent woman, consistently striking in her colourful headscarves tied in a knot at the back of her head, out the front of which large looped earrings would glint in light. I imagine them courting, a striking good-looking couple, the attraction between them palpable in Zainal's voice as he speaks of her all these years later.

'She was twenty when she came,' Zainal says. 'We met and became friends and got on, you know ... I was still at school ...' he grins. 'We got married sometime in the nineteen eighties.'

We go on to talk about his family history on the island a little more. Zainal's face shows traces of emotion when he briefly speaks about the tough living and working conditions he witnessed his parents endure during the days his father was employed on the phosphate mine. 'It was very tough then,' Zainal says quietly, looking away, then he moves the conversation on.

Zainal's parents left the island after the Australian Government closed the mine in December 1987, taking the resettlement scheme offered by the government as they tried to depopulate the remote territory. Zainal stayed, the couple living off Farida's wage (by this time Farida had already started teaching) until Gordon Bennett and others were successful in purchasing and reopening the mine in the early 1990s.

'*Selamat siang*!' I hear someone call, and turn to find Nek Su – my Cocos interviewee-to-be – wave as he goes to prepare for prayers.

'*Siang*, Nek!' I exclaim in surprise. Neither of us, I suspect, would have thought we would bump into each other here. Zainal and Nek Su exchange more greetings in Malay that I do not understand, punctuated with much laughter.

'*Jumpa lagi*, Mak Greta,' Nek calls affectionately (my Cocos name meaning, literally, 'Mother of Greta'), then goes off to wash before he enters the mosque, and Zainal turns back to me, still smiling.

'It is good to be so close together here,' Zainal tells me. 'It is like one big family. Some people say, "Oh, it is too close and everybody is right next to each other, but I think it is good. It is the best place to bring up the kids, they are so happy here with the opportunity to mix with everyone, and the parents don't have to worry where they go or who they are with because everybody knows each other.'

I turn the conversation to questions about Zainal's faith and his role in the community. Zainal tells me that being President of the Islamic Council is only meant to be a two-year role, but he has been asked to continue on into his fifth year. Zainal tells me does not mind the responsibility, as he is passionate about his community, but he hopes one day to see a member of the next generation in the role.

I think about watching the sunset down at Flying Fish Cove, and the silence through which the call to prayer used to travel in waves over the water. I ask Zainal if he has experienced any prejudice from other islanders toward the Muslim population.

'No, not so far. Being Christmas Island, we ignore that,' he says with a shrug and grin. 'We continue on, we have our own way of life. People have their own point of view, but not in an aggressive way, just "Oh, that is your view, that's fine, that's how you feel".'

'But what about the call to prayer, Zainal?' I ask. 'That was one of my favourite memories, hearing the sound travel over the sea. Were the mainland tensions toward Islam the reason that the call to prayer is not being played at sunset anymore? Did those prejudices make their way over here?'

'Oh, that,' Zainal answers. 'No, that's because the audio is broken. Actually I must fix that, I keep forgetting. It has been a few weeks now.' I laugh in relief and at myself reading so much into a technical issue. With the obvious exception of attitudes toward asylum seekers, the 'live and let live' attitude of most Christmas Islanders was something I really enjoyed and respected. To learn the mutual tolerance and acceptance of diversity among most islanders is intact is very reassuring.

I venture to pose a question I had always wanted to ask when I lived in the Christmas Island community: I ask Zainal if he ever wished there was more integration between the white, Chinese and Malay populations.

'I like the different, distinct communities,' Zainal answers. 'There is harmony, when there is a big event, we all join together. I suppose it has maintained our culture, otherwise it gets too mixed. It gets to a stage maybe in two or three generations that you tend to lose step with your culture, so it is good that everyone looks after their own community and when we come together as an island, we celebrate. I think that is important.'

Zainal's answer surprises me. I always had thought of integration as something inherently good, presuming that the Malay community wished the white community would make more of an effort to mix. I see that for Zainal, in his leadership role, the distinctness of the communities helps him maintain the cultural integrity of the Christmas Malay people.

Zainal tells me that the current generation of young people are mature and responsible, but when the island's casino was in operation it caused a lot of challenges for the Islamic community, with large numbers of people flying in and out and the increase in the availability of alcohol. Zainal tells me that it is part of his role to look after the community so, at that time, he and other members of the Kampong began to meet regularly with police so any problems could be quickly addressed. Though things have settled with the casino's closure, and the new generation of young people have a greater connection to the mosque and their Islamic inheritance, the strong links and regular meetings with the police have been maintained.

The conversation shifts to Zainal's own children, who have recently moved to boarding schools on the mainland to finish their education, beginning with their daughter Farzian receiving a scholarship in Perth. He tells me Farzian and her sister were horrified when Zainal and Farida suggested moving to Perth to be closer to them, the girls adamant that they wanted to maintain their connection with Christmas Island, made possible by returning to see their parents in the holidays. Thinking of the way the family straddles their lives between mainland Australia and Christmas Island, I ask Zainal if he considers himself to be foremost a Christmas Islander or an Australian. 'If we talk with islanders, we are Christmas Islanders,' Zainal says, 'but I consider myself an Australian because of one thing: our Australian citizenship. In time that is going to be our future for our kids.'

'And what do you hope for the future of the Christmas Island community?' I ask. Zainal tells me that he wants his daughters to be able to come back and find work and for the operations of the mines to continue.

'I am hoping it will give us another twenty years so that another generation can have the employment and will stay on the island and enjoy what I am enjoying now.' I look at Zainal's face, his dusty hi-vis work wear, the sense of calm he seems to inhabit, a wholehearted pleasure in his way of being in the world. I had never thought of the mining industry as something giving Christmas Island vitality and holding the community together. I only saw the devastation the extraction of phosphate wrought on the tropical ecosystem, the moonscape the mines left behind. Zainal's statement throws up an inner conflict in me, but I try to stay with him, try to really think about what the phosphate mines mean for him and the Christmas Malay people.

I start to become aware that the interview has been going for well over an hour and realise that Zainal must need to get back to work, though there is so much I would like to ask him.

'Before we finish,' I say, 'let me ask you about the sea.' I tell Zainal that I had first become aware of him at the memorial service for the Christmas Island boat tragedy, that I was incredibly moved by his speech and the stories he shared. Though I worry I am being intrusive, I really feel the need to ask Zainal if continuing to live overlooking such a perilous site for so many people impacts on him and whether he is troubled by his memories of that day.

'I didn't think it had any impact on me,' Zainal says, 'but then after a while the reality dropped, tears every time someone mentioned it. It doesn't really have me mentally ill, you know, but it's a tragedy. I have friends who have suffered, who still have those memories, but I don't have that. Though when you start talking about it, it flicks pictures up in my mind.'

I want to ask Zainal more about this, but I get the feeling my wish to go over what took place during the time of the boat tragedy is not a need Zainal shares. Zainal no longer seems troubled by the topic nor particularly interested in continuing to talk about it. I sense he has reached a peace with what took place and largely managed to let his troubling memories of the boat tragedy go. I am amazed to see the calm in his face after witnessing the initial impact of his experience of so much trauma. I leave space, but Zainal does not elaborate, so I let the topic be.

'Do you think the way the ocean is always present here affects how you experience your life?' I ask.

'The sea is why I decide to stay,' Zainal answers. 'In fact, from my verandah, you can see the water.' As Zainal speaks about his lifelong connection with the ocean, I visualise his day through the lens of his swimming goggles, watching the fish dart through bright fingers of coral in the early morning, see him tying his dinghy out at the buoys in the bay in the still of night. Not to fish, just to sit. The calm. The space. The quiet. I can see how out there in the lightless enormity of water, an expansiveness beyond horizon, how cares could relent to the dark liquid lull; how there might be enough air to let each worry float up and out, dissipating into a vast star-rich sky.

14. Walking Backwards Toward Light

Driving back to the cottage after interviewing Zainal, I feel an enormous sense of wellbeing wash over me, a distinct sensation that both in my being here, as well as through these conversations, something in me is beginning to soften, to heal. This is strange, because I did not know Zainal at all during my time on Christmas Island, nor was our conversation intense or particularly emotional. *What is it?* I wonder. *What exactly is happening here?*

I make myself some lunch and then flip open my laptop, sitting in the cool air of the air-conditioner, skimming over emails and social media sites. An article that an advocacy group has posted catches my attention and I click on the bold heading that reads 'The Nauru Files: cache of 2,000 leaked reports reveal scale of abuse of children in Australian offshore detention' above an image of children whose faces are obscured, standing behind wire. A sick feeling rising in my stomach. As I skim the screen, it becomes clear that the report released by the *Guardian* newspaper contains over two thousand files of documented claims of abuse of asylum seekers in detention on Nauru, a 'client state' of the Australian Government and an offshore island where our nation continues to detain asylum seekers who arrive in Australian waters.

Among the two thousand files, more than half of the claims in the report are about abuses alleged against children. As I continue to read, 'The Nauru Files' reveal details of children self-harming, receiving death threats and being violently assaulted as well as sexually abused. In 2011, when I was teaching children detained on Christmas Island, I was required to count in and out scissors and sharpeners, so my students didn't self-harm with school equipment. At this time, I remember thinking surely our nation had hit a moral rock bottom, but it seems, five years later, we have discovered a whole new level of low, a darkening of our collective conscience.

I find this striking, the synchronicity of the report's release coinciding with the week I have returned to this complex and beautiful place. Accompanying the report is a video that I click on and wait in 'island time' for the internet to upload the file. Once the video is uploaded, I find myself listening to teachers who worked on Nauru speaking of their affection and care for the asylum seeker children they taught, then watching these same students start to drown in the tedium of detention and self-harming, the workers' emotional struggle with their sense of powerlessness in it all. I am awed by the courage of these women in the face of the *Australian Border Force Act 2015*, but the tremor in the teachers' voices is a sound I recognise, and I am caught off guard.

After five years, it is sometimes difficult to recall the day-to-day detail of what it was like teaching children in detention, but hearing the heartbreak of the educators employed by the Red Cross and reading their faces, images and memories start to flood in. I dig into my bag next to the couch and rummage around for my external hard drive. I plug it in and begin searching among my files for a submission I made to the *Forgotten Children* report in 2013. The *Forgotten Children* report was a damning document submitted to the Australian Parliament by the Human Rights Commission in 2014. It reported on a ten-month investigation into eleven Australian-funded detention centres, revealing the widespread sexual assault, self-harm and severe mental disorders in child detainees.

I find the file with my submission and open it, looking at the photos I had taken as evidence and read my answers to the inquiry's questions, remembering my fear of the possible consequences over what I had revealed. Though I had ticked the box for my submission to remain confidential, my grave concerns regarding what my actions would mean for my relationships with people on the islands, and whether they would affect my ability in the future to return to a place I loved, were real.

As I read through my comments, I am consumed by memories and emotions that are hard to confront or contain.

> Witnessing the effect detention had on children on Christmas Island was one of the most confronting experiences I have ever had. I really thought that as a nation we cared about the Rights of the Child, but my experiences over the three years I was in the Indian Ocean Territories showed me a very different picture. Children came off boats full of joy and hope, they would sing, laugh, play and joke. What I found would happen within two, three, four months, let alone when it was over a year, is that children began to shut down. Some students stopped wanting to eat, others would not sing or play, and one intelligent and articulate six-year-old student, who had thrown her arms around me in gestures of warmth and happiness when she first arrived, in the end would sit at the entry to the detention centre rocking slightly with a vacant look in her eye.

And then ...

> My main concern is actually for the unaccompanied minors that I taught. In the absence of families, these

> students formed strong friendships, which I imagine helped to fill the gap the absence of families created. It was not uncommon when returning students to their detention facilities to have the Serco officers meet them at the gate arbitrarily separate them (they would say 'right you and you there, you lot over there – you lot pack up your stuff, you're leaving'). It was distressing to see the seeming arbitrariness of who was going and staying, and the complete insensitivity to breaking up friendship groups for these young men. It was all they had. To see the distress on their faces was heartbreaking. I don't know if they even got to say goodbye to each other.

I read on, right to the end, and all the powerlessness I experienced as a teacher on the islands rushes back. Alone in this place, I find I have no means to guard against it. Sitting in the walls of my accommodation, I feel raw, broken, the sense of immediacy in the memories the report has conjured betrays the fact that years have passed between the time that I taught asylum seeker children and now. Sitting in silence, I wonder how to hold on to the weight of what I know, how to respond. An old rage stirs in the memory of my muscles, a surge of anger at my own impotence that even now there seems to be nothing I can do to prevent the tide of pointless suffering that I witnessed here, and that evidently continues elsewhere, on other islands. Things have not improved for asylum seekers for all my and others' lobbying, protesting, submission and letter writing; instead things have become so much worse.

With a new resolve, I turn off the air-con and get back into the car, heading toward the top of the island, toward Phosphate Hill. The sound of frigatebirds, the clatter of their calls, curls in my ear, the sound bending as though coming through a long pipe. As I turn up the slope toward Poon Saan, golden bosun birds trail their opulent tails over the car's roof, but the day has clouded over, so their flash of brilliant colour is muted. After the Poon Saan shops, I turn left, put the car in first as it starts the steep ascent up the slope, past the hospital, climbing until the car reaches the top of the hill and a signpost points right, its white letters against blue reading 'Refuse Centre' and 'Sports Ground'. Though the detention centres at Phosphate Hill spill out over both sides of the road , there was never any signage during my time here to point people in its direction, nor any wording to indicate the camps even existed. (Phosphate Hill Processing Centre was the original site of detention; the dongas across the road originally used for construction workers employed at North West Point detention centre were later added to the detention facilities as numbers of arrivals grew.)

The time I spent at the Phosphate Hill detention centres is a memory I have needed to come at slowly, like walking backwards toward a searing light, a place I have needed to inch toward in increments, glimpsing the turn-off to the camp like a hook in flesh as I raced past. Driving in, I can almost hear the young men's footfalls as the students crossed the road from their accommodation in Construction Camp to the huddle of dongas that formed our makeshift classrooms. I drive in at walking speed as layers of faces and experiences fall and settle gently on my head and shoulders, pushing through skin, pulsing in my blood. On my left, an area cordoned off with the bright bodies of life rafts comes into view, then beyond that the rows of dongas that formed administration and our small school. I keep driving to the end of the road, pulling over at the cricket club. My presence instantly attracts the attention of two men sitting there, so I round the cul-de-sac a little more until the car is out of sight, park on the curb and grab my camera.

This would have been a risky move a few years ago, but the detention centre now sits like a ghost town, beige and rusting behind pool fencing and cyclone wire. Shade cloth designed to screen the walkways from the eyes of media and passers-by has begun to rot and fall away in great swathes. Beyond the fence, row upon row of dongas sit above the red-brown soil; in the distance dense jungle obscures views of the ocean. As I photograph the detention site, a car comes around the cul-de-sac and slows behind me. I feel my body tense, sense that I am being watched and, for a moment, an old guilt, an old fear, comes over me. A man in hi-vis wear comes out of the toilets at the back of the club, sees me with my camera and takes out his phone and makes a call. But despite the islanders' seeming defensive reactions to my presence, I am not a threat. The Phosphate Hill detention centres have been closed for over a year. There is nothing for anyone to defend anymore, no shroud of secrecy to be maintained. Just stillness where this interface between the community and asylum seekers was once a source of tumult and anger, tension and resentment. Now there is only absence, space and silence.

At first, the sight of the compound fills me with sadness as well as a familiar, vague sense of stress at being watched. Then I experience a shift – with an immediate sense of elation I comprehend that for the first time I am on this island on my own terms. My shoulders have rounded, drawing me into myself, so I consciously push them back. I raise my body up and stand straight. I don't need to be accepted here, this is no longer my home, I am only here for ten days. I feel myself expand, take up space. I step up, step into the right to be where I am in this moment, the right to tell my own story. I feel a serious and pressing need to make sense of what has happened to me and others in this place, to understand my forever-altered life, and this detention centre has everything to do with who I have become.

Living in the Christmas Island community, the pressure to turn a blind eye, to keep things light, was oppressive. It was as if a great gravity was making this small world stay in the orbit of the status quo, though the dark underbelly of nationalism simmered and boiled at the periphery of our vision. However, this time I find I have the confidence of not only my sense of connection to this powerful place through body and memory, but also the newly found freedom of being someone simply passing through.

I look out across the tennis courts that were annexed to Construction Camp and find myself unexpectedly filled with a rush of happiness. In March 2011, only days after rioting at the North West Point detention centre saw police open fire on asylum seekers with rubber bullets and tear gas, the families at the Phosphate Hill detention centres rallied to try to create as normal as possible an environment for the children imprisoned there. A massive Persian New Year celebration was organised, also known as *Nowruz*, and at the last minute I was asked to come along. Looking through the cyclone fencing, I can clearly visualise the scene. Over a basic table had been laid many offerings, symbols of hope for the new year: sweet dried fruit for love, green sprouts for renewal, apples for beauty and health, garlic for self-care, vinegar for wisdom and patience. *Nowruz*, a time to let go of sadness and hardship, a time to wipe the slate clean.

The site conjures a memory of being surrounded by one or perhaps two hundred people on this small court, then without its net, and the incredibly warm welcome extended to me by my students' parents. I felt as though I were a guest of honour: the joy and excitement of teacher and parent finally meeting was obviously deeply reciprocal, the sheer humanity of us being face to face. The students took my hands and dragged me from adult conversation onto the improvised dance floor, where we moved and laughed by candlelight, me sweating heavily under my cardigan but reluctant to remove it and expose my shoulders, lest I risk offence when my hosts had been so generous. In the corner, a pasty Serco guard slumped in a plastic chair tried her hardest not to seem interested, pushed down the corners of her mouth that, despite her best efforts to control her face, seemed to want to break into a smile.

I can still see the whirling Afghan dancers, the call and response in the moves of large groups of Iranian men and women, but most of all I remember the young men. In tight jeans and brandishing coloured silk scarves, the Iranian men were flamboyant and breathtakingly sensual, arching their muscular bodies and circling their hips in a way I have never seen men move before. I felt a strange sense of gender role-reversal watching this highly charged and sexualised performance, yet it was a dance also overtly playful and teasing, the men vying to outdo each other and court the women's – and perhaps even the men's – gaze.

Today an afternoon haze hangs over the carpark and there is no trace of the lives crammed into this small nexus from different parts of the globe. I follow the fencing, cross the road and walk toward the site of the old school. The car that had pulled in behind me has gone, the man with his phone has joined his friends at the club, and everything in me has gone quiet, become finely tuned to this moment.

I walk to the security checkpoint at the front of the compound. To the left I can see the mounted spotlights and high wire fencing – the barbed wire since removed – around the enclosure where they had detained the asylum seekers who had arrived after the announcement of the Gillard Government's proposed (but never realised) Malaysia Solution. The people inside were not permitted to leave the small space or mix with other detainees, nor the children able to receive any schooling. I can picture the strange young guard who checked our ID, searched through our bags and teaching equipment, gave us our identity tags, took our phones and signed us in. In particular, I recall his strange personal-empowerment speak, as he read self-help books through his long days in the tiny room guarding the compound, the way I nodded politely, with my phone stashed in my underpants, later photographing what I saw with a slight shake in my hands.

I can see there are workers on ride-on mowers moving through the grounds, so though the gate is unlocked I decide not go in. Signs affixed to the detention centre boundary read

> NO TRESPASSING – IT IS AN OFFENCE UNDER SECTION 81 OF THE CRIMES ACT FOR PERSONS TO ENTER OR REMAIN ON THIS LAND WITHOUT LAWFUL CAUSE.

More buildings have been erected since the time I had worked at Phosphate Hill, so it is difficult to make out which dongas were the classrooms where I taught. The spaces where we played sport and ate lunch do not exist or are no longer visible. Peering in between the fence posts, I see that a child's playground has finally been erected, standing new, bright and unused in the centre of the camp.

Initially I had taught children between the ages of six and nine who had been bussed from this centre to the island's school. My role at the school had begun in February 2011, only weeks after the Christmas Island boat tragedy. The air had hung heavy over the island or, perhaps more accurately, had sat like a silent reservoir beneath us all. I had felt up against it, waded against the weight of it, but life went on.

As the young children were frequently and suddenly transferred without notice, there was no roll for me to check. I chose a child to count the bags for morning tea, then we would count each other, and that was the way we would know we were all there. The young students were Iranian and Afghan, many from the Hazara minority group fleeing ethnic cleansing in Afghanistan. The Hazara children were gentle and wide-eyed. The Iranian children were the opposite of everything I had expected from a refugee. Urban, bold and educated, I had not anticipated I would need a quick wit to hold my own with students who had so recently made such a dangerous journey.

Rather than trying to control this spirited group, I learned to go with them, to become playful too. I taught them the hokey-pokey: 'You put your right arm in, you put your right arm out,' we sang, enjoying our new song and building on our English. I demonstrated the actions to the line, 'You put your bottom in, you put your bottom out.' Mouths and eyes open wide, the children stared at me speechless. Finally, I had outdone them! I laughed and showed them again. Through such a simple song, a light-hearted act, despite the oppressive regimes many of the students had fled, they began to understand that in this space we were safe. These were bodies with which we could move and play and, in doing so, find a way past fear and shame. With each new boat, the children passed this message on to each other, teaching their classmates the hokey-pokey in a strange rite of passage we came to love.

I put my students' work into the newsletter: a six-year-old's painting of being rescued by the Navy, the Australian flag like a sun on her horizon. Another student depicted her garden in Iran in lush bright lines. I scribed their proud sentences of newly acquired English to include as captions underneath the pieces of work. Nikoo's words read: 'First of all I painted a blue colour for the sea, there is a fish in it. There are little boats and there is something wrong with them and the Navy is coming to help them. I have drawn mountains with a sun, this is the Australian flag.' Beneath Fatemah's flowers I also pasted her words, 'My painting is about the farming in our village where we used to live. We had some flowers in our garden that is why I painted flowers. Next door to our house there was a yard with two big flowers. There is a butterfly next to the tree, she is flying to sit on the flowers.'

The day after the newsletter went to print, I was called into the office. The deputy principal told me there had been a mistake, that it was not to happen again. I was told if I wanted to include my students' work in the newsletter, I would have to speak to an administrator first. I understood they were telling me my students' work was not to appear in the newsletter again. I walked away confused. I was doing what I always did as a teacher, including my children's work in the newsletter so they had a sense of a tangible audience, a motivation and purpose for acquiring and applying language skills. This had always been encouraged by my principals, yet here I felt like I had done something wrong, that I was being somehow provocative. At staff gatherings, on my lunchbreak, even socialising away from work, it was becoming clear that my day was not to be mentioned, the students were not to be mentioned. My class full of children bursting with life was not to be spoken of, never to be named.

Around halfway through my time on Christmas Island, there were fewer young children arriving by boat, so I started to teach the mostly male unaccompanied minors inside Phosphate Hill Processing Centre. These were older students and young adults whose families had saved and borrowed money to send the young men on their own to Australia to find a better life, often in the hope of saving their lives. Like the younger children, these students were also predominately from Iran, Iraq and Afghanistan, and though they were in their teens and early twenties, they laughed and went along with my will to sing through our days. We wrote poetry, scribed reports, played cricket, made pikelets and recycled paper as we built on our varied levels of English.

Yet in the walls of these rusted, ageing buildings are sad memories too: the young Hazara teenager broken-hearted at his separation from his mother, placing a love heart with 'I Miss You' on his sheet of newly made paper; a struggling Iranian teenager who sat by the perimeter fence desperately needing to be alone, my insistence that the student join the class out of my fear he may try to self-harm if I left him unsupervised. The holes in the floor, the broken tables and computers. The unspoken question of missing funding. But of all these memories, there is one moment in which I felt my world as I had known it finally fracture, like a faultline rippling at speed between what had happened before and the choices I made after, where the border between 'me' and the 'you' of asylum seekers warped and finally dissolved, and I felt myself becoming porous, my future no longer wholly separable from the fate of those young men who shared their lives with me.

Beneath the pandanus, the young men were already waiting, many in matching polo shirts, all in white Dunlop sneakers. 'Thirty-seven today,' the guard said. 'Hossein is having his interview and Ali N. is at Medical.' Someone wrote this down on a form attached to a clipboard, then the group divided itself into three as teachers and assistants walked toward their rooms. In the class I was working in, Barb was running an extension program for the students who had already acquired some English and had attended school in their country of origin.

'Hello, good morning,' the boys greeted us. 'How are you this morning?'

'Very well, thank you,' I replied. 'And you?'

We all enunciated clearly, felt the staccato consonants and wide vowel sounds slide around our mouths as we formed our immaculate sentences. I liked the students' playfulness and warmth. Some smiled shyly then looked away, others, like Mehdi, seemed to be constantly performing. Loud and boisterous, wearing a thick gold chain and bright orange t-shirt, this Iranian-born student liked his English raw and raucous, but he was always respectful. Like his friends, he was grateful to be here, grateful for something to do to break up the monotony of his life in detention. There were hundreds of asylum seekers crammed into this makeshift camp, originally built to house workers building the North West Point detention centre, and only a handful of places at the school. While the students remained imprisoned in the country they longed to be a part of, these young men were at least able to build their English language skills in the time that they were here. The students could feel this was a new beginning, however different from the one they had dreamed of.

Some of the students and I were working in small groups on a project called 'Thonglines', while Barb took a majority of the class. This involved the students writing about their journeys in short poetic forms, so we could scribe our creative works onto the blank sole of one of the thongs that regularly wash up on the island. The thongs were going be used to create a collaborative artwork for display. I had gathered scores of these colourful and discarded pieces of footwear, combing the island's few beaches.

For me, each rescued piece had become a layered metaphor, something lost or discarded, turning up on the unlikely landfall of this tiny island. The thongs scattering otherwise pristine beaches were confronting and we didn't want to acknowledge them, yet each piece had made a long journey, been sculpted and changed by its time at sea, to arrive at this chance intersection in our lives. Each thong had a unique imprint, a life and story pressed into its sole. Wound together with wire, carved with knives into pieces of art, broken or barely worn, each piece came like a floating question. When laid together alongside others, the thongs became beautiful, both in the synchronicity of the form and in their diversity.

In the preceding days I had run something of a crash course in short forms of poetry, focusing on haiku. Many of the Iranian and Afghan students had come from a tradition immersed in verse, lives lived in the heart of Persia. The challenge was not the form, but the language, the only translators being the students themselves. We had Farsi-to-English dictionaries, English-to-Farsi dictionaries, Dari-to-English dictionaries, and thesauruses. We drew, we mimed and laughed – we made do, and the poems they produced were startling in their pared back facts, both banal and profound in their raw expressions.

Students were transferred off the island without notice, before I could record many of their names, or before they could paint their hard-earned words. I typed these students' poems up at home, printed and pasted what they wished to say on the best thongs, on the brightest or the most beautifully sea-formed. Day to day we did not know which students would remain in the class, so I worked harder, faster, tried larger groups, to help as many students as I could to finish. Today in my rounds I had missed one student, now I noticed he was struggling. I saw him hunched over his desk, paper on one side, pink thong on the other. He stared at his page.

'Do you need a hand?' I asked. The student looked up, his body remained curled over his grey plastic desk.

'Ah, maybe,' he said. 'I am not sure.' I looked at the stark sheet of computer paper the young man was curled over, saw he had written two lines.

'Do you mind if I have a look?' I said, and the student sat up and passed his sheet of paper to me. I wondered if he was new in this class, and whether he was finding the task overwhelming. Though grouped according to their competence in English, the students still represented a huge range of abilities within each class, and their experiences of schooling could be very varied. 'What is your name?' I asked.

'Mohammed,' the student replied. 'I am from Afghanistan.' Mohammed was lean with black hair and pale skin. He appeared young, perhaps fifteen or sixteen. His eyes looked intently at mine, then back at the page. There, in shaky handwriting, were written the words

> The sound of firing
> many people fall down.

I knew I was out of my depth and did not wish to press students beyond what they were wanting to say, nor beyond what I was able to constructively respond to. None of the staff were given any specific training or support while working with asylum seekers, so I often worried my intuitive responses to the students' needs may have unwittingly caused harm to those who had experienced such severe trauma. I looked back at Mohammed, holding the half-formed poem between us.

'That is very powerful,' I said, 'and very sad. Do you want to paint the words on their own, or would you like to include an illustration with your work?'

Mohammed looked intently at me, like he was searching for

something, so I waited in the silence next to him, waited for him to find his words.

'I am sorry,' he said, 'my English is not very good.'

'That's okay, that's what I am here for.'

Mohammed smiled weakly back at me, but he was unsettled, and I was not sure what he wanted.

'Can I ask you something?' he said finally.

'Of course.'

Mohammed picked up his ballpoint pen and began to draw quickly, in rapid movements, onto a piece of lined paper. I wondered what it was that seemed to be so pressing, pushing him up against all the challenges in his ability to simply say. On his page he drew a picture of people in a park, some holding something.

'The women and the children, they go to the park. It was a graveyard, but they are playing cricket there,' he told me, and began drawing again in rapid, small strokes. I watched. I waited. He was drawing a truck, there was a door on the back of the truck and it was open. He drew men coming out on a ramp at the back of the truck, he gave them guns. He began to repeatedly point with the tip of his pen at the men at the back of the truck.

'Please can you tell me?' Mohammed asked, 'because I cannot understand. I just say to you as one person asks another so I can understand my life, what happened.'

'Sure,' I said. I held his gaze.

'The men,' he pointed again at the blue figures at the back of the truck, 'they jumped out of the truck and they shot all the women and the children in the park. I just stand there, but all around me the people fall down, crying, dead, dying everywhere. Why? Can you tell me, why did this happen? I don't understand. Can you tell me why they did this? How can this be allowed to happen?'

Mohammed's eyes looked directly into mine. He waited. He wanted me to give him something to make sense of what he could not hold. I wanted to ask if the men were white, but I didn't. I stayed with his question. I tried to find something, I dug deep in the silence, would not turn away, would not play it down.

'I am so sorry,' I said eventually, while I felt a strange ripping sensation through my body. The day turned silent. 'I don't know why. That is terrible. I don't know why.' We sat together with the weight of his question while the class moved and whirled around us. He nodded.

'What should I write for my last line?' he asked eventually. I looked back at his poem.

'Well, what happened after the people fell down?'

'I was just standing there.'

'Then that is what we need to write,' I said. Mohammed added his last line and we read the poem in silence, together:

> The sound of firing
> many people fall down
> but still I stood there.

'I think that is it, I think you should leave it like that, Mohammed, perhaps a comma after "still". Well done, that's a strong poem.' Mohammed curled back over his desk and added the comma. I stood up, saw another student with his hand in the air.

From the demountables at the Charlie compound, I look out toward the remnant rainforest at the camp's periphery. Life in the Phosphate Hill detention centres was a struggle, and many students were scarred by unimaginable trauma. Yet even so, for me, the glow of the pared-back, honest nature of our relationships pushed through the dark details of many of the young men's lives. The students appeared to me as luminous, the sense of their irrepressible humanity shone around me, their sheer will for vitality. In the time we spent together, our classrooms were filled with playfulness and drama, our laughter becoming a shared language, yet as their teacher, I was consistently treated with respect and kindness. Despite the often overwhelming nature of my work teaching in detention, standing here, I can't but help feel I was gifted something priceless and I am filled with emotion and a deep sense of gratitude.

The council workers have finished mowing and are packing away their gear. There is nothing more to see, so I turn to leave. Without the students' bustle and energy, the buildings are lifeless, so I walk back to the car and drive away from Phosphate Hill, heading back down the steeply sloping road toward Poon Saan. The ocean curves improbably high on the horizon, the rainforest arches over me, lush and green. As I drive, I feel a sense of peace, of calm, yet also the soft sorrow that takes the shape of loss, the absence of each of the faces of so many young men I knew so briefly but so intimately, our lives meeting for a month, a week, a day.

15. An Island of Hungry Ghosts

Apples, oranges, hand towels, fake money, pressed shirts, coloured flags, sweet biscuits, plain crackers and a pile of twenty or thirty new pairs of shoes. This is what it takes to placate the dead during the Festival of the Hungry Ghost. Late morning, I walk around the small mountain of goods contained by black plastic bags and cardboard boxes in the front courtyard of the Poon Saan Club, a 1950s-style building of stark concrete softened by an entry of architectural curves that forms a nexus of the Chinese community on Christmas Island.

Alongside these items are two large wooden tables adorned with an array of rectangular metal catering trays containing delicious-looking Asian dishes covered in plastic wrap, each pierced with ten or so sticks of incense. As I walk around the remarkable scene, a woman moves toward a third smaller table that is lined on the right side by a row of bowls. Each bowl is piled high with white rice, skewered with a lit stick of incense and accompanied by a large plastic spoon, a small container of what looks like sauce, and a teacup. An enormous silver teapot sits off to one side. Behind the teapot stands a red container filled with sand in which large maroon and silver joss sticks decorated with elaborate golden dragons have been arranged, along with more incense sticks. The woman brings over another handful of lit incense sticks and begins to add them to the others in the red container. She then places incense around the table of offerings, moving her hands in a circular motion through the smoke in what seems to be an act of prayer.

A man who looks to be somewhere in his early sixties, with black hair and olive skin, has been watching me from the shade of the club's porch. He walks over and stands beside me as I photograph the event and we begin to chat. I introduce myself and he tells me he is the president of the Poon Saan Club. The man gestures toward the tables of food and offerings, says everything I can see is for the people who were buried but do not have a grave. He tells me the shoes have been left out so the dead can be happy on the island, but sometimes it is difficult because you do not know what the dead want.

'Unless they come to you in a dream, maybe then you can learn what they want. This time now is the only time we can talk,' the man continues. 'The only other time you feel the dead are there is when you see shadows. When you see a shadow on the side of the road, you slow down. It is the spirit letting you know you might have an accident; you see the shadow and you know to slow down.'

I am pleased that my return to Christmas Island has coincided with such an intriguing festival. The Festival of the Hungry Ghost (also known as *Zhongyuan, Yu Lan Pen* and *Zhong Yuan Pudu*) draws its origins from Taoist and Buddhist traditions. It is believed that during the seventh moon (around August/September), restless spirits are released from the underworld to roam the land. It is the most important festival in which offerings are made to the deceased in Chinese celebrations, and includes honouring not only one's own ancestors, but also those unnamed transitory ghosts that have made their way from purgatory to the earthly realms. The two-sided attitude many Chinese people hold toward spirits is expressed in this ritual commemoration: both an attitude of awe and respect as well as a fear of getting the other world offside. The offerings made to the wandering ghosts are both an expression of compassion toward those spirits that may be experiencing ongoing suffering and also a utilitarian act of self-preservation.

The Festival of the Hungry Ghost is a series of ritual acts in which bad luck can be averted, and peace and prosperity are ushered in for oneself as well as for family, one's business and the larger community. It is an important time of bringing together diverse elements of a society in a united wish for peace and goodwill, as well as a rite of renewal. The communal element of the Festival of the Hungry Ghost is palpable for me as I look up and see a growing number of people from the island smiling and talking together in and outside of the hall. Inside the door to the Poon Saan Club, I see a lean older man talking together with a mother and her two young daughters. The man has given the brown-haired pair of girls triangular paper flags decorated with red-and-yellow snake-like dragons. The girls are intrigued by their gifts, turning them in the light from the window, taking in the colourful design. The pair look up and the group smile; their bodies lean in toward each other, the scene framed perfectly by an open sliding door.

Three years after my return to Christmas Island, while I was writing this book, I was fascinated to hear about the film *Island of the Hungry Ghosts*, directed by another former island resident, Gabrielle Brady, who worked with asylum seekers in detention as a torture and trauma counsellor. I found Brady's film excruciatingly painful to watch, her journey very much paralleling my own. Brady, presumably playing herself, documents the film's main character becoming incredibly affected by the stories asylum seekers shared with her, compounded by the trauma of witnessing the needless suffering of detainees as a result of Australia's border policies. For Brady, like me, this combination of events results in her difficult decision to leave, despite the sense of abandoning the people caught up within this inhumane system. What is also fascinating, however, is that one of Brady's structural elements in the film is the way she weaves the influence of Chinese culture on Christmas Island through ritual scenes, interspersed throughout the larger narrative about Brady's experiences of detention. As the title *Island of the Hungry Ghosts* indicates, several of these scenes are about the Festival of the Hungry Ghost.

As I watched the film, it dawned on me that Brady and I were at the Poon Saan Club on the same day at the same time, the same people appearing in our different mediums for recording what we saw during the ceremonies (my photographs show the same people in the same attire performing identical ceremonies to those documented in Brady's film footage). I realised I could actually recall seeing Brady setting up her camera, getting ready to film, though at the time I had no idea who she was or why she was there.

In her documentary, Brady indicates that she believes the rituals performed as part of the Festival of the Hungry Ghost were not only setting free relatives of the people gathered there, but also freeing the souls of those asylum seekers who had died on Christmas Island. At the same time the film also portrays the way Chinese Christmas Islanders work to facilitate the safe passage to the other side for the spirits of Chinese indentured labourers who died on Christmas Island, far from their home country, buried in anonymity in unmarked graves. As scenes of the island and its rituals flash before our eyes, we hear the distinctive voiceover of a Chinese Christmas Islander. He states '... the first people who arrived on Christmas Island one hundred years ago were not given a real burial, so we need to pray for them. For a month they are in the world of humans. They are Hungry Ghosts.'

I am only half aware of Brady, who is now filming the young girls with their new flags, framed by the sliding door. Near the door there are people beginning to form a line, so I walk over and join the queue of people inside the hall. One by one we are given a large incense stick to light. When my turn comes, I place my stick in the sand where the islanders' collective will for peace visibly grows, becomes expressed as a strange, rich scent filling the hall of diverse animated faces, smoke weaving out of the door, reaching with tenuous tendrils into the humidity, gesturing toward the glistening horizon of sea.

The crowd continues to grow, and sounds of conversation in several languages fills the air. I am reluctant to go, wishing to see what happens next, but I have been invited to the home of an old acquaintance for lunch. As my previous sense of isolation from the community on the island (largely due to my work with asylum seekers) has started to melt away, I start to see Christmas Island with a fresh lens, notice there is a general sense of peace, an absence of latent tension and anger in people, so different from the time I was here six years ago. Driving down the hill, I pass my old home in Silver City. The dated aluminium building in which my family lived was one of the silver cyclone-proof structures that inspired the suburb's name. It sits on the corner with its magnificent views of Flying Fish Cove, though I can see someone has levelled the garden I had tended with so much care, and I worry about the red crabs that had made their burrows among the fernery. A man and a child come out the back door, so I don't stop, instead turn left. The phosphate chute comes into view, its structure filling my windscreen, its industrial angles disjunct against a steep hillside graced with tropical greenery and backdropped by ocean.

Pulling up outside my friend's home, I see Tai Jin House sitting royally at the top of the sea cliff in the distance, resplendent in sun, framed by the blossoms of pale frangipanis. Laughter mixed with the sound of familiar voices spills down from the verandah high above. I pause as I open the door of the car; everything feels so tranquil on this stunning tropical morning, so calm. I wonder if I have judged this island too harshly, if I am wrong about its pervasive dark heart. Perhaps my own lens has been skewed by my particular view through a veil of human suffering. With the closure of the Phosphate Hill detention centres and the scaled-down operations at North West Point, perhaps this place has reclaimed a measure of what seems like a former innocence, a side of this island I was previously simply unable to see.

16. Living with the Goddess of the Sea

Blue, blue, blue! To be immersed once more, steeped deep with colour! In front of me the terrain of coral reaches as far as my eyes can see, saturated with a brilliant azure hue. Blue like thick glass; blue, a diffuse net trapping liquid light. Jo swims in front of me, her long flippers sending up bright white bubbles, two small ascending waterfalls of luminescence.

After my trip to the detention centres at Phosphate Hill, I called Jo to catch up once again, and over dinner at The Golden Bosun we decided to go for a snorkel from the jetty on what will be my second-last day on Christmas Island. I want to spend as much time with Jo as I can before our paths part again, and I am also very keen to get in the water now my biopsy dressing has been removed.

The cloud has dispersed as we head off from the jetty, lighting up splayed swathes of colour, textured fingers and stilled frills, coral everywhere growing its small moons and wide planes. Then it stops. With a shocking abruptness, all abundance ceases and what opens out to me is a watery desert, a terrain of lifelessness and desolation, the skeletons of staghorn corals lying bleached and at strange angles like a field of bones. The part of the reef that once looked like a forest viewed from the air now appears more like a war zone in miniature.

I swim to the surface and Jo swims up to meet me. I pull the snorkel from my mouth, breathless.

'Jo, Yvonne said there had been some bleaching but I didn't

know it had been this bad. This is devastating!'

'Actually, it's not as bad as it was,' Jo says. 'You should have seen it in April. After the bleaching the cove turned white. It was terribly beautiful, a bleached moonscape – all that life so suddenly wiped. The coral is starting to come back, it's much better than it was. The thing is, we don't know yet exactly what we have lost.'

As Jo speaks, I think of the islanders that cranked up their air-cons at night so they could sleep under heavy doonas, those who left their air-conditioners on while they set off for a six-week holiday so they didn't have to remove the mould on their walls on their return. Though the reasons for coral bleaching are multiple and complex, I can't help but despair at many of our choices as humans, the lack of urgency expressed in what we do, especially when on the island what is at stake is right in front of us. I wonder what it takes for us as people to change our ways.

'Do you think the reef will recover, Jo?'

'Well, it's amazing how resilient it has been, so maybe. Whether the soft corals and things like that will return, I don't know. The problem is, if we get another heatwave and it happens again ...' Jo trails off and I get the feeling neither of us wants to go down that path. We bite on our snorkels and duck back into the warmth of the water, past the graveyard of staghorn coral to where life once again pushes up lush and insistent.

Soon the sea floor drops away into a sapphire darkness and I hover over the sea cliff, floating in a dream-scape, gazing down into a depth I cannot understand. To my surprise, once again a white-tipped reef shark, all sinew and s-bends, streamlined and curving sensuousness, cruises past. I feel its one eye on me, scanning, watching. Once it has passed, I push down into a cloud of life, a school of blue-and-yellow angelfish rendered cinematic in watery light. The silence. Down here I feel like I am breathing, as if in all this stillness, all this abundance, is a place where I could make a home, where I could stay.

After our swim, Jo drops me back at my cottage and drives up the slope to her place in Silver City to have a shower and get changed. As the sun begins to glow golden, lowering itself into thin cloud shapes just above the horizon, she returns. I open a bottle of red wine I have kept in the fridge, pour myself a glass, but Jo declines as she has to teach the next day. Instead I make her herbal tea and we talk, looking out at the frangipani trees, their fat leaves silhouetted against the darkening sky, the silver bosuns ferris-wheeling raucously between the palm trees. Jo is perhaps five years older than me, a quiet and capable woman, humble by nature, yet I feel I have much to learn from her unfailing attentiveness to the world around her. I am grateful for Jo's friendship, which has grown since I left Christmas Island, the two of us meeting for coffee when she has been back in Perth or messaging each other from time to time over the sea. Our common bond is forged by an interest in each other's work as artists, and the often unspoken connection we have through our experiences of teaching asylum seekers, though at different times in the Phosphate Hill detention centres' history.

I tell Jo a publisher is interested in the poetry manuscript I wrote while living on the Cocos Islands, and that I am waiting to hear back after our meeting and my second edit, though I add it is early days. We toast our glasses, chatting excitedly about the collection and the possibilities that might lie ahead. I ask Jo what is happening with her own work. Jo is a visual artist, and her distinctive linocuts adorn the walls of the cottage where I am staying, textured works of pattern, movement and colour conjuring rock pools and beaches, temples and people. In the kitchen, the owners have hung one of Jo's prints depicting a temple scene, which I have found myself poring over, holding my morning coffee. The work's play of shadow and light depicts a woman placing sticks of incense in a large urn. Behind her a banner decorated with images of dragons adorns the wall, and a large red flag curls in on itself.

'I get very inspired by the natural environment and people,' Jo says when I ask her about the print. 'The cultural side of things really stimulates me. I am fascinated by places like Ma Chor Nui Nui, the temple that is out by the resort. It is a cultural and religious site, yet when you go there you are actually surrounded by this wild seascape. There is something quite powerful about the ocean there, something difficult to explain, but when I am there, I appreciate why it is that islanders built a temple on that site to honour the Goddess of the Sea.'

As we sit looking over the water, we talk about the ruggedness of Christmas Island, its awe-inspiring energy, both brutal and exhilarating. Jo tells me that she experiences the island as something raw and elemental, as if the middle ground has been removed.

'There is not a buffer here,' Jo tells me. 'You come up against things, the boat accident, everything. It is not very often that you are really up against things in such an immediate way – a way that affects you directly – on the mainland. I think you can be very removed in a suburb of the city.'

Jo tells me that years ago, before she had children and long before the place became known as the notorious detention centre site, she and her former partner used to spend time walking around North West Point. Following fisherman's tracks and slashing through jungle, they would spend hours finding their way along the cliff's lower terrace. Jo tells me that an image stays in her mind, lit and vivid, of stepping out from the jungle into a clearing at the top of a cliff where a stunning vista of water opened before her.

'It was one of those days when the ocean was absolutely crystal clear, completely glass-like,' Jo says. 'We stood on the top of the cliff with the jungle all around us, when all at once a huge pod of spinner dolphins swam by, leaping out of the water, turning in the air. There was not a single ripple other than where the dolphins leaped from the water. It was almost like they were they were leaping out of the water because they knew we had come out there at that moment. It was magical!'

We begin to speak about the detention centre, and I ask Jo if she too feels like there has been a shift in the culture of the island since North West Point detention centre had been scaled down and the family detention facilities at Phosphate Hill closed. She tells me it is as though there has been a collective sigh of relief across the community – like a simplicity, a lightness has returned to Christmas Island, a shift back to the place she used to know in 1995 – twenty-one years ago. Twenty-one years. I hold the figure in my mind, taken aback, I had no idea Jo had been here so long. A time before *Tampa*, before Children Overboard. Before. It now seems almost impossible to imagine.

Jo tells me about her experiences of teaching in the early days of mandatory detention. Jo started working in 2003, two years after the *Tampa* incident, in which Australian troops famously (and controversially) boarded the Norwegian freighter MV *Tampa*, when Captain Arne Rinnan tried to bring 433 rescued asylum seekers into Australian waters. The *Tampa* incident became a turning point in Australian federal politics, marking a new era of a hardened stance toward asylum seekers and greater emphasis on border protection.

Jo's work began at the family detention centre at Phosphate

Hill in the shadow of these recent events, teaching English to Vietnamese asylum seekers before the North West Point detention centre was built. At this time, the detainees were essentially two groups of extended families. Many members of the family had been businessmen and women and professional people who were frustrated at their lack of entrepreneurial freedom. They had started distributing anti-communist leaflets in Vietnam, and it was this action that threatened the government and ultimately forced them to flee. Jo tells me about the incredible vegetable garden made by the asylum seekers, brimming with flowers and produce. A little baby was also born in the camp, and Jo was able to bring her own baby daughter to meet the young family so their children could play.

'I stopped working when Ruby was born but used to take her up there to visit the Vietnamese people in the detention centre and they loved it. They loved it because it was a little baby being brought in and they spoiled her rotten and sewed little clothes for her. I have still got the little white cotton outfits they made for her. It was a really special relationship.'

Jo tells me a young couple even got married in detention, and she was able to lend the bride her wedding dress for the ceremony. The couple's wedding photos were taken with a disposable camera. Yet in all this life-fulness, Jo tells me she also struggled with witnessing the effects of long-term detention on the detainees.

'The families were in detention for two years up at Phosphate Hill and the children were in detention as well – they were released to go to school but locked up again every night. It is an unnatural living environment and the conditions bred problems. I worked with the Vietnamese asylum seekers for a year, or two years maybe, and I saw people go mad. I think detention has caused so much damage to so many people. If you have to do it for a short period of time, to process people during the initial stages, I can accept that, just for a couple of weeks at the most, but I have seen the damage it has done, it is a terrible thing to do to people. It makes people go crazy; it makes them give up hope.'

The sun has sunk below the horizon, and Jo and I sit in silence for a while, warm breeze on our skin. At the end of the low headland, frigatebirds angle between the palm trees, haunting the air, speeding past in groups of twenty or thirty birds, silent and unafraid.

'You asked me last night about the ocean,' Jo says, turning to me. 'About whether it affects the way I experience this place. I have been thinking quite a lot about your question. It made me consider how the ocean here links me to other places, especially with the asylum seekers that come, but also through all the objects that wash up. On Greta Beach, though all the rubbish brought by the tide is bad for the ocean, if I can take the environmental factor out, I find it amazing that all these objects have been used by people. To me it can almost bring you closer to other people – we are actually not that far removed. I think in Australia there is such a sense of wanting to shut ourselves off from the rest of the world and protect our borders and all that, but on Greta Beach there are these little bottles that were used for shampoo or hand cream, or toothbrushes. They are like small, washed-up stories.'

Jo goes on to tell me about one piece of flotsam that really spoke to her. It was an old toothbrush, something usually shunned not only as rubbish, but as dirty, unhygienic. Yet she was so struck by its human imprint that she ended up using it in her artwork.

'It was like it had been used for so many years that the handle had bent right back and the bristles were worn down to almost nothing, they were splayed right out, and I am not sure why, but it made me think of an old Indonesian man, you know, brushing his teeth and he had probably been using the same toothbrush for ten years or something; at least, that is what I imagined. I often turn over the kids toys washed up on the beach and think about who has played with them, and then something like a tiny shoe arrives, and it can't help but make you think of all the people making that journey by sea.'

I get up and turn on the light so I can see Jo's face better as the last light disappears from the horizon.

'Oh, it is getting late,' Jo says. 'I'd better get back, otherwise my kids will think I have abandoned them! But before I go, let me tell you one more story I think you would really appreciate ...'

I drain the last sip of wine from my glass and pull my chair toward Jo, willing her on. Jo tells me the moment had taken place earlier in her time on the island, before the asylum-seeker issue became significant for the community, before there was even a general consciousness of refugee people and their families drowning at sea. Jo had walked along the coral pebbles at West White Beach, turning over shells, looking at flotsam, when a dark rectangle had caught her eye. Jo walked toward the strange object and, once closer, realised she had found a rickety old suitcase lying washed up on the shore, its small form stark against the white bleached coral. Jo pulled on the case's salt-encrusted clasps and, though they were rusty, she found she could open them. She lifted the lid of the old case and peered inside. There, framed by the case's battered edges, were two items only – a folded black suit and a polished pair of men's shoes.

17. Turning Back

In the cove on this, my last morning on Christmas Island, boats sit bright as a pin. The vessels are all primary colours and child's toys hues: reds, whites, blues and clean lines, by the dusty phosphate tower beneath a single palm tree on the island's headland. Before my drive down to Flying Fish Cove for the final time, I had driven up to Tai Jin House and placed the coral pebbles I had inscribed around the plaque commemorating the 353 people who had died aboard the SIEV X. The flowers I had placed earlier beneath the rocks had gone, but I reassured myself it was just the wind and walked up toward the house's gardens, which tumble in a shout of colour from the sheer limestone cliffs. I felt still, quiet, as I picked bright sprigs of bougainvillea. Placing the purple foliage among grey pebbles, I felt a sense of grounding and release, as though in this act of honouring, something in me was being restored.

Now, sitting by the water, taking in my last moments at the cove, I feel relieved and surprised that my return to Christmas Island has been so peaceful, so pleasurable. I had anticipated this half of the trip as something of a necessary ordeal, yet I have felt there has been a place for me on this island this time around, a place not only held by the island itself, but by the people who crossed my path.

Walking along the pebbled beach to the jetty, I am filled with a strong sense of happiness and wellbeing. I can see a Zodiac speeding in from the large blue ship, the *Ocean Shield*. All at once it dawns on me that this vessel that has remained on the periphery of my vision my entire stay is, in fact, a Border Force ship, and that it must be Border Force officers who are being brought ashore. Reaching the end of the jetty, I take a closer look at the boat and the penny drops. The great white arm on the back of the ship is lowering a beautifully crafted red-and-white Indonesian-style fishing boat. At the edge of the port's cliff face, two more fishing vessels have been placed ready to move. These are turnback boats. The vessels are not old boats left at the port after asylum seekers had arrived; these are new vessels designed to push people fleeing persecution back to their perpetrators. I begin to shake, my body racked with fury. Taking the camera slung over my shoulder, I start to photograph the boats. It is then that I suddenly understand that the orange vessels stacked in the prow and placed in platforms built into the side of the hull are not only life rafts as I had presumed, but also turnback boats. These cruel, cramped vessels on which asylum seekers are pushed back to Indonesia after being removed from the fishing boats on which they arrive make asylum seekers incredibly sick, as they offer no windows and little to no ventilation.

I notice a woman waiting in a bus on the jetty is watching me as I photograph the boats. I register she is probably there to transport the Border Force officers to accommodation in Settlement. I can see a port worker in high-vis work wear waiting for something by the rail, so I approach him, pushing down my anger, and say hello. We chat and I ask him if he knows anything about the boats, and the young Malay man confirms the bright vessels are used to turn back asylum seekers at sea.

'The Indonesian Government was getting angry,' he says, 'because they knew the orange boats were from Australia, so the Australian Government made some boats to look like Indonesian fishing vessels. We have some Vietnamese workers at the port and they say they are good boats, top boats, top of the range for fishing.'

I thank the young man and walk back along the jetty, feeling utterly betrayed. Things have not changed out here in the middle of the Indian Ocean. I walk briskly back to the car and find my phone and, despite my latent anxiety about the threat of the *Border Force Act*, begin posting pictures of what I have seen, determined to make what the Australian Government does to vulnerable people visible by any means available to me. It is then I remember glimpsing orange vessels similar to those on the *Ocean Shield* up at Phosphate Hill, but at that time I had assumed they were also life rafts. I start the car and drive up the hill through Poon Saan to the top of the island, turn off at the road to Phosphate Hill. And there they are, fenced off with familiar government warnings about trespass: three more orange turnback vessels, a tractor and a crane. I sit in the car at the side of the road completely enraged, trying to slow my breath, to calm down. With shocking clarity I see that the suffering of asylum seekers has not ceased in this border zone, it has instead become completely silenced, the lives of already marginalised people now entirely hidden from view. This is why I could never stay. Here on the island's peak, I feel suffocated by the palimpsest of dark acts that have occurred here over generations, made possible by the remoteness of a landmass surrounded by wild and unforgiving sea.

18. Between Islands

Not long after my return to mainland Australia after living in the Indian Ocean Territories, I was walking down my suburban street near Fremantle when I noticed a car parked at the side of the road displaying a 'FUCK OFF, WE'RE FULL!' sticker prominently on the back window. The words were framed with the iconic image of Island Australia. We often associate the idea of our 'island home' with unity and togetherness: in our unofficial anthem we sing we are one, and that we are many, raising our voices in seeming unison. Yet when we are celebrating our 'one-ness', we are actually drawing borders around bodies – scribing lines between people – demarcating the 'in' of the Australian and the 'out' of the un-Australian. This idealised singular image of ourselves and our landmass can all too quickly slip into expressions of exclusivity and hostility, into Fortress Australia, as the car sticker on the back windscreen in front of me had shown.

Pausing in front of the car, much to my surprise, before I registered what I was doing, I had ripped the sticker from the back windscreen and taken off down the street. Heart beating hard in my chest, I crumpled the thin plastic strip into a ball before throwing it into a park bin. I had seen for myself the dire consequences for those who do not fall within the embrace of our definition of 'Australian', in the geographical violence played out in the name of border protection. I could not let the inherently hateful slur go.

Australia's defensive and inward-looking gaze and the ways in which this plays out in border zones like Christmas Island first became apparent to me in the Indian Ocean Territories at the memorial service for the Christmas Island boat tragedy, the same one where I had heard Zainal speak. I think back to when I first heard news of the tragedy on 15 December 2010 while driving my car home from South Beach in Fremantle. Our worldly possessions were already on board the cargo ship, the *Queen Mary*, heading for Christmas Island. I can still feel the incredible shock as the news came over the car radio, followed by an unexpected wave of grief; some of the children who had died such terrible deaths that day would have become my students.

My family and I arrived on Christmas Island three weeks after the tragedy, and the silence on the island about what had happened that day was disturbing – people simply did not talk about it. Though I worked closely with several people who witnessed the tragedy, in the twelve months I spent living on the island, I never heard anyone speak openly about what they witnessed on that day. Teachers (including me) were also not told which students had been affected by the tragedy nor given any guidance as to how to support the students who survived. I remember one morning at the start of school hearing a teacher shouting angrily at a young asylum seeker student to line up properly, her tone deeply unsettling. I later learned that this student – nine-year-old Seena Akhlaqi – had only days before returned from his drowned parents' funeral, held on the Australian mainland.

Despite the deeply distressing circumstances in which fifty asylum seekers drowned, I was grateful for the knowledge that the ceremony to mark the tragedy would take place during my time on the island. I saw the memorial service as a moment that would help the island heal by allowing a space for the islanders' and the asylum seekers' shared grief, bringing people together as they experienced their shared humanity in the face of adversity, brought together in the honouring of each precious life.

The memorial service took place on 5 March 2011 at the island's recreation centre at the top of Phosphate Hill. The large hall was filled with flowers (no easy feat three thousand kilometres from a nursery). Thick sunlight sat between the leaves visible through the large, open roller door of the recreation facility, behind which, only metres away, you could see the pool fencing that marked the border of the Phosphate Hill Processing Centre. Islanders gathered in the large building, women embracing and chatting in low tones, men sitting silently and stiffly in white plastic chairs. I glanced around restlessly, wondering when the asylum seekers would arrive, wondering how the survivors must be feeling on this difficult day. As the hall rapidly filled up, I glanced at my watch – nine forty-five – the ceremony was about to begin. I was worried, anxious there would not enough chairs now for the refugee attendees when they arrived, wondered why the bus was running late for such an important occasion.

A local member of the Chinese community stepped up to the microphone and formally opened the proceedings. I began to feel sick. *Where were the asylum seekers?* I turned around, craning my neck, to see if anyone was going to ask the MC to wait, hoping those from the *Janga* were perhaps just outside in the door and I had not seen them. But the faces behind me looked sad but calm, no-one looked overly troubled by the start of the ceremony. I glanced again at the door, but there were no asylum seekers waiting politely in the building's foyer.

The Minister for Veterans' Affairs and Defence Science and Personnel, Warren Snowdon, was introduced. He laid his akubra aside, stepped up to the microphone and announced from behind his moustache:

> We are honoured to be present today on behalf of the Australian Government to acknowledge and thank the Christmas Island community for your efforts in the aftermath of the crash of SIEV 221. ... I can only imagine the sense of helplessness you must have experienced wanting to save these people, but [instead were] powerless to support the emergency effort except through land-based support. The rocky landscape where this occurred is also notoriously razor sharp – meaning even land-based support was fraught. I want to commend the skills and bravery of Border Protection Command personnel involved in the rescue effort.

The Nation's 'Border Protection Command': why didn't the minister simply say 'Navy'? Why was he being insensitive to this tragic context by using polarising titles, and by 'these people', did he mean asylum seekers?

While these questions raced through my mind as Snowdon continued to speak, it began to dawn on me that the seeming insensitivities in the minister's response to the tragedy were no accident – they had been strategically thought through. With a growing sense of shock and disbelief, I began to comprehend that asylum seekers were not going to be directly referred to, they were being erased from the narrative of grief.

Suddenly I understood with a terrible clarity what was unfolding. The asylum seekers were not coming, they had not been invited to a memorial service about their own loved ones, and they were being carefully edited out of official versions of their own story. Sitting in that flower-filled space, I was awash with shame and rage, consumed by my own powerlessness to stop what was happening. I wanted to leap to my feet and shout at the room full of officials, the crowd of islanders, *Why on earth do you think we are we all here?* But instead I sat simmering mutely in my hard plastic chair. I was new in town, I was not even there on the day the tragedy occurred. I had repeatedly learned in my few weeks on this isolated island I had no right to ask difficult questions. The minister asked for a minute's silence.

As the service continued, some of the subsequent speakers did seek to acknowledge the death and suffering of asylum seekers, and several islanders explicitly sought to humanise the people on board the *Janga*. This included Zainal's profoundly moving speech in which he recounted the heartbreak of what he witnessed:

> I cannot stop seeing the eyes, the faces, of the people on the boat as it was dashed against the rocks, the father desperately clinging to the boat with one hand and with the other clutching his child to his side. Then a child swept from the arms of the mother. It was horrible.

Zainal went on to recount how he made eye contact with one little girl holding on to a piece of wood amid the debris of the broken boat. Though they were only metres from each other, the dangerous swell meant Zainal could not reach the child in order to save her from drowning. With a choked voice and tears falling in a steady stream down his face and onto the podium over which his body curled, Zainal shared that, later that same day, he discovered the little girl's body washed up on the shore of Ethel Beach.

Letters of thanks written by asylum seekers to islanders, medical staff, Immigration and Serco were also read out. We signed books, left flowers, wrote messages of heartfelt sadness, coming together in our sorrow and grief as an island community. Yet these gestures were completely overshadowed by the absence of the very people who had lost family and friends. Department of Immigration and Citizenship (DIAC) records report:

> Discussions between the Shire and DIAC leading up to the memorial on 5 March covered the issue of attendance of the survivors ... Over several days DIAC's advice changed from the survivors [sic] would be transferred off the Island before the event, then they would be here and DIAC would facilitate attendance. Finally in a couple of days before the memorial Fiona Andrew [Assistant Secretary to the Department of Immigration and Citizenship] advised that she was advised the best interests of the survivors would not be served by their attendance and that this was the advice from her medical team.

When mourners are denied the right to their grieving process, their ability to come to terms with their grief can be significantly impaired. In psychology, this phenomenon is described as 'disenfranchised grief'. Disenfranchised grief occurs when significant loss is experienced (for example, the death of an ex-husband), but the person's loss is not publicly acknowledged or socially supported because society's 'grieving rules' do not recognise the mourner's grief as real or legitimate.

The memorial service on Christmas Island on 5 March 2011 overtly demonstrated that the Australian Government had made the decision that what would be remembered about the boat tragedy would be the government's and Christmas Islanders' version of events; that is, the witness of Australian citizens. These events would be relayed by selected government officials and islanders alone. These recollections and contributions would be communicated in a way that completely controlled input from non-citizens (asylum seekers) who were deemed unworthy of the right to attend a memorial, even when that memorial was about their own loved ones. This act was made all the more insidious by the fact that those related to the deceased were literally a matter of metres away, imprisoned within the Phosphate Hill Processing Centre compound, within hearing distance of the service. The decision made to exclude survivors of the boat tragedy from the service portrays the acts of memorialisation as rituals to allow for the mourning process of islanders, while carefully minimising and stage-managing asylum seekers' grief.

Yet the lack of meaningful commemoration not only impacted on asylum seekers, it also had a significant impact on islanders who were involved in the rescue effort on that day. On my return to the islands, one islander, who wished to remain anonymous, shared her reflections with me, looking over the ocean near Rocky Point (the site of the tragedy) in the following way:

> It is hard. It is hard to see babies die, to see people die and not be able to do something. Most people's instinct is to rush in and do something, and everyone's instinct there that day was to do that and they were completely unable to, we had no power to do anything but watch and I think that makes people feel powerless, but also question what it is all about. You question lots and lots of things after an event like that, you know – we are so protected in Australia, away from the universal tragedies that occur globally. It does affect you. You may not be able to fully understand in what way, but I think a lot of the community, a lot of people have had to ... how can I

> explain ... the first few weeks were quite traumatic, people were getting counselling, or not, or simply chatting about it between themselves trying to process as best they could, and then you have to get past it, you have to keep moving, but then what do you do with it when you are at that point, what do you do with that information and that sort of scenario? What do you do with all that grief? I guess you have to put it somewhere and deal with it whenever you do, like any tragedy in anybody's life, I guess. I don't know ... I think the worst thing about it was there was this whole ... it became politicised and they [the asylum seekers] were whisked away, never to be seen again, and normally there would be a bit of a debrief after that, it might go on for a while where survivors and rescuers and people gathered together and talked, but it was just wiped, this one.

Even in the most brutal acts of silencing and marginalisation, if we look closely, we can often find traces of resistance and presence, even in the silence itself. Of the five letters of thanks read on the day of the memorial service and printed in the local newsletter, *The Islander*, only one letter thanks the Navy and police, a brief sentence of seven words added almost like an afterthought, 'Residents on the island who witnessed the incident tried to save us throwing life jackets and ropes. And so did the Navy and police.' Every heartfelt expression of thanks is directed toward those who lived and worked on Christmas Island, while a striking silence remains toward those whose role was to help avert disasters in Australian waters: the Royal Australian Navy. I look at these letters and go back and read my record of Tom's recount of what took place on 15 December 2010: 'We knew the

Navy was around the corner at Ethel Beach. We thought they must be coming at any moment. Another Navy vessel was further out to sea. No-one came. Until the boat was in pieces and spread across the coast, nobody from the Navy arrived.'

A coronial inquest into the tragedy records the testimony of an unnamed Iranian survivor who lost his wife and child when the *Janga* sank, which raises disturbing questions about the violent logic of the border. He states:

> How long do you think a wife and a child can exist in water like that, even with a life jacket? ... We actually owe our lives, and the reason we survived, is the people of the island, not the Australian Navy ... We have suffered enough and we can't sleep during the night because as soon as we shut our eyes, all these scenes and memories come to our eyes ... Who's going to answer for that?

Another survivor, interviewed in 2011, adds another more devastating layer to the seeming lethal indifference to the drowning asylum seekers:

> I don't know what happened, but one speed boat it came to save only one of the people, one person, then going back to the Navy boat, smoking and looking, but then staying there for a while before they came back. They could have picked up seven or eight people at one time [but] they didn't do so. It seems they didn't care about us. If they had been quicker, only by two or three minutes, they would have saved the people ... We owe our lives to the people of Christmas Island, not the Australian Navy. The life jackets they threw us made us to survive.

I would venture to suggest that the silence in the asylum seekers' letters, the seeming omission in their statements of thanks, speaks volumes about what took place at Rocky Point in the early morning of 15 December 2010.

While letters from asylum seekers were included at the memorial service on 5 March, the letters provided by the Department of Immigration and Citizenship and security company Serco were all *exclusively* expressions of thanks to the islanders and the Department of Immigration and Serco themselves, rather than expressions of the inconceivable grief and trauma the survivors must have been experiencing. This makes it hard to believe there was not some 'stage managing' around what asylum seekers were invited to express. Fortunately, the island's Shire President, Gordon Thompson (an active advocate for asylum seekers on Christmas Island), was able to approach several asylum seekers directly about what they wished to say on the day of the service. Gordon was also able to share something of the asylum seekers' specific experiences of loss so we get more idea of them as people, a small sense of their stories.

One of the letters that Gordon read out at the service was a letter from Ramin. Ramin lost his wife and son as well as his brother and brother's wife the day the *Janga* sank and was caring for his orphaned nephew. Ramin's letter is full of gratitude, yet through his words we can finally allow our hearts to break over what happened that day. Ramin's raw devastation and sheer humanity shine through each of his words. Though he could not tell his story in person at the March service, thanks to Gordon's efforts he could at least share his story on his own terms:

> I don't know how to bring forward my feelings and thoughts to you. It's amazing that people who live together here have such a big heart and that everyone tried their best to help other humans. This is not me just saying this to you. It's my family, my relatives over there in Iran and here in the camp. Here on Christmas Island we have met the kindest people on earth. From my heart I appreciate your help. I hope this never happens again. Some people, they like to hide the facts, the differences between people cause them to hide the facts. I wish I could talk in your language to Australia and Iran and all the countries how it is here, how kind you are. This is an island in the middle of the whole ocean and facilities might be limited, we appreciate the limited things here, we are grateful. I hope one day if we get the honour to be Australians, we'd like to meet people like you in our life. We lost wife, kids, a lot of people. That much effort for a sudden thing is a lot. We come from the worst place in the world, the worst human acts and we come to you, the most kind. I am so happy to have met people like you. Even if we don't end up staying in Australia, I appreciate meeting you.
>
> 'Anywhere we go the sky is blue, it's the people who make the place beautiful.'
>
> (Iranian Proverb).

As I sit here typing Ramin's words from my copy of *The Islander*, I feel the awful tension between his outpouring of gratitude and the fact that he was not permitted to attend the memorial for his wife and son, their lives unmentionable even by our own government. I also think of Tom's recount, how he shared that some of the islanders threatened to throw rocks at the struggling boat. I think of my colleague who was at Rocky Point helping with the rescue on the day of the tragedy, months later wanting to call a work cocktail 'Refos on the Rocks', of the threats some islanders made to burn down the SIEV 221 memorial if it was placed at the site of the tragedy near The Golden Bosun pub at Rocky Bay. Ramin's words are humbling, the choices of my fellow islanders and my nation's government deeply disturbing. Are the spite and hate that steep these acts, these expressions of inward-looking protectiveness, what it means to be truly 'Australian'?

After the Christmas Island boat tragedy, survivors of the mass drowning and families of those who died filed a class action against the Australian Government. This class action was lodged against the Federal Government for its failure to rescue asylum seekers in the hours (and, here I stress, it was almost *two hours*) between the time the *Janga* was first sighted off the coast of Christmas Island and when it was smashed against the rocks, as well as other seeming systemic failures that were believed to have contributed to the large numbers of those who drowned. Justice Geoffrey Bellew ultimately ruled in favour of the Australian Government, but the NSW Supreme Court summary gives some confronting insights into whose lives matter at sea; would we accept this ruling if those who died were British citizens who found themselves in trouble in Australian waters? It reads:

> The Commonwealth had no control over the risk that a SIEV, if not intercepted, might be shipwrecked on the coast of Christmas Island due to factors such as poor weather, poor navigation or running out

> of fuel. Further, the Commonwealth did not put the plaintiffs at any risk of harm and, in particular:
>
> a) could not, and obviously did not, direct those in charge of the vessel to navigate a particular route to Australia;
> b) did not control the weather;
> c) did not control and, on the evidence, knew nothing at all about, the level of skill of those operating the vessel; and had no control over the primitive nature of the vessel ...
>
> ... on the information which was made available to him at about 06:00 on 15 December 2010, Commander Livingstone did not know, nor did he have reason to suspect, that SIEV 221 was in distress ...

To someone who has lived through a wet season on Christmas Island, the judge's statement that Commander Livingstone 'did not know' that the *Janga* (SIEV 221) was in distress is breathtaking. During the wet season, the glassy waters that surround Christmas Island turn hostile, large swells smashing against the jagged limestone cliffs that rim the island, sending dramatic spumes of spray over rocks and buildings. Supply vessels often cannot moor for months due to the treacherous seas, so islanders find themselves with gin and no tonic, conditioner and no shampoo, as basic supplies run alarmingly low. The dangerous maritime conditions in the wet season are a well-known reality of living on this remote island, so how could the Commander Livingstone – a man whose vessel would have been circling the island for months – not know that *Janga* was in distress?

Equally revealing is the way other sections of the report continually refer to the asylum seekers as acting illegally, yet under the 1951 Refugee Convention it is legal to seek asylum in Australian waters when fleeing persecution in one's home country. Though this right is stipulated through international rather than federal law, the right to seek asylum is still a point of law; surely this is something we can expect a specialist in Australian law to have understood. The report concludes: 'Those on board could have protected themselves simply by not undertaking the voyage in the first place'. This statement is an overt – even nonsensical – denial of the rape, torture and murder enacted by repressive regimes that repeatedly force asylum seekers to flee their home countries.

What we witness in this transcript is not the enactment of justice, but instead what appears to be a ruthless example of 'wishful sinking'. Consistent with a history of not wanting to accept people of non-white appearance in our country, the Australian Government appears to be complicit in allowing asylum seekers to drown in Australian waters as an informal strategy of deterrence; letting people die becomes an invisible, extreme enactment of our nation's prejudices. The decision to seemingly let asylum seekers die appears to be upheld by a similar expression of systemic racism evidenced in Australia's legal system. The Christmas Island boat tragedy was perhaps not a 'tragedy' after all, but an event that reveals something far more sinister about our nation's psyche.

The series of events that played out during the Christmas Island boat tragedy were far from an isolated incident. The circumstances of the sinking of the SIEV X in 2001 in which 353 died (and to whom Christmas Islanders and Canberrans made such affecting memorials) was also highly contentious. One only needs to do a quick internet search to see the way in which the Australian Government was implicated in the drownings in reputable news sources such as the *Sydney Morning Herald* and the *Guardian* as well as articles published by the Australian Broadcasting Corporation (ABC). There have been repeated calls for a judicial inquiry into what took place in 2001, but in a rare bipartisan move, both major parties opposed an inquiry. As a result, details of exactly what the Australian Government knew about the SIEV X and its sinking remain unclear.

In the book *Dark Victory*, authors Marian Wilkinson and David Marr delve into this controversial period of the Howard Government, raising concerns that the Australian Government may have been complicit in the sinking of the SIEV X. This perspective is shared by author, activist and psychologist Steve Biddulph. In an interview with Geraldine Doogue on the ABC in 2011, Biddulph said:

> Nothing about the SIEV X voyage was normal ... because we came to know many of the survivors of the SIEV X and they told us what happened; that they were bussed in a fleet of buses halfway across Indonesia, the buses were blacked out, you couldn't see in or out, and they were escorted by motorcycle escort, they were kept at the hotel belonging to the chief of police in Bandar Lampung. Worst of all, they were loaded onto the vessel at gunpoint. The vessel was very decrepit and these were people that were very sensible people and they saw that it couldn't possibly survive a voyage. And one family tried to get off and the father was pistol-whipped by a policeman and forced back on.
>
> During the voyage, in the early hours of the voyage, it was shadowed by an aircraft. And the most disturbing feature of it was that when the boat did eventually sink

> in very heavy seas, that the following night, when many of the people still were afloat, still surviving clinging to wreckage, two military vessels ... appeared on the site of the wreckage. How they found them in the dark in a storm is a huge question. And many of the people thought they were safe, and they thought they can just swim towards these boats. And the boats turned their lights off and sailed away.

Among the dead were 146 children.

It is also relevant to remember here that the Norwegian captain of the MV *Tampa,* Arne Rinnan, unwittingly made political history when he attempted to save the lives of asylum seekers aboard the sinking *Palapa*, which the Howard Government subsequently refused to allow to enter Christmas Island. More recently, on 10 June 2013, border patrols spotted an unmoving asylum-seeker vessel fifty-three kilometres from Christmas Island. It was two days before a mayday and full-scale search was launched. Sixty men, women and children drowned – there were no survivors. The Royal Australian Navy refused to retrieve the bodies from the water for the families of the deceased.

However, the racially based violence directed toward asylum seekers was not limited to the government's physical actions (and inactions) but was also expressed through legislation. In August 2001, in the days directly following the *Tampa* crisis, the Howard Government sought to excise Christmas Island and the Cocos (Keeling) Islands from the migration zone. This move was deliberately designed to strip asylum seekers of their right to seek asylum by claiming the new arrivals had, technically speaking, never set foot in Australia and therefore were no longer entitled to access Australian law or claim asylum in our country. The excision of the

Indian Ocean Territories was an aggressive expression of racism by the Howard Government that actively sought to punish asylum seekers for arriving by boat, while inflaming a climate of fear.

In *Against Paranoid Nationalism*, Ghassan Hage describes the way in which the Howard Government marked a resurgence in what he describes as 'white colonial paranoia', a fearful protectiveness that had been largely marginalised since the advent of World War II. Hage argues that the shift toward Australia's self-concept as a 'multicultural' nation in the 1980s, as well as the Mabo ruling in 1992 acknowledging the lawful ownership of land by Indigenous Australians prior to colonisation, alienated many white Australians. Howard played on a nostalgia for a return to 'Australian' values, a fantasy of 'changing back' to an unquestionably Eurocentric Australian culture.

I can't help but wonder, had events not been cast so darkly across the globe over the weeks to come, whether the Howard Government would have been so extraordinarily successful in spinning this divisive narrative, a fearful story that has largely gripped the nation since. Yet within weeks of *Tampa*, on 11 September 2001, 2,996 people died in the wake of the terrorist attack on the Twin Towers in New York City. John Howard was in Washington, DC, on the day of September 11. Up until that time he had been struggling in the polls and a Labor victory seemed likely. On that terrible and fateful day in 2001, Howard must have realised September 11 was his moment. The enactment of the excision legislation, though hastily drafted in response to *Tampa*, and the legally dubious act of the military seizing the Norwegian freighter off Christmas Island, were seemingly vindicated in the light of a perceived new threat – the Middle Eastern 'terrorist'. Our struggling prime minister gave the order for Australian troops to join the USA in the wars in Iraq and Afghanistan, framing himself as the man in charge of rescuing the nation. On his return to Australia, Howard set a surer foot on our country's tarmac, armed with the politics of fear and the excision's enactment. The announcement of the opening of a detention centre on Christmas Island was made within weeks of the devastating events at the World Trade Center. Soon after, Howard would famously announce his historic words, 'We will decide who comes into this country and the circumstances in which they come.' Our country's leaders' commitment to framing asylum seekers as potential terrorists began.

Through the Howard Government's excision of places like Christmas Island and the Cocos (Keeling) Islands from the migration zone, our nation gave birth to a near-fiction, to 'un-Australia': an in-between space, a place that both is, and is not, 'Australia'. The somewhat bizarre nature of this relationship was apparent to me every time we flew back to Christmas Island. My family and I were required to board our plane at the international airport, yet we were not required to show our passports. When filling out our incoming passenger card for the Department of Immigration, with the assistance of the flight attendant, we were instructed to fill out our card as residents returning to 'Australia', with the country where we will spend most time abroad being 'Australia'.

These strange rituals become expressions of our nation's sometimes seemingly irrational, even pathological, will for disassociation. The disowning of places that challenge our sense of sovereignty as white Australians create shadowlands, 'no-go' zones, spaces often barely known that haunt our national psyche. Through white Australia's disowning of places like Fitzroy Crossing in the Kimberley, as well as the decision to legally excise places like Christmas Island and the Cocos (Keeling) Islands from our sovereign obligations, we distance ourselves from the violence that continues to allow our own privilege. We turn our eyes away from the fact that what we have has come at a cost of the lives of those at the border, for both 'non-citizens' at the watery edge of our nation, as well as the mentally excised spaces that are the home to many First Australians, the latter cutting us off from our centre, our country's heart.

For Christmas Island and the Kimberley, this distancing seemed to come as an active denial of the extreme and sustained violence that continues to play out in these regions, but on the Cocos (Keeling) Islands, it did not seem as straightforward to come to this conclusion. My need to return to this atoll in the middle of the Indian Ocean was not so much about what I had witnessed in this similarly excised world, but instead a vague need to address what I had experienced as an unsettling silence, particularly when inquiring about the atoll's history. As I flew the nine hundred kilometres from Christmas Island to the Cocos (Keeling) Islands on 6 August 2016, I thought my work was largely done in the Indian Ocean Territories, that perhaps while I was back among friends, I might still learn a thing or two, and yet little did I know there was still so much more to the story ...

Cocos (Keeling) Islands

'What the map cuts up, the story cuts across'

Michel de Certeau

19. West Island (Pulu Panjang)

I have two distinct memories of my first arrival on Cocos (Keeling) Islands in January 2012. The first is looking down from the plane at the view of West Island, where we were to live for the next two years, and bursting into laughter. I had never wanted to live on the Cocos (Keeling) Islands. As someone with a strong and consistent need for personal space, the idea of living on an island with a population of around ninety people, on a landmass half a kilometre at the widest point, terrified me. However, after the death of my father at the end of 2011 and Massom's attempted suicide, I reluctantly conceded I could no longer sustain my work with asylum seekers on Christmas Island. Yet the idea of returning to my former life on the mainland after all I had witnessed in the Indian Ocean Territories seemed impossible. My response to this challenge was to accept my husband's initiative to apply for jobs on the Cocos (Keeling) Islands, while simply and actively going into denial. Surely West Island is not as small as people said, I decided. Friends are exaggerating for effect, to make a good dinner-party story. Or perhaps I misheard the conversations of Christmas Islanders: surely, they were actually discussing one of the other twenty-six islets on the main atoll, not West Island where I was to live. In reality, I was sure I would find my new home was actually of a reasonable, habitable size.

My denial was so successful that I had forgotten about other people's descriptions of the atoll until the plane came in to land. I looked down to see a landmass that looked more like a sandbar than a place to make a home. West Island was even more marginal than Christmas Islanders had described. Looking down, I had no idea how I was going to cope with this new situation, but here we were, descending rapidly into another great adventure of miniature proportions.

My second memory is walking alone for the first time on the atoll, along the reef just past the runway. In the still of early morning, the sky was imbued with the deepest of blues. On the shore, palm trees reached lean bodies toward the clear curve of a wave, their trunks forming a gentle arc over brilliant white sand. From turquoise waters that appeared more like a shifting sculpture of glass, two turtles lifted their curious heads. A few metres from where I stood, an egret stepped cautiously, gracefully with her long yellow legs through rock pools, looking for eels curled among the coral. There was not another human to be seen.

I could barely comprehend the beauty in front of me, let alone understand that this paradisiacal place was my new home. After witnessing all the suffering and injustice on Christmas Island, as well as my father's slow cruel death from liver cancer, I could not make sense of my life, of why I had been given so much in a world marked by relentless and incomprehensible suffering. I broke down, falling onto my knees on the sand, my shoulders wracked with sobs as I was consumed by a wave of gratitude and confusion. I cried with the relief of realising that, despite my doubts, I *could* live here, that I had been gifted something extraordinary, almost unbelievable. Yet I could not reconcile my good fortune with what I had learned other people had to endure, nor could I understand what it was that I was supposed to do, given my new insights into what my country was capable of. How should I respond to all that I had seen? What was my responsibility to the asylum seekers I knew now?

More than four years later, I turn these memories over as the aircraft arcs over the atoll. Today, having left Christmas Island in the late afternoon, the passengers and I do not arrive until sunset. The sun has already been consumed by the vast liquid horizon, rendering the lagoon subdued, soft-hued, the islands transforming into dark shapes on a wide and shifting pastel palette. Over the lagoon, a full yellow moon begins to rise. As the passengers and I bounce along West Island's tarmac, the aircraft's window frames two pilots standing beside a large military plane backdropped by a lush forest of palm trees catching the last light. An ornate bronze rooster runs manically away from the plane toward the trees' protection. Today, arriving seems ordinary and surprisingly tranquil. I am grateful for the mundanity of the moment – forklifts and foyers, slow queues and the slightest glimpse of moonlight leaning on the black expanse of the sea.

After making my way through Border Force checkpoints, I see the welcome sight of my friend Emma, who is picking me from the airport. Waving at familiar faces, I make my way toward her and we hug briefly before I throw my bag in the back of the ute in the pub carpark. Emma drives me and my pack one hundred metres down the road to where their home sits a few metres past the oval, its wide verandah looking west out over a shifting expanse of Indian Ocean. Soon we are sitting on their wide deck in the balmy tropical warmth, drinking beers like no time has passed, though the addition of a tub spilling with children's toys and a bright plastic swing hanging from the rafters stand as small markers that, despite all the evidence to the contrary, time has indeed moved on.

In the morning, Emma and Pete's kitchen is abuzz with energy. They are about to head off on holiday to Canada and mutual friends have moved in as they are housesitting while Pete and Em are away. The couple's little boy has the gentle nature and tousled bleached-blond look of his surfer parents. He runs through the house with Pete and Emma's curly-haired toddler, fists grasping pieces of toast, faces painted with Vegemite.

Pete is a big-hearted and well-liked high school teacher and surfer who came here for work and then stayed on the atoll after he fell in love with Emma. Emma has lived on the Cocos Islands with her family on and off since she was a child. Now in her early thirties, she has established her adult life here on the atoll. Also a keen surfer and accomplished artist, Emma runs a gallery made from an old barge formerly used on Home Island before it was unceremoniously dumped among the coconut palms near North Point at the end of its working days. Emma and her dad lovingly restored the old boat, and the Big Barge gallery is a testimony to their strong work ethic and meticulous aesthetics. Emma and I had worked closely together on the atoll as I was the art teacher at the district high school and Emma was an artist-in-residence on the same campus, once again using washed-up thongs for art, this time converting them into a beautiful mural of a traditional Cocos Malay *jukong* (a small, wooden boat with no keel) sailing on the lagoon. Emma became pregnant a few months before I left, so I had never quite got my head around her being a mother. It feels remarkable to see her home like this, full of the bustle and life of young children. Watching the kids run around, and witnessing Pete and Emma patiently and tenderly talking with their young daughter, I begin to process that this striking young couple have become a family.

I pack up my things and Emma drops me at my accommodation another few hundred metres down the road. As I haul my pack out of the ute once more and wave goodbye, a vague sense of elation begins to rise at my return to this small paradise. Knowing my time on Cocos is going to be limited, I have planned ahead. In forty-five minutes, I need to be at the school, where I have volunteered to run poetry workshops with the older students. Placing my pack by the wardrobe, I dig around for pens, paper and my teaching notes, hearing the familiar chatter of white terns and crash of rolling surf, the sun reaching into the room between frangipani blooms. Armed with books and a tentative lesson plan, I run down the road toward the school. The swell looks magnificent in the early light and there must be turtles bobbing between the sets, but I cannot stop, don't want to be late, cutting down a path between two houses to save time.

When I step into the familiar space of the small dim staffroom, I am greeted by a handful of faces I remember well, all busily readying themselves for the start of the school day.

'Hello Mak, welcome back!' Nek Namira calls as she continues making herself a sweet instant coffee from a small packet she keeps in her pigeonhole.

'Hi Nek!' I am happy to see this friend with her irreverent sense of humour continues to keep things lively in the school library.

'Hello, Mak!'

I turn around as Pak Yati, one of the older male education assistants, comes in the staffroom door. 'Pak! It's been a while!'

We laugh at the surprise of seeing each other again. Pak Yati was instrumental in helping to translate my poetry into Cocos Malay when I was on the islands, a gentle and affable leader in his community with a passion for fishing.

'Wow, I heard you were coming,' Pak says. 'How is your family, how are Greta and Pak Greta?'

We chat for a while about our families while I start to register the many unfamiliar adult faces coming and going as everyone prepares for their school day. I am taken aback that there seem to be so many new members of staff; there are hardly any teachers and no administrators here I recognise and, for a moment, it dawns on me how the Cocos Malay community must experience West Island. West Island houses the largely white population of public servants and teachers that come on two- or three-year contracts, while the Cocos Malay population of around five hundred people live almost exclusively in Bantam Village on Home Island. As a West Islander, I didn't really experience the transience of the white population directly, as most of our friends came and left in approximately the same time frame. Now the warm but distant way with which the Cocos Malay inhabitants largely related to us *orang putih* makes sense: there would be little motivation to invest in friendships with the white population if you knew in a couple of years they were almost certain to leave.

Pak Yati makes a coffee and walks over to the classroom with me. He works as an assistant in Pete's room, where I am about to teach. The faces of many students I recognise from my time teaching art on the campus turn to look at me as I walk in the door. I notice some of the girls, now a few years older, have started to wear colourful *tudung*s, or headscarves, some decorated with ornate silver jewellery. The bright cloth both contrasts with and frames their dark eyes and olive skin, making the young women seem even more beautiful than before. Considering the almost three years I have been away, the students are surprisingly warm with me, and I am moved by their openness, especially as these students are high-school aged, a time when many older children become less demonstrative. The students ask me eagerly for news of my daughter and I update them, then we take our places and the class begins.

At first I am self-conscious teaching in front of Pete and

Pak Yati. I have never mixed my worlds of teaching and poetry before – it feels strange. However, once I get the students writing and sharing their work, we all settle and get into our stride. After they have been writing for some time, I ask the students to read their work to each other. They are shy but excited, and much to my delight, almost all the class members choose to share what they have written. I can see many students seem slightly taken aback by the work they have produced, perhaps surprised to find themselves enjoying, and relating to, poetry.

As I start to relax, I begin to feel more comfortable about sharing my own work with the students. I read a poem called 'Pinggiran', meaning 'margin', to the class.

'Some of the phrases are in Cocos Malay that Pak Yati and Mak Sofia helped me translate,' I explain after I have read the short work, 'to try and show how we move between languages here on Cocos. For example, the phrase *kehidupan belum tentu*. Who knows what that means in Cocos Malay? Who can translate the phrase into English?'

'Life is tenuous,' one capable student replies, and he looks slightly astonished, his mouth open in an expression of surprise as he angles his head like he is focusing intently. His eyes look straight into mine. Some of the students have gone quiet, and I am not sure if it is the experience of hearing creative works in their first language that has caught their attention, or whether they too experience their own mortality strongly in this island-scape. Either way, I sense a shift in the room, something has changed in the small crowd of faces looking back at me. In a school system where we were continually pushing the students to speak in English to increase their employment prospects, my gesture back to them in their first language feels like an intimacy, a gesture of respect that it seems is being returned.

Leaving the school, I am buoyed by what the students and I have shared. To return the poems I wrote on the island to these young islanders, and have the works openly received, is incredibly satisfying. The school's new principal had hoped I would work with all students from years one to ten during my time here; however, we compromised on focusing on upper primary and high school students as I felt these students would get the most out of the sessions. Before coming to the Indian Ocean Territories, I had offered to go into the schools on both Christmas Island and the Cocos (Keeling) Islands to run poetry workshops and share my work. I was upfront with both schools that my work spoke to the issue of asylum seekers among other themes, but my focus was to share my love of poetry with students and to get them writing about the unique place where they lived. While initially I was told that Christmas Island District High School would be happy for me to come into the classrooms and share my work with the students during my visit, none of my subsequent emails or messages were ever returned. I never got to work with the Christmas Island students or share with them poems about their island home. For me, this was disappointing but not at all surprising, the disparate responses a telling reflection of the contrasting cultures of two very different island populations.

Once back at my accommodation, I start to unpack my things. The space is beautiful, filled with light, yet alarmingly close to the rooms beside me. Yet I can't hear anyone around, and the view from my window is of hibiscus glowing red, the foliage of banyan trees and frangipanis framing a bright slice of foaming sea. The day is getting warm and my excitement at being back is beginning to grow. Throwing my sarong across the bed to make it feel more like home, I walk to the bathroom to put on my bathers. In that lit space, as I slather myself in suncream, once again the mirror confronts me with the disturbing brown mass that is growing on my shoulder from which the biopsy was taken. I had been successful at putting the threat of cancer out of my mind, but here in a new space again on my own, I am forced to face this frightening possibility once more. A sick feeling rises in my stomach. I can't deal with it; I don't know what to do. There is nothing, nothing that I can do. I realise my results must be ready, that I am supposed to visit the clinic, which is about a five-minute walk from my accommodation. *Not today*, I think, *not today*.

I examine my shoulder in the mirror in the bright sunlight coming through the blinds, but its mutated shape only makes me feel more anxious. I pull a t-shirt over my shoulders, taking the disturbing sight from my view, pull on my shorts and try to push the ominous feeling of my pending mortality away. There is so much to celebrate here, I can barely contain my joy, my sheer elation at having returned. In this watery place I feel more grounded than ever – to be back on these islands on my own terms is incredible. I walk outside to the shed where the accommodation's website said guests could access a range of bikes. Beside a small laundry there are a stack of metal frames, and I go into the small building to have a look. On closer inspection, two of the bikes have flat tyres, one is a child's bike and another has a chain stiff with rust. *Too bad*, I think, *it's rust or nothing*, and I pedal my way, straining against the bike's resistance on the low boardwalk through the tropical garden. Once out on Airforce Road, I hit the trade winds howling over the runway and am forced to confront the fact that my idyllic memories were of Cocos in the doldrums, not in this howling wind that throws sand in my eyes, pushing me back, even as I strain against the rusty chain to propel myself forward.

Though the situation is ridiculous, I can't bear the thought of not being able to get to the bright waters at Pulu Maria, and I strain against the chain and wind, telling myself it is good, I am wearing off the overconsumption from Christmas Island, which is just as well, considering I am in a place where you spend half your life in a bikini. I strain and strain, eyes stinging, sweating into full sun, until I finally hit a grove of lush palms that line the road along the rest of the island. Palm fronds clap their hands loudly as wind tousles their lacquered canopy, but down here the breeze is calmed and a moist shade falls across my skin. I stop and take it in, the luminous green of coconut upon coconut, palms iridescent with life, picturesque as a garden. The thin sandy track winds between the coconuts' layered trunks, the most ancient palms reaching high into sky, long poles pushing into blue. A car comes bouncing along the track toward me and its passengers wave, snapping me out of my brief reverie. Pedalling again, I find I move faster without the wind's resistance, until through the gloss of fronds the view opens before me.

The tiny island of Pulu Maria pushes above the sea, almost a caricature of itself: a small contained mound of white sand rising from turquoise waters, covered in a jostle of coconut trees, at the foot of which the slightly dilapidated remains of a *pondok*, or hut, sit just out of view. Further out, the large arc of South Island helps create the atoll's distinct horseshoe shape and, further still, toward the end of the of islets' curve, Home Island suggests itself in the thinnest of lines. A section of the atoll only two metres above sea, this densely populated island is a ghost terrain from here, a wisp of sand barely visible above the salt spray of the lagoon.

I breathe slowly, take in the scene I have committed to memory. I step out from the shelter of the trees toward the water only to be hit hard once more by the wind. Fish gather around my toes in the shallow water; a small reef shark swims by. From here I can see a crowd of kite surfers carving lines of wake into the ruffled surface of the water further round the point. It is not the serene moment I anticipated, but it is enough to get my bearings. I have missed this place like one aches for family – here is a landscape of water where I was held. In the atoll's shifting liquid embrace something in me was made whole. In the elbow of these islands I found a place to belong.

After my ride out to Pulu Maria, I join Trish (my friend who I had bumped into at the airport on my way to Christmas Island) and her family for dinner at their home. Their children spill out over the verandah, giggling and talking; bright toys escape down stairs. We sit looking out over a lush garden of dense greenery through which the ocean shifts and glints in the last of the day's light. The table is filled with salads and fresh fish, warm bread and wine, and I am filled with gratitude at being welcomed into their family. Being here with Trish and Tony, I experience an irrational sense we are simply picking up where we left off. For a moment it feels like I have returned, as though I never really left, my old life about to resume. As we eat, I am struck by the openness of their children. It is in the gentleness of their faces, the animation in the lit windows of their eyes. The boys emanate the glow of those who know they are loved, articulate with a tongue born from being listened to fully, repeatedly.

After dinner, as I am about to head off, Trish offers to lend me a less-rusted bike that she has stored in her shed. I feel excited at the idea of being able to get around more easily, in a way that I used to: riding along the beach at night coming home from friends' houses, whizzing alongside the runway at sunset after a game of tennis, pedalling slowly on the way to work in the early morning, the sky wide and always an expansive sense of space and light.

Trish wheels an old silver mountain bike into the yard and I thank her once again for her generosity. I wave goodbye, deciding to ride the long way back to my accommodation. My shadow speeds before me under the streetlights, morphing and moving. I watch this second self for a moment, so clear and sharply defined, before the lights end and the image flickers, then slips away.

As I ride, I can feel myself starting to settle into a fresh way of inhabiting my old home. I am discovering a newly found sense of intimacy at being grounded, being sure, in and through the place itself. I feel steeped in the atoll, close as a lover, held as a friend. The wind is warm and gentle on my skin, night air fragrant with the scent of salt and blossom. The moon has risen over the palms and its light catches the edges of thin cloud, is scooped into the smooth curve of a wave until it breaks, lit whitewash pure as snow. Turning the corner, I ride into the blackness until the runway lights come into view, colourful and strange as an abandoned party, the lagoon invisible but darkly present behind. As I ride onto my old street, on the right my old home glows warmly, flickers with light from a television, volume turned down low. I feel strangely reassured by the life that continues at Number 23 without me; perhaps deep down, I want to know that I will leave.

Once back at my accommodation and in bed, I find myself staring at the cheap sea-themed prints on the wall: striped umbrellas, nautical knots, shells on yellow sand and frangipanis in white wooden frames. The pictures are both relevant and irrelevant to where I find myself today (few nautical knots, plenty of sand, but not a yellow grain to be seen), causing me to feel slightly disorientated. I try to familiarise myself with the alien space of my temporary home. Looking though wardrobes and cupboards, I begin rifling through the reading material beside the bed. There are brochures for motorised canoe adventures, glass-bottom boat tours as well as kite surfing and scuba-diving. It is disconcerting seeing my former home through the lens of glossy brochures, so I pile the pamphlets together and stash them in a drawer out of sight. As I do, I glimpse the bright blue cover of a book that I instantly recognise. I stop, pull it out, sit up and begin to flick through the thick pages of *The Clunies-Ross Cocos Chronicle*, an iconic text that recounts the atoll's history from the perspective of the founding family who ruled the tiny atoll from the early 1800s until the late 1970s. I never quite got around to reading more than a few pages of this book when I was on the islands, despite my interest in the atoll's history. Something about the tone of the *Chronicle* always made me feel uncomfortable. Glancing through the text again, looking at the series of black-and-white photos, I experience the same sensation. *The Clunies-Ross Cocos Chronicle* has a distinct air of 'boys' own adventure', all pilots and sailors, boats and planes, brimming with images of self-assured white men with moustaches.

I stop reading, struck by a thought that part of me is aware, however unconsciously, of why I am here on the atoll. My need to go back to Christmas Island to come to terms with my experiences was all-consuming, compelling, a drive both deeply personal and inescapably political. By contrast, the two years I spent on the Cocos (Keeling) Islands were largely peaceful – it became a time to recover and heal. I had good friends and plenty of time to begin the slow and ongoing process of unpacking what I had experienced, through both my external studies at a university on the mainland, as well as the daily alchemy that saw me turn my most difficult experiences into poetry.

The chance discovery of the *Chronicle* in my room has scratched at an itch, this time more political than personal. I think back to Pete Ch'ng's reflections on the history of Christmas Island, when at the end of our interview he said, 'I think Australia can still be a great country if it wants to be, or we can choose to be a mediocre country that stumbles along. But I think at the bottom of our history is race ... and if we don't face that one ...'

On the Cocos (Keeling) Islands there is an overriding culture coming largely, but not only, from the Cocos Malay people, of 'live and let live'. Conflict is avoided and grievances rarely stated, but this culture has led the atoll's history to remain largely a vague mystery for most white people on the atoll, including me. My experiences back in the Indian Ocean Territories this time around seem to be repeatedly teaching me that to understand my own place in the story, I need to properly map the layered and complicated worlds where I have been.

The Clunies-Ross Cocos Chronicle prompts me to follow a lead I had been avoiding in my own desire to avoid conflict. I pick up my phone and search for John Clunies-Ross on social media. My phone thinks for a while (the internet, as always, is on island time) but sure enough, eventually the image of a tanned middle-aged man with wavy hair, dressed in a tropical shirt, appears. I am unsure how he will feel about being asked to be interviewed. During my time here, I had tended to deliberately avoid this larger-than-life, irreverent character with a well-established reputation as a barfly. I can't recall if we even spoke when I lived on the atoll, despite West Island's tiny population. Yet I have always thought there was more to John Clunies-Ross than he would have people believe.

John Clunies-Ross – or Johnny, as he is more commonly known – is the sixth-generation incarnation of a line of men sporting the family name. The original John Clunies-Ross was born in 1786 on the Shetland Islands in the north of Scotland, an incredibly beautiful and changeable island-scape, in which it was not possible to be more than five kilometres from the sea.

This seemingly fearless young man with a love of the ocean set the tone for his descendants, embracing this wild terrain with its tumultuous and often violent ocean, becoming a capable seaman with an appetite for adventure.

It was this seafaring ancestor who formed a working relationship with Alexander Hare, the atoll's original coloniser, working on his employer's sailing vessels and, through this connection, in 1826 found himself living on the Cocos (Keeling) Islands. Not much love was lost between the two men as they jostled for power, not only over this tiny arc of sand in the middle of the ocean, but also over the acquisition of the labour force of illegally kept slaves predominantly from Malaysia, but also Indonesia, China, Papua, Africa and India – the original ancestors of the contemporary Cocos Malay population. History has been told by the winner, and much has been made of the cruel and decadent habits of the losing coloniser. From 1834, the Clunies-Ross family began to lay claim to the tiny atoll of the Cocos (Keeling) Islands and its inhabitants, a family dynasty that continued for five generations. Under this feudalistic regime, the Clunies-Rosses were successful at establishing a coconut plantation for the production of copra, utilising the labour provided by the Cocos Malay inhabitants, as well as maintaining a significant family estate. In 1978 the Australian Government purchased the Cocos (Keeling) Islands, yet despite the end of the family legacy, the most recent incarnation of John Clunies-Ross has decided to stay. I am intrigued and wish to understand the reasons why Johnny remains on such a tiny landmass when the balance of power has shifted. What are the implications for the population as Johnny continues to live with the people his family once ruled? What does his presence mean for the lives of the Cocos Malay community and what does the history of this tiny outpost, also excised by Howard in 2001, tell us about our nation?

I check the time – nine p.m. Though this is well out of my comfort zone, I take the chance: the worst that can happen is Johnny will refuse to meet or simply ignore me. I message Johnny, requesting his time for an interview, giving him a very clear out. To my surprise, I get an instant response: a matter-of-fact 'fine'.

'Come early,' he writes, 'when I'm having coffee, before I head out to the clam farm.'

'Great,' I respond, 'I will set my alarm.'

'Don't bother,' he responds, 'open your blinds.'

20. The End of the Line

Johnny is right, the next morning the sun wakes me at six thirty and the sound of the swell pours in thickly through the windows. All night its roar and sigh sang in my sleep and, as I open my eyes on this cloudless morning, the ocean foams and shimmers in pale morning light. The white terns have woken and their early arguing and chattering filters down through high branches of figs and banyan trees. I make a bitter cup of International Roast coffee from a thin foil packet I find behind the kettle and carry it down to the seawall.

As I walk along the asphalt that leads to the water, my presence startles a rufous night heron resting on the road. She flies up, wide-winged and long-legged, into the branch of a frangipani tree. The swell is slowing in day's gentle light and the white terns begin to wheel, setting their neat sails to the sky. Climbing down the concrete of the seawall, I move coral pebbles to make a spot to sit where I had often sat outside our other former home here, what was previously the deputy principal's house. This long building with its large wooden deck has grounds that ramble down to the sea, though it is harder to connect with what once seemed like our own private beach, as someone has felled the tall coconut palms that graced the shore.

Down on the beach, caught between coral rocks and coconuts, the remains of what seems to be a Sri Lankan sleeping mat have washed ashore. I unroll it, and though it is frayed at the ends and seems melted in the middle, its colours are bright, the geometrics of its yellow-and-blue pattern clear. The Australian Border Force, once it has intercepted vessels in Australian waters, detains those on board on its own ships, and routinely burn the beautifully coloured fishing vessels out at sea for reasons that are not always entirely clear. This mat appears to have drifted from one of these burned boats, and that is why its fabric looks partly melted. Putting the bright runner down, I wonder what story it has to tell, then sit looking out toward the water. Sure enough, one, two, three turtles poke their heads above the surf. One distinctively curious turtle reaches his stumpy head high repeatedly between sets to look at me, then just as quickly he is gone, becomes a drifting distorted shape before melding perfectly with the reef below.

My coffee is repulsive, but the morning is stunning, alive with colour and movement. Over the roof behind me, a small flock of terns are lit gold. Whirling above their white forms, the slightly larger, darker shapes of common noddies wheel against the blue. My whole body is singing, every cell alive to my return. It is as though the ocean, the birds, are being breathed in through my skin. Salt pulses through my blood, spills in watery traces from my eyes. I am filled with such a sense of wellbeing that it makes me cry. I sit feeling clear, feeling calm and incredibly grateful to be alive. It is at this moment I remember again the ominous mark on my shoulder and my sense of resolution is clear. I will not find out my results while I am on the atoll, I do not want to know. I need to be here, fully present in every sense, and the future, whatever it may hold, can wait. My whole body palpably softens with relief. I have never felt more certain. Drinking in the scene in front of me a moment longer, heart brimming with happiness, I turn and take my cup back to the house.

I am early, so walk the short distance to Johnny's home along the beach even though the tide is high. After walking behind a row of houses perched on the seawall, I climb down several rows of sandbags and hobble over coral rocks, finally reaching the water. There is a small fringe of sand above high tide, but every so often a surge of swell rushes in and I am sent running up the rocks, until the wave recedes and I can make my way to the shore once more. Toward the end of the small bay, she-oaks sigh at the water's edge, and beyond them palms stretch their lean bodies in a gesture like longing toward the sea. I make my way past the front of the medical centre and several tourist bungalows until I am looking up at a massive banyan tree the ocean is threatening to claim. Finally, I reach the grounds of the motel where the shore has been dramatically eroded. Rows of palm trees have fallen head first into sand, where they are slowly being reclaimed by the tide. I scuttle up the bank, hauling myself up with a thick matt of roots, then cut through the grounds to Johnny's place across from Cocos Autos.

Making my way toward the faded fibro home, I am not sure what to expect – if Johnny will even be awake or if he has remembered that I am coming. Reassuringly, his white ute is parked out the front, back number plate at strange angles, tray loaded with an odd assortment of boxes, ropes, tools and bags. A red inflatable boat sits parked by the front door. The TV is on, so I call out, open the flywire door and look inside.

In the front room, on a large flat-screen television, the Olympics is being discussed loudly by two men in tracksuits holding fat microphones. Above the television there is a picture in a frame made from driftwood of Johnny's son, Jack, jumping from a jetty with two girls in bikinis. An assortment of objects covers the shelves, coffee table and floor. In the far corner there is a kitchen obscured by a cupboard and a wide black bench.

'Coming,' Johnny calls from what, in most houses, would be

a large pantry, but here seems to be a very small office. Johnny comes out naked from the waist up, all barrel chest and beer belly, in a pair of black stubbies.

'Want a coffee?'

Real coffee? My day seems to be taking a turn for the better.

'Oh, yes please.'

'Cup or a bucket?'

'Cup's fine,' I smile.

'May as well get dressed,' Johnny says as he pulls on a red cotton t-shirt lying on the lounge, and then he hands me a large steaming cup. I am buoyed by such good fortune, close my eyes, breathe the aroma of fresh coffee in and try to look like I am feeling relaxed about being here on my own with him.

We chat for a bit about who has had babies and things that have changed or stayed the same before I grab my folder and find the consent forms I need him to sign. He seems a little taken aback by this and I am quick to assure him it is a formality. I am keenly aware of the damage the media has done on the islands and I want to earn his trust. I tell him I will type up the transcript and that he can change anything he feels doesn't seem right. Johnny seems reassured by this and we chat for a while about the anger caused by an SBS documentary about education, the unfair slant it put on many people's words and its misrepresentation of a complicated situation. I wonder if I am in danger of doing something similar, whether my words will cause hurt, anger or a sense of betrayal. I finish my coffee, find my questions and turn on the recorder.

I ask Johnny about his childhood and see his shoulders stiffen, his tone becomes perfunctory. He tells me he was born in Singapore, 'back when that was the closest hospital'. His mother had lost her first child, and I wonder how long this was before Johnny was born. I imagine him as a small boy running through the kampong, barefoot and free-range, living a life of incredible privilege. Yet Johnny's childhood on his tropical island home was short-lived. As with generations of Clunies-Ross males before him, Johnny was sent away to Europe to study, his turn at age four. Johnny was first flown to Ireland to start his early-childhood schooling, then when he was primary-school aged, he was sent to England where he was joined by his mother. Johnny would return to visit the atoll every second year and his father would visit in the year between. I want to ask more about what it was like to grow up in such an idyllic setting surrounded by family, only to find yourself whisked so far away at such a young age, but everything in Johnny's body language, the way he averts his eyes and flattens his tone, tells me not to go there. Johnny's response causes me to wonder how the physical and psychological distance from what that very young Johnny Clunies-Ross loved so much has shaped the man sitting before me today.

'How was it when you returned to Cocos?'

'Oh, it was like Narnia.' Johnny visibly lightens and becomes animated. 'You get into this tube and it flies and you get out here and, you know, you pinch yourself for the first few days and then eventually you start thinking of it as normal, just in time to get back on the plane to go to some institutional place where you have to wear shoes again.'

I glance down at the broad brown feet pointing toward me from under the coffee table.

'I was expected to come back here,' Johnny continues, 'I was the eldest son, I don't think it was ever talked about. I studied boatbuilding, with the concept being that I would pick up the new technologies, fibreglass and welding, and bring them into the community. So I did that, and when I came back to the community

I was put through rapid apprenticeships. I worked with the Cocos Malay bush crew, which is the biggest mob, picking up coconuts and clearing up the plantations, then moved on to boat and machine maintenance and then ferry driving and stevedoring.'

'Did you stay from that point on,' I ask, 'or have you come and gone from the atoll since then?'

'Well, when I was in my twenties we had the big fight with the Commonwealth about my family owning all the land. So the old man sold up, which basically left me without a job so I had to leave for Perth. The old man technically went bankrupt because the Australian Government fought with him for so long.'

There were rumours on West Island that the Australian Government had been incredibly aggressive in its treatment of the Clunies-Ross family in the acquisition of the Cocos (Keeling) Islands in the late 1970s. Hearsay during my time on the atoll was that the Australian Government had also deliberately orchestrated events that ensured the failure of the family's shipping company, resulting in the estate's bankruptcy, in order to force the family off Home Island and gain exclusive power over the atoll. Certainly, as I found myself later finally reading *The Clunies-Ross Cocos Chronicle*, the implication that the Australian Government conspired against the Clunies-Ross family is clear. Somehow this history helps makes sense of the irreverent figure before me, his strange mix of cynicism and straight-upness, his consistent distaste for authority.

I ask Johnny if these rumours were true, if he feels the Australian Government was aggressive in the way they took over the atoll.

'Oh yeah, they were spiteful and mean,' he answers. 'I think if people did things in their own name, they would not have done anything quite so nasty, but they were doing it on behalf of the Commonwealth, and most of the people I bumped into around that era who heard about what happened apologised to me for the behaviour of the government toward me and my family, so it was not a very nice time.'

As Johnny speaks, my mental picture of this family's feudal regime starts to alter, taking on another dimension. Here, in this version of the story, the ruler becomes the underdog, the master the victim, and I don't quite know whose team I should be on: that of the Clunies-Rosses, the Cocos Malay community or the Australian Government. Was it possible, or even appropriate, that I resist the urge to take sides?

'What about the Big House?' I ask him, referring to the family mansion, Oceania House, on Home Island's waterfront. The estate was once surrounded by extensive walled gardens made possible by importing soil by boat from Christmas Island nine hundred kilometres away. Since the family was forced to sell the estate, the gardens have become ramshackle and uncared for, far from their former glory. 'It's a shame to see it so run down ...'

'It is not part of the community anymore. We used to have New Year's there and *Hari Raya*, parties, and a fair amount of produce came out of the garden for the community – ah, times go,' he says with an air of grief and resignation. 'To run a private house like that is stunningly expensive and you need staff. You can't have a house like that without at least two people helping you keep the dust out of the place, and so that is eight thousand dollars just in dusting. Then the toilets break, the whole thing becomes ...' Johnny's voice trails off. 'It is built as a manager's residence who has got a lot of labour in a third-world situation where the labour is not worth a lot of money. We had, like, seven gardeners, four house girls and could call on all the tradies as well.'

In this moment, my impression of Johnny alters again. The shift in understanding and allegiance I am experiencing is confusing and fascinating. With this statement, the seemingly harmless man sitting before me has unapologetically admitted the labour conditions his family created for the Cocos Malay inhabitants were incredibly inequitable, 'third-world' in Johnny's own terms. I wonder if Johnny comprehends that he has conceded that his family, rather than freeing the slaves that had belonged to Hare, instead grossly underpaid the Cocos Malay people in their care in order to support the family's privileged lifestyle. Indeed, in *The Clunies-Ross Cocos Chronicle* it proudly states that every Cocos Malay woman was required to serve an 'apprenticeship' in the Clunies-Ross household, working as a family maid in order to 'learn the domestic arts'. I try to look as unflustered as possible about his remarks. I know if I directly challenge Johnny I may lose his trust, he may close up, and there is so much more I want to understand.

'Do you think you will always live here?' I ask.

'Yep, my boots are already buried, mate,' he says as he puts down his coffee. 'Not on Home Island, mind you, there's heaps of room in Mum's box. He cremated her, so ...'

Johnny reaches over and tops up my already large coffee, 'You can brush your teeth with this stuff ...' he says.

I decide to ask Johnny what I have wanted to know all along: *why stay*? Witnessing his family being forced from the atoll, losing their business, home and the Cocos Malay workforce, why return – why is it that Johnny chooses to stay?

'I don't have a concept of living anywhere else,' Johnny tells me. 'I would be lost in the suburbs. If I get in a situation where I can't see very far, like if there are hills blocking the view, or a house or a tree, I get a bit twitchy, this is a much more natural environment for me. During the day I can see the moon, I have a point of reference. I keep an eye on the moon. I generally know the moon phase over the next couple of days, and then you find yourself in an environment where you don't know what phase the moon is in, you don't even see the bloody thing! The city is a construct; this is real.'

Though days glide past in a kind of dream on this slow-paced tropical island far away from the lived reality of modern life, I can't help but agree. There is something honest and exposing about each islander's dependence on the natural world and each other that pares things back here, confronts you and makes you honest with yourself while forcing you to be tolerant of, and largely accountable to, others.

'Here everyone knows who you are and you have a responsibility to the greater community outside your door,' Johnny continues. 'It is the freedom – you have your own boat, you can go fishing and catch your own food, which some people find quite confronting, but if you can't catch your own food, you have a distance from it. And it is a great place to have children, an amazing place to have children. Everyone loves your children as much as you do, pretty much, and they disappear for hours on end and they come back okay and probably have a new shirt on. I was a single parent for a while, everyone on West Island was really supportive of me, and my family were two doors down and I suppose at this end of my life it is more about relevance and how you fit into the puzzle.'

'I am only now reintegrating with the Home Island community, there was a long period where it was politically incorrect to be integrated, there was a resentment in the community. I really enjoy my friendship with the Homies [Home Islanders] and, you know, we just take the piss out of each other all the time and it is quite robust in that way.'

'Your father must have been devastated when he left,' I say.

'Oh, it broke his heart. He won't come back, it is too much.'

I ask how Johnny's long connection with Cocos affects him now. He tells me there was a heavy pressure on him as he grew up to take things over, including the Clunies-Rosses' own on-island magisterial system, set up to resolve island disputes. He tells me it was almost a relief when his time to take on the role of ruling Home Island never came to pass. Before the acquisition of the atoll by the Australian Government, Johnny's father would get up every morning and walk around the kampong, establishing a time when anyone could approach him for advice or help. Johnny was slowly seconded into that role, and he believed people from the Cocos Malay community came to see him as a figure to confide in.

'You were the father of the community; it was more than paying the wages. The social fabric was polished and maintained by my family.'

I ask Johnny if part of him wishes he could have taken on that responsibility, that role. He skirts around my question, expressing his frustration at the co-op, the council, the business sector and the skewed political system that sees the islanders having to choose between political candidates in the Northern Territory.

'There is no statesman, no spokesperson. No one person,' he laments.

'So being able to perform that role would be a satisfying one?' I ask.

'Well, I think it would be politically effective as well as satisfying – to say this is the community's view on that, we have had our discussion and here we go. I mean, it's a heavy one, but having said that, if the authority line was clearer and someone said, "Look, I have to deal with the Cocos Islands, who do I deal with?" and the line of authority was clear ...'

Johnny starts becoming agitated as he discusses his frustration with government organisations, and as he does, I begin to notice he starts to use the term 'us', referring to himself and the Cocos Malay community. This is an interesting shift, so I encourage him to speak more, trying to work out what the implications of such an identification could be.

'The wider community can be very bullying. Parks Australia, they believe they are in the absolute right, but there are ways and means of doing it without being white colonial bastards.' I look up to see if there is any sense of irony or play in Johnny's expression but can read none.

'And that tends to be the track, you know: we are right – the tree-hugging university – you guys don't know what you're fucking doing, and this is the way we are going to go. There has been a fair bit of that going on. We had a barney with Fisheries because they wanted to put fish limits in, which doesn't really suit us – if we have a wedding, it is open slather. Everyone goes out and supports the wedding, catches fish, we eat more, we eat *gong-gong* and everyone puts in for two households and they fish day-long. And they say, "Oh no, you can't have them because we have introduced catch limits," which is foolishness. They haven't listened to us. I have had two years of previous conversations with Fisheries and they haven't listened to a thing we have said.'

There are so many things to tease out from this statement, the least of which is the fusion between Johnny's sense of self and the Cocos Malay community. It is true the Cocos Malay people elected Johnny to council, but this and other statements he has made during the interview, as well as the repeated use of the term 'us', referring exclusively to himself and the Cocos Malay inhabitants, indicate to me that for Johnny Clunies-Ross, the boundaries between himself and the Cocos Malay people are not clear. Johnny identifies with the Cocos Malay community, but do they identify with him? Is he speaking for the Cocos Malay people simply as a councillor, or are some intergenerational habits of appropriation resurfacing as he takes on his leadership role?

I look at my phone and realise that Johnny and I have been talking for almost two hours. I feel like we are only beginning to touch on some of the most important questions of his role on the islands, yet I am beyond trying to take in any more. I did not appreciate that listening could be so demanding, the constant act of being out of my comfort zone, reading the situation, the person, trying to think on my feet. Reluctantly, I turn the recorder off and pack my things away. We continue to chat for a while longer about the role of Fisheries, bureaucrats and climate change.

'Yes, well none of that has been proven beyond doubt, has it?' Johnny says.

'You don't believe in global warming?' I ask, both surprised and not surprised by the possibility.

'Well, the jury is out, isn't it? They say they have asked all the scientists, but they haven't asked all of them, so there isn't consensus, no-one can say for sure one way or another. If you asked all the scientists, of course you are going to get a range of opinions, but they can't ask everyone. They haven't asked me, for example.' Again, I wait for a hint of irony, but there is none, perhaps just a hint of self-consciousness.

'But you are not a scientist, Johnny,' I say.

'Well ...' he seems a bit taken aback at my directness and I try to hide my astonishment; surely he must be joking, but I am not convinced, I don't think he is. I understand that, for all the humbling blows his family has taken, Johnny Clunies-Ross remains a big fish in a very small pond. I take the conversation back to safer ground. The interview has gone so well and I am really enjoying getting to know this complicated and sometimes contradictory character better. I ask Johnny if he will take me out to see his clam farm. I had never got around to seeing it during my time on the islands and had heard his collection of creatures was really something quite unique.

At my suggestion, Johnny jumps up to get his things together. I ask to use the toilet before we head off and he points toward the hallway.

'The centipede is dead, by the way, I haven't gotten rid of it yet,' he calls as I get up off the couch. Once again, I am not sure if he is joking but soon see its scaled form, the length of a ruler, lying on the lino in a back-to-front 'S', its head disfigured, I am guessing, by the force of one of Johnny's thongs. As I continue down the hall, a small ginger cat jumps from a bunk in one of the bedrooms and begins to smooch my ankles emphatically. It follows me into the tiny room and, unsure what to do, I go to the toilet with the door half-closed while the cat continues to rub its face passionately over my feet. The cat follows me out as I wash my hands in the bathroom's greying sink under which a chipboard cupboard slowly buckles, returning to the earth.

I give the cat one last pat and walk out with Johnny to the car. Johnny has had to wire the driver's door shut as the police complained about him driving around with it open, so he has to enter the car from the passenger side and I follow in behind him. As we drive off, I can see the road running beneath my feet through several holes in the rusted floor, and I smile to myself, happy to be here, happy that Johnny has been willing to give me a window into his distinct, even if idiosyncratic, view of the world.

As we head along the one and only road that runs along the fourteen-kilometre stretch of West Island, a Cocos Malay man comes toward us from the opposite direction in a large roadwork vehicle. There is only enough room for one vehicle on the asphalt, so Johnny veers off into the grass, sending feral chickens flying madly into the palm trees. Back on the bitumen, an opulent jungle fowl sways his magnificent, richly plumed tail as he walks quickly to get out of our way. Palm trees lean intimately over us along the road, sheltering us from the trade winds that continue to hammer the atoll.

We turn into the farm and bounce along the white sandy track until Johnny pulls the car up in space cleared between low coconut trees. I get out of the passenger side so Johnny can get out of the car, and turn to see an array of rectangular ponds lined with thick black plastic. White PVC piping carries water between the tanks, and several metres away, through the greenery, I can see the swell rolling in.

Walking up to the first pond, I am taken aback by the sheer brilliance of the sight in front of me. The stark black pond reveals itself as a luminous, fleshy terrain. The bubbling water is filled with vibrant beings. Each creature is about the size of two large cupped hands, voluptuous and patterned with iridescence: electric blues, greens and browns, each clam holding its own unique and intricate design.

'These are about thirteen or fourteen years old,' Johnny tells me. '*Tridacna derasa*, or smooth giant clam. They are quite rare.'

The clams close slightly as I move toward them. They are larger than life, improbably bright, a living, breathing palette of fluorescence that somehow senses my presence.

'They change colour depending on where you stand,' he adds, and we walk around so the angle of light changes. It is hard to grasp that these are living creatures, each being like a rippled sculpture in its own right.

'Over here are a different type. *Tridacna maxima*: burrowing or small giant clam. These are the ones we sell the most of, but they are much younger, only a few years old. You've got to watch the heat too. It can be a killer.'

I am taken completely by surprise once again, this time by the sheer quantity of creatures as well as the diversity of colour and design. Considerably smaller, the burrowing clams fill pool after pool, tightly packed together like a piece of luminous abstract art. Johnny lends me his camera and I photograph them, homing in on line, pattern and contour.

We walk back to the first pool with the large clams and I become aware that I can see right into the body of some through a small hole, and it is hard to avoid seeing the vulva-like resemblance in their shape, their long and rippled fleshy slits. I don't mention this as I lean over the pond, but it is like the man reads my mind.

'So if you've never had the opportunity to have a lesbian relationship, here's your chance,' Johnny calls over his shoulder as he grabs a container from the ute.

I laugh, refusing to blush, 'Yep, only on Cocos!'

'And what happens on Cocos stays on Cocos,' he says, smiling wryly, and goes off to flush out the PVC piping. I dip my hand down into the water and gently touch the side of an ancient-looking clam with patterns in shades of brown and intricate as lace. The sensation is different to what I expect, more resistant, rubbery, not as supple as it seemed to the eye. The clam does not slam shut, as I feared, but closes slightly, as if politely asking me to go away. With growing confidence, and rudely ignoring the clam's seeming request, I touch another and it feels strangely intimate. I find myself filled with a surge of tenderness for these exquisite sentient creatures.

Johnny returns from his pipe work and gets inside the car through the passenger door, so I follow. Soon we are bumping our way past his beehives in polystyrene stacks, past a rusting old bus among beach cabbage until we bounce off the white sandy drive and onto the road.

The strong silent presence of the clams lingers in my mind as we leave. Palms flash past the car window as I keep a lookout for the herd of resident wild goats, until Johnny takes a sharp left, turning off the main road and onto the track out to The Farm. In a previous life, before my time on the atoll, The Farm had been an abundant market garden of sorts run by another local man, providing the island with a small bounty of much-needed fresh produce. However, a cyclone had arrived and destroyed the entire area. The farmer's wife left the farmer and then the embattled farmer left his farm, and the once bountiful hub of activity became a shell of itself, a few sheds and a stand of fruiting lime trees the only trace of a small chapter in the West Island's history. Johnny, along with Trish's husband, Tony, are working to try to restore The Farm back to a productive space.

About fifty metres in, we pull up to an old greenhouse where Johnny takes me to see his hydroponic garden. Once inside, the old structure is green with new life. Zucchini vines weave their way through beds, and tomato plants are staked between kale, orchids and chilli. In this unfolding show-and-tell, Johnny pulls his traps containing newly drowned rats out of tubs of water, then leads me out to a field that was once a plain of beach cabbage, where a crop of dwarf bananas have been planted, blue bags tied tightly over their ripening fruit. It is heartening to witness a modest abundance returning to this weed-ridden block, to see care and attention breathing life back into a space that had once helped feed an atoll.

We climb into the car and head back to Johnny's place. I feel at ease next to him in the ute now, the asphalt continuing to whiz visibly by beneath my feet, palm trees and surf a blur of blues and greens outside my window. With the sun on my face and wind in my hair, it strikes me what an incredible privilege it is to have time and the means to talk to people whose lives were on the outskirts of my own during my brief time on the atoll. I wonder how I will tell Johnny's story, whether that is even possible and if it is my place to do so. How will his story be challenged or affirmed when I finally sit down to talk with Nek Su? The Clunies-Ross legacy is a complex one and I am not here to umpire. Perhaps all I am doing is bearing witness to a series of moments, picking up fragments to hold to the light. Perhaps all we ever have are these weathered shards, only ever the idea of a whole; we tessellate, place pieces together and hope that a picture, a story, will form.

21. Quarantine

All morning the military planes have been arriving. The great hiss of them after they land, their long insect whine, again wakes in me a familiar rage. I get up from the table where I have been reading, grab the bike Trish has lent me and set out toward the runway. As I arrive, the mighty craft turn their grey bodies. The noise deafening, drowning out the existence of all other sounds. They are dull and angular, menacing and enormous, and with the sight of them, the sound of them, memories come crowding into my mind.

When we first arrived on the Cocos (Keeling) Islands in January 2012, the arrival of asylum seekers was almost unheard of. No Navy vessels hovered on the horizon and no Customs officers scoured the sea from shore. The Australian Border Force had not even been invented. There was no camp in which people could be detained and few military planes arrived growling on the unfenced runway. Islanders were happy to discuss what was happening on Christmas Island nine hundred kilometres away, their conversations consistently framed by compassion. On the whole, I experienced the perspectives of Cocos Islanders as refreshingly welcoming and open. After my experiences on Christmas Island, it came as an incredible relief to experience a population so tolerant and accepting.

On 16 May 2012, on a warm starlit night, came the first of what was to be an influx of arrivals over the next few years. The police station, never normally lit, glowed with a strange orange light. The airport was unfamiliar, eerily radiating from within. Airport staff milled around inside, looking like shadowy strangers, silhouetted by the stark fluorescent lights. People I knew – in a pre-Covid world – pulled white paper masks down over their faces, against perceived threats from the new arrivals.

The community was intrigued. The asylum seekers were housed in the pub that also served as a cyclone shelter. I worried what would happen if some West Islanders couldn't order a beer. A community cricket match was organised to welcome the new arrivals – the sporting locals were excited to see how the Sri Lankan men bowled. From the bus window, the Cocos Malay schoolgirls pressed their faces to the glass, looking at the young Tamil men through the window, giggling and pointing, uncharacteristically animated and loud.

Though my time on the Cocos (Keeling) Islands was far more peaceful, and my witnessing of what happened to asylum seekers in the name of border protection on the atoll largely distant, as more boats arrived, I became increasingly concerned as the tone of the island changed. West Islanders wanted their bar back. Johnny Clunies-Ross approached the media, complaining that locals, excluded from the pub by the makeshift camp, could not access the wide-screen television to watch the State of Origin game. Another temporary camp was opened at the island's old quarantine station. The locals got their pub back, but people were unsettled. The Cocos Islanders had seen what had played out on Christmas Island, the price the people paid as their small community was swamped by fly-in fly-out workers, Serco officers, media, customs officers and Australian Federal Police. Cocos Islanders were used to flying under the radar, being far from the mainland's gaze. No-one wanted the influx of officials, the spotlight or territorial enactments unsettling their daily lives. Most of all, no-one wanted a camp.

At tennis on Wednesday nights, I would hear nurses whispering behind their hands. I strained to make out their hushed conversations about the people they had treated, asylum seekers whose legs had been crushed between boats during rescue operations and other details I could not hear. On West Island's oval, where games of cricket were once played, asylum seekers were now made to sit in straight lines with their heads facing the runway as they awaited their charter planes for processing on Christmas Island. A Serco officer walked close to the men's bodies along the long and silent rows, his presence a clear effort at intimidation, forcing the men to avert their faces from the road, from the islanders' view. Life jackets, passports, pieces of boat and children's shoes washed up on the atoll's shores. On the horizon, thin plumes of smoke rose where Customs burned the bright fishing boats on which the asylum seekers had arrived.

I felt saddened that the tolerant and accepting community that I lived in had started to exhibit similar signs of fear, and occasionally even hatred, as the community I had left on Christmas Island. Was this what humans did when placed under pressure, when faced with the reality of an influx of vulnerable people in their own backyard? To try to counter this, all I could do was wave. Hearing the charter planes warming their engines, I would race from my desk out onto the unfenced runway outside my home, holding my arm high, moving my hand in a slow-motion salutation, willing that even one act of goodwill or welcome could counter at least something of the prejudice they may face. But I wanted so desperately to do more.

It is 10 February 2013. I am bumping along a thin line of asphalt that winds through tall palms, ute loaded with tubs of paintbrushes, crayons and children's toys. Though it is only nine-thirty in the morning I am already sweating into the humidity. On the steering wheel my fingers grip and loosen, nails dig into plastic, body restless. As I look out over the surf peeling in sun along the atoll's outer reef, the Serco officer's rebuttal rings in my ears: *You need to fill in a form, you need to go through Immigration in Canberra, you need to give us forty-eight hours' notice.* But we both understand this is a farce. On Cocos, not even Border Force gets forty-eight hours' notice as to when the asylum-seeker boats will arrive. *We are not here to entertain them,* he states dryly as I try to argue, lips forming into a thin pale line, his tone becoming final. *They are not to be rewarded for coming by boat.* The Tamil children who had arrived on the island only the morning before had watched us curiously from within earshot in the shade, angling their heads, reading my face, as tension rose in our adult voices. Month after month, the officer and I go through this routine. The children watch me walk in with my tub of toys, and children watch me carry them out.

I am not so easily dissuaded. In the months or sometimes weeks between boats, I work on my Tamil. I stand in front of the mirror and roll the language's new sounds around on my tongue. *Vanakkam, eppadi irukinga?* I ask myself. *Eppadi irukinga?* Oh, *naan nalla iruken,* I answer nonchalantly, but it never sounds quite right, so I play the phrases back on my phone's app, trying to form the strange sounds correctly. *One day the guard will be gone,* I reassure the strained face staring back in the bathroom mirror, *It is just a matter of time, don't give up, it's just a matter of time ...*

On 3 April 2013, a boat arrives in the lagoon on the Cocos (Keeling) Islands with around eighty asylum seekers on board. I hear from other islanders that Immigration has been caught off guard, that they do not have enough officers on the ground, enough clothes or food, the camp brimming with their sudden bodies. I know this is my chance. Loading the ute with my tubs of toys and art materials, I drive along the winding line of asphalt once more, beneath lush palms that sway under cottonwool clouds, until I arrive at the wire-fenced paddock that marks the beginning of the Quarantine Station. Pulling up under the frangipani tree next to the administration building, I feel my heart quicken in my chest. As I step out of the car, the people from the boat watch me curiously, shyly, so I wave, their faces brighten, smiles flash across their strikingly unfamiliar faces. Children look at me and then at their parents.

I walk up to the foyer where the glass doors have been opened to the breeze. Several officers sit inside at trestle tables with individuals or pairs of new arrivals, talking quietly and filling in a variety of forms. I can't see the Serco officer anywhere. My heart beats emphatically. I push away the guilty feeling that I am doing something wrong.

A lady in a Department of Immigration–issue brown shirt approaches me, and I explain I am a teacher at the local school. I tell her what I told the Serco officer, that I taught asylum seekers on Christmas Island, and I would like to offer my skills, I would like to help.

'Oh, thank you for coming in – except we don't really have much you can work with,' she apologises.

'That's okay,' I reply. 'I have brought a couple of things with me, paints and teddies and so on, they're in the car. I just wanted to check with you first.'

'Great, then,' the woman says. 'Are the trestle tables outside okay? It is a bit windy, but we don't have any other room.'

'Perfect, thank you,' I say.

Walking back to the car, I try to process my unexpected good fortune. No-one has asked me for a single piece of documentation, demanded any kind of notice, or asked me contact anyone in the nation's capital. I am stunned.

Returning with my tubs of resources, I see the man in the blue Serco shirt walking toward the foyer. He looks toward me and the young Immigration officer who has come to help. The Serco officer's expression seems to hold a mixture of anger and defeat. I wave; he turns his gaze away. The immigration officer carries the tubs out to the tables, watched by fifty or sixty curious eyes in the shade, as well as from the makeshift field where the children are playing soccer. Some of the younger children start to walk at our sides. I look down and smile into their eyes, and the children beam my warmth straight back. 'Look, look!' an older boy calls, pointing into the clear tub. 'I can see a toy!' Soon more and more children begin to run over as we place the tubs down and I try to think through the logistics of the situation. The officer helps me set up trestle tables where the children will need to sit shoulder to shoulder in order to fit. I laugh to myself at the irony of being told I could not work with the five or six children that had come on previous boats, but here I am being gifted twenty-eight young people crammed onto three trestle tables, more children than I really know what to do with.

As the young man returns to the building, the parents come around and settle small groups at the tables, rearranging seats to avoid conflicts and speaking to the children in hushed tones. Soon the children look up at me expectantly and I can see it is time to begin.

'Hello, my name is Reneé,' I say, pressing my palm into my chest. 'Can you say "hello"?'

'Hello,' they respond, enjoying the word. 'Yes, hello!'

'We,' I indicate with my arm moving in a large horizontal circle in front of me, 'are going to do some drawing together. I will give you some paper,' I hold up a blank sheet, 'and some crayons.' I wave a red crayon in the air, quickly deciding to abandon all ideas of painting. 'We are going to draw with the crayons on the paper,' I say, quickly sketching a red smiling face onto white.

'Yes!' the children call, 'Okay, we can!'

The parents help give out the paper and we break the crayons into pieces. It must be the imminence of Easter, as it is hard not to think in this act we are aiming for some kind of miracle hoping so little will go so far, and despite my lack of sainthood, the scene reminds me of Jesus breaking up his loaves and fishes. Yet in this process, the women and I are relieved to find there are in fact enough crayons to go round. The children begin drawing bright shapes, palm trees, turtles, peacocks and gardens on their pages, while the parents stand around, quietly watching and settling any small disputes that arise. Seeing the children happy and occupied, I stand back from the scene for a moment and try to take it all in.

Elderly asylum seekers sit beneath the shade of a dense tree, hoping to avoid the rising heat of the day. I notice one old man has withered legs and a pair of crutches. Many of the Tamils have very dark skin, striking in shadow, and unlike the Iranian and Afghan asylum seekers I knew on Christmas Island, many of the people's limbs are noticeably thin. Despite the number of people, the air is quiet. In the distance, the ocean implies itself in small aqua winks between the fleshy growth of beach cabbage

Spread around us are the small asbestos dwellings that used to house the Quarantine Station staff back when this site held elephants, giraffes and other exotic creatures, making their own slow migration to the mainland, bound for the Perth Zoo. These days the buildings are worn with neglect, locked and disused, except for a handful of dormitories that have been converted for the arriving Sri Lankans and small houses for immigration employees.

'Hello, excuse me, Miss.' I turn to see a Sri Lankan boy around nine or ten at my side.

'Hi,' I reply. The boy is smiling widely, standing tall, with quick, intelligent eyes.

'Excuse me, Miss, my name is Zaahir. The guard told me you are a teacher. Miss, are you a teacher?'

'Yes,' I say, 'I teach art at the school here.'

'Have you taught in other places in Australia?' Zaahir asks in immaculate English.

'Yes,' I respond, 'at lots of different schools.'

'Oh, good,' he says, his eyes lighting up even further, 'because I am looking forward to going to school in Australia. I want to be a pilot. I just wanted to ask if there were any schools that you could recommend, good schools that would help me to become a pilot.' I laugh, taken aback and impressed by his wilfulness and spirit. Then, as another feeling arises, I pull a mask down over my face so he cannot see.

'Don't worry,' I say, willing him every good thing in the world, 'most of the schools are good in Australia. Whichever school you go to, if you study hard, you will get to be a pilot.'

Zaahir beams excitedly back at me. 'Thank you, Miss!' he says, running off happily to join the soccer game.

As I watch Zaahir laugh with his friends, I feel a wave of sadness and anger wash over me. I know from here the Tamil people will be transferred to Christmas Island. In the detention centre on Christmas Island, the accommodation has become overcrowded. The government does not seem to be able to keep up with the unexpected increase in the number of arrivals from Sri Lanka. As a result, and perhaps due to pressures in the diplomatic relationship between Australia and Sri Lanka (that insists on Australia agreeing the civil war in Sri Lanka is over), Australia had begun to 'fast track' the Tamils back to their home country. This means the due process of making a claim is glossed over, many

Tamils not even being given an interpreter, not necessarily told their rights, and instead being quickly assessed and more often than not, put on a plane and returned to their perpetrators. It has become well documented that many Tamils who fled Sri Lanka by boat have been imprisoned, tortured and even murdered on their return.

Zaahir runs off to join his friends and now I can let my face fall. I try to hold the tension within me, the gap between his hope and what is likely to happen after I leave the Quarantine Station. I hold it, then I place it to one side, appreciating there is so much to do in this moment.

A small child comes up to me and shows me a beautiful drawing of a home with steps and a palm tree.

'Is this your home?' I ask.

'Yes, in Sri Lanka,' she responds

'It is a beautiful drawing.'

'It is for you.'

'This is for you too!' the boy behind her calls before I can respond, handing me his picture of a large green dragon.

'Mine too!' adds another, then all at once I am handed paper after paper of brightly coloured sketches. I thank them, trying to acknowledge each one.

As the remaining children begin to finish, I distribute puppets and toys, which a small group of the older children start to draw. Some of the boys get up and begin a game of cricket. Several of the mothers and I watch, standing next to each other in silence. We had been catching each other's eye from time to time as the children were drawing and now most the younger children have finished the activity, we can relax as they run off to play. I am grateful for the women's help, for the gentle way they settled the children as they worked.

One of the mothers stands close to my left shoulder, and I realise we must be about the same age. I turn tentatively toward her, and she smiles briefly back at me, then we look out toward the tables at the remaining children. I wonder if she speaks any English.

'Hi, I am Reneé,' I try. The woman turns to me.

'I, Jahanara.' Jahanara looks thin and worn. She is wearing a bright red cotton floral dress. Jahanara does not smile or frown but stands upright. Her eyes have a striking intensity.

'Thank you,' she says, gesturing to the children.

'No problem,' I respond and immediately worry that this phrase would be difficult to interpret. We stand together in silence for a while, neither moving away. 'Were you frightened on the boat?' I ask suddenly, then at once regret my directness and look down. But Jahanara turns toward me, nodding once, slowly, her eyes fully focused on mine.

'Fifteen days, two days no ...' Jahanara shows me an action, cup to mouth. I nod.

'Two days, you had no water.' Jahanara gestures with her hand to the children at the tables, takes her finger, trailing tears from eye to cheek, waits.

'You had no water, the children were crying.'

'Yes.' Jahanara is calm, contained, she watches my face.

The world grows silent, distils, colours glow warmly on the periphery of my vision. When I move my body, it is like pushing through liquid glass, the day falls silent. Slowly I turn my whole self toward her, pulling from something deep inside, and she waits, she waits for me, everything paused. In that moment I cannot see anyone else: the old people, the children, the immigration workers, the ocean, the cricket game. All other detail is simply erased. With all the will I can muster, I try to find the language to speak truthfully as one woman to another.

'As a mum,' I show *us* (hand to her, hand to me), 'when your children are sad,' my finger tracing eye to cheek, 'it is so hard.' I place my hand on heart, my expression pained, turn my face fully toward her own. Her eyes look deep into mine. Strong eyes, sharp eyes, fierce with the love of a mother. I stay with those eyes. I simply stand and hold her gaze. She does not flinch, does not look away. We hold the silence together.

22. South Island (Pulu Atas)

Returning from the runway, I pack up my books and the notes I have started to make from *The Clunies-Ross Cocos Chronicle* and put them away. My interview with Johnny has raised more questions than answers, and I am trying to think through all Johnny has told me while waiting for Nek Su to return from his trip to Christmas Island.

Finding my phone, I begin to scroll down though my emails, checking there is nothing that requires an urgent response. My pulse suddenly quickens as I register my inbox contains a message I had not expected to receive until my return to the mainland. In the subject line is the title of my manuscript. My chest tightens. This is the moment; this is the publisher's response to the revised manuscript I had been working on with the publisher's editor, the same poems written about the islands which I had excitedly shared with Jo. My whole body tightens while I simultaneously try to push down the rush of elation that this could be my passport at getting my work into the world, to tell the stories from this very place that so need to be told. This second time around, the publisher's response has come in a matter of weeks, and I cannot tell if this is a good or bad sign. Trying not to overthink it, I quickly open the message and it takes a moment to let the content to sink in. The email is so considered, couched with such tactful restraint that I have to read it a second time to understand it is a rejection. Despite hours of feedback and weeks of editing, the answer is a definite 'no.' The publisher has chosen not to run with my work.

Weeks ago, when I left Perth for the Indian Ocean Territories, I was so worried about this moment playing out during my return the islands, that the rejection of years of work on poems written on the Cocos (Keeling) Islands would floor my confidence and take away from my ability to carry out my current research. I feel my eyes sting and a balloon of pain swells in my chest. But to my surprise, from somewhere deeper, something else kicks in and overrides my devastation, makes my body stand straight, makes my eyes blink back the tears, urging me to sharpen and focus. I think of the turnback boats I discovered on my last days on Christmas Island, I think of all the people I met in my three years out here and the way their stories stay in my body, I consider all the faces and memories returning to me, so many stories that remain untold. I can't afford to be shattered, this is not a time to be undone. For all I know I may even have cancer, so the time to rise above is now.

Turning my attention back to my phone, I begin to search my emails, aware that I can find what I want in my records somewhere. I scroll back to December 2015 and there I find it – the email from the director of another publishing company that shortlisted my manuscript for an award the previous year. At the top of the email is her email address. I find my laptop, thinking I'd better do this properly, and send the director my concise request. I tell her my manuscript has been refined by my work with their competitor's editor and is looking better that when it was shortlisted for the publishing house's award. I didn't want to waste the director's time or mine, but would she be interested in publishing my work? Should I send my revised manuscript through? The response I get is immediate. 'Yes, I am interested,' the director writes, 'send your manuscript directly to me.'

Even though I am buoyed by the interest of a second publisher,

I understand this is only the beginning, there are no guarantees. The publishing company and I will need to start the process of reviewing the manuscript all over again. I feel at a bit of a loss in my small room. The trade winds are blowing a gale again, and new guests have arrived in the room next to mine, which causes me to feel restless and slightly claustrophobic. I walk outside, trying to work out what to do, when I see Trish running down the road toward me.

'Oh great, you're here!' she says, catching her breath. 'I've just decided to take some leave. Do you want to go to South Island for a couple of days? Could you be ready in an hour?'

As I step out of Trish's 4WD at the south end of West Island and start to cart the tents into the boat, the full force of the trade winds hits me. The water has been whipped into an aqua blur and everything without weight has become airborne. Trish reverses the boat trailer into the liquid colour, all around us the palms have become manic, clapping and flicking their fronds in a frenzied cacophony. Once the boat is immersed, Tony winds the trailer's cable, easing the boat down until the water takes its weight. Before he can bring the boat back to the shore to load, Trish's arms are piled with kids and bags, waiting in the shallows. Quickly we fill the tinnie with our few possessions, Trish tucking the young boys with expert efficiency under canvas tarps. Tony waves with his familiar broad grin as he drives back to the bakery, disappearing into lush greenery.

As we begin to plane across the lagoon, the sea spray, in what I experience as something akin to a personal attack, violently soaks my hair. Trish's children huddle further beneath the tarp in the tinnie's hull as the water cascades around their small bodies, but they don't look worried or complain. The ocean is frenzied, foaming, mad! I look toward Trish at the stern of the boat, wondering if she is thinking of turning back, but she is a picture of confidence, senses sharp, highly present, her body awake and tuned to the lagoon. Her straight back and narrowed eyes remind me I am with a woman well acquainted with water, who lives with the sea, her manner both practical and practised. There is nothing to fear, the water in this part of the lagoon is only about a metre deep even at high tide, I let go and enjoy the wild ride.

Shortly after we arrive on South Island, Trish's friends follow; the window of high tide that makes movement between islands by boat possible (at times only just) is brief. This marginal, salty inundation will soon start to recede, leaving the thinnest veil of water over clusters of coral, interspersed with a sea floor drying to desert, a rippled landscape of blinding white sand. Once we arrive, it is all hands on deck, putting up tents, unpacking supplies, laying out bedding beneath the coconuts – though, despite our will for shade, we are careful not to place our bodies directly beneath the heavy fruit. The sun has begun to ease itself toward the water, behind the tiny islands of Pulu Blan and Pulu Kelapa Satu, disappearing quietly into cloud.

The ocean has already begun to make its rapid retreat, so by the time I have finished readying my sleeping spot, I look up to see the boats are already marooned on the shore, rendering them as strange installations on wide swathes of white. Trish's friends have two older children, and the small gang acquire head torches, roaming among purple hermit crabs the size of small fists as they search for coconut husks to place on the fire. Once lit, though we don't need its warmth, the light draws us in and we sit, resting after the hustled process of arriving, boats slowly coming out of shadow, silver bodies gently shining in the light of the rising moon.

The families head to bed early, and as I hear their canvas-muted conversations give way to sleep, I wander out onto the now vast expanse of glowing sand. The wind has stilled and an almost silence, a new calm, settles over the water, between the trees. Alone – I lift my face, my hands to the pale night light, turning my body in all that air. The shallow water whispers back. I barely feel real, toes digging into dampness in this liminal watery moonscape, this in-between place that disappears darkly, seamlessly into sea. I am on an abandoned film set, light directional, cinematic, glancing off the gloss of coconut fronds, the trees' long bodies swallowed by shadow. An army of horn-eyed ghost crabs are stationed in position, standing on their own silhouettes across the newly birthed land. In all this absence, all this presence, I breathe. I breathe and become air, breathe and become silence, exhaling, losing the sure boundary of this thing called skin.

The next day we wake with the sun. We are becoming tidal, living finely tuned to the long liquid breaths of the lagoon. The morning has painted itself in gentle pastels, colour resting on fat clouds stacked over the islands in billowing towers. Where late last night thin trickles of water ran silently over sand, at dawn the channel between islands is a swift rush of crystal-clear sea. I sink into the surprise of cool water, feel the salt close over my head, zip-locked into the membrane of this place. My cells sing to the water, *I am here, I am here, do you remember? Do you know my name?*

As the sun rises higher in the sky, we become happily trapped, marooned as the ocean once again retreats from the lagoon. White terns and dark noddies wheel in the sun while the water retracts to a briny veneer. In the glassy shallows, fish hide behind small moons of coral as the sea leaves steadily, swiftly, departing in a long liquid sigh. Around me, tanned children run around saturated in light, inhabiting their idyllic lives. Palms pile into forts, coconuts are cracked for a late breakfast, little feet race between crabs carting their small spiral caravans. I wander away from the camp, ready for a little space, out toward the southern point of the island. Walking along the island's edge, I stop to read the broken lines from others' lives washed up on the shore: a white prayer hat, a schoolchild's cap with a map of Indonesia printed under the spread of an eagle's wings, two backpacks empty but for their cargo of sand.

The sun is high, and the wind has once again become ruthless, relentless, bearing down on a flat and sandy space robbed of resistance. Many Cocos Malay islanders call South Island 'Pulu Atas', meaning top, or windward isle, and as the trade winds blast every last trace of moisture from my face, I can certainly see why. I battle it out for some time on the shore until I see the rise of lush undergrowth further inland and relent, retreating into young palms under the wide arms of figs. Out of the wind, the *wheet, wheet* of white terns catches in the canopy, their tiny bright eyes watching the fact of me stepping below. I arrive in a small bay whose deep shape keeps the wind at arm's length. Here the figs stretch out, casting thick shade over glassed pools of water. Under their seemingly ancient limbs, sand and light are soft, the low ceiling of foliage holding a moist hush. So quiet. On the shore, brightly coloured rope washed off from boats has caught in the trees' wide weathered roots, creating perfect ladders for a montage of crabs to climb. They look at me, surprised, from stalked eyes held high.

Rachel Carson, the late groundbreaking marine biologist and nature writer, tells us once the Earth had enormous tides surging hundreds of metres. The waters would rise, flooding valleys and lowlands, climbing hills, only to tumble back in huge flows to where they had begun. As the Earth evolved, the moon gradually moved away from us, a pale child slowly but surely leaving home. Its pull is subtle now, expressed in increments kind to life, kind enough to let a purple crab carry her sacred cargo of eggs; you can almost feel the weight, the effort it takes to hide hundreds of small black pearls under her low-riding body.

I step once more into sun, walking past the southernmost point of the island, leaving the shelter of the lagoon behind for a view of the atoll's outer reef. Lines of motion that have pulsed for miles through the liquid arc of the Earth reach their foamy crescendo here – waves roar, curling and crashing into layers of weathered rock. A turtle eyes me as it breathes between sets, its brown body a splayed silhouette in the lit wall of waves. On the reef sits the prow of a wooden boat, the ominous V of the broken vessel heightening the drama of the swell. Along the back of the island, flotsam and driftwood pile for miles. The multiple ledges created by hundreds of washed-up logs catch washing baskets, children's toys, toothbrushes, thick arms of rope and piles and piles of bright thongs. A white-faced heron attempts to angle herself into invisibility. Red hermit crabs scuttle amid the debris; five take shelter under a discarded high heel.

My eyes are snapped sharply back to the side of the point from which I have come by a snake-like movement that jolts my whole body. I turn and realise what I have seen is, in fact, an eel moving between rock pools, coming in and out of vision as she scours the reef. Her liquid movements are a wonder to witness as she feeds and curls, all action and intent. As my gaze follows her, she wraps her body around several small knolls of reef, raises her head, watchful and alert, then moves to another, carving a path from sea to shore. As the eel reaches the edge of the ocean, she carves a path over the sand and, to my surprise, moves completely away from the water – half serpent, half fish, silver and glossy, weaving, glistening across the sand's semi-dry surface. She is right on the border, zigzagging between the dual worlds of land and water, fluid and strong, an inhabitant of in-betweens, always watching, reading, pushing her muscular body into sand, carving out her sinuous path. Back and forward she goes in the littoral zone, swimming through shore, slipping in and out of the clear lip of lapping sea. Then suddenly I am the one seen and the eel becomes a magician, quicksilver, becomes one with the water. I search for her body, eyes scouring the rocky shore, but her art is honed – she leaves no trace.

A day passes slowly on South Island. The world is pared back to light and dark, heat and shade and the out-breath, the in-breath of the sea. On the second evening, during the window of high tide, Trish heads back to the mainland to pick up Tony after his shift at the bakery. He arrives with warm buns, a lime tart and a fresh catch of fish. Our meal feels decadent amid the sparse conditions of camping. In the light of the fire, watching their faces as they talk, I am filled with so much love for this small family. After being together again, it seems improbable that it is only a matter of days before my old friends disappear from my life once more. All night I lie in my tent beneath crisp stars, listening to shoals of fish leap from the black water's flow, imagining the glistening arc of hundreds of tiny silver bodies in moonlight, the sleek shadow of a shark in their wake.

Just after dawn, I emerge from my tent to a perfect morning. The wind has dropped and the lagoon is glassy, reflecting voluptuous clouds with perfect symmetry. This is how I remember the atoll, inverted, continually reflected, water unrippled and brimming with life. The crystal quality of the light. I stand, cleaning my teeth, feet in the shallows. Fish nibble at my toes. But there is no time to reminisce. The window to leave at high tide is brief, it is time to be on our way.

23. North Keeling (Pulu Keeling)

While on South Island, Trish and I organised a time for me to interview her. I want to find out her perspectives on Cocos life as a long-term West Island resident, but in particular how her experiences as a park ranger have influenced her impressions of this fluid and changeable world. When we meet on the following Monday, Trish has just returned from a trip to North Keeling, an uninhabited atoll twenty-five kilometres north of the Cocos (Keeling) Islands' main atoll.

I arrive at Trish's place at about four, in the brief space between when Trish finishes work and the time for baths and showers and preparing food for her large family begins. We sit on the bed in one of the boys' bedrooms so we are able to shut a door, while Tony entertains the four boys in the lounge.

'How was North Keeling?' I ask, smiling, suppressing my intense jealousy that Trish's work frequently takes her to a wild space few people in the world ever get to see.

Named after Captain William Keeling, who is recorded as having sighted the atoll in 1609, North Keeling is the remotest of the remote when it comes to islands. The Cocos (Keeling) Islands are already part of Australia's most isolated territory, yet this tiny C-shaped ring, yet another twenty-five kilometres from islands' main atoll formation, is that one step more removed again. Accessible only in the company of Parks Australia officers, and without so much as a jetty on which to land, North Keeling, though small, contains an astonishing abundance of life.

Of Pulu Keeling National Park's twenty-four bird species, eight are listed as being of special conservation significance, and fourteen are listed for special protection under the Japan–Australia, China–Australia and the Republic of Korea–Australia Migratory Bird Agreements, including the red-footed booby that has an estimated population of around thirty thousand breeding pairs. North Keeling is also home to greater and lesser frigatebirds, the endemic Cocos buff-banded rail and the exquisite red-tailed tropic bird, (or silver bosun bird, whose elaborate breeding displays I so enjoyed on Christmas Island). Green turtles and the critically endangered hawksbill turtle also nest on the island's shores. The Cocos (Keeling) Islands, more broadly, hold significant historical and scientific value as they are the only coral atoll that Charles Darwin visited, playing a key role in the evolution of Darwin's theory of coral reef development. North Keeling gives us clues as to what the larger atoll must have looked like when Darwin visited in April 1836, and it serves as an important seed stock and gene pool for rare species that have become absent or threatened on the more populous areas of the Cocos (Keeling) Islands.

After 1944, in the brief period when the Clunies-Rosses gave way to British rule, Cocos Malay people accessed North Keeling frequently for hunting, bringing down thousands of the naturally friendly and curious birds, presumably for barter with the influx of soldiers during World War II. In the 1970s and 80s, increasing access to the island, as well as new technologies in the design of both boats and guns, meant that the population of birds on the atoll was becoming massively depleted, and the Australian National Parks and Wildlife Service (now Parks Australia), intervened. In July 1986, a seabird-hunting moratorium was introduced. Since the moratorium, the birds have thrived on the small atoll, their feathery bodies once again filling the sky, making North Keeling the internationally unique and ecologically vital rookery that it is today.

Trish and the other Parks officers make regular trips out to North Keeling to collect data, check on the wildlife and maintain the small amount of infrastructure on the remote site. Trish tells me that these visits always make her feel incredibly humble, keep her in her place, especially as she takes the comparatively small vessel, the *RJ Hawke*, over an area of impossibly deep and open ocean.

'You go up to North Keeling and you feel really small, really insignificant because it really belongs to the wildlife out there. It was a big demon for me, the ocean. Coming from being a ranger in Kakadu, I thought I was pretty invincible, and when I applied for this job, I thought one of the only things I can't really do is drive a boat in the open ocean, and that is what I am going to have to do. It really was about confronting demons for me, and that was a big demon: facing a wild and wide, open sea.'

I think of Trish on the dinghy in the howling trade winds on our way to South Island. It is hard to imagine she had not always felt so sure, that her confidence was a life skill, a courage, she had to grow.

'North Keeling also makes me glad that there are places that are not managed just for people,' Trish continues. 'As a ranger at Kakadu, I worked in a national park rich in diversity that had threatened species and this suite of habitats. Then I saw the way this unique place brought in all of these tourists that came to visit, and you have to build infrastructure for humans. You had people walking through rare and sacred sites, and you couldn't help but see that the park was clearly managed for tourists. Whereas on North Keeling, there is none of that: there is no jetty, there is no anything, there is nothing there. So it is nice that there are a few places left in Australia that are managed for conservation rather than the enjoyment of humans. It is such a wild place, it's like something out of this world. Where we camp on North Keeling is about twenty metres from the beach, the waves are so ridiculously loud that you can't really have a conversation. You feel pretty vulnerable when you are staying there, at the mercy of the big unpredictable ocean.'

Trish tells me it makes her really understand a little of what it must be like for the asylum seekers who make their dangerous boat trips over the Indian Ocean from Sri Lanka to Australia, such as the groups that made landfall on North Keeling itself.

'Tell me about that again,' I say. 'I can still picture the plumes of smoke rising from the signal fires the asylum seekers lit on North Keeling when Ash and I were sailing on the lagoon. What happened when you got there, after the Navy had arrived and taken the asylum seekers away?'

'That was in twenty twelve,' Trish says, 'when we had that influx of asylum-seeker boats on Cocos, and a group of about thirty people came ashore on North Keeling. I remember reports in the media said that it was about ten days before the signal fire was picked up on Home Island. We have some equipment up there and little shelters where we stay, and the asylum seekers were using some of our camping gear and food supplies to simply stay alive. I was quite grateful that we had those resources up there because I would not like to think what might have happened to the people otherwise.'

Trish tells me that when she and the other Parks officers went back to assess the site and check whether there had been any introduction of invasive species from the asylum seekers' boat, they found traces the brief visitors had left behind. Among those traces were messages written by the asylum seekers on the bins and huts, such as 'Australia please take us', 'We are 32 people',

'Sorry we take your things' and 'Sorry Australia'. I love this story, the unexpected interface that occurred between two very different groups of people, but I am also struck by that fact that asylum seekers, under such incredible duress and owning so little, would think to apologise for the small liberties they were forced to take.

'For me, that moment of discovering the messages became a really personal and emotional side of my job that I never thought I would come across,' Trish says, 'and it was important for me to try and communicate that experience to the people who lived here. So we put a little article in the local newsletter not trying to colour it either way, only to say they had come ashore and used our things and were very grateful. Their messages are still there and it is actually part of the interpretive tour that I do now, so every time I take Border Force people or a school group up there, I always show them the notices, I show them because it is part of our history.'

Trish goes on to tell me about another boat of asylum seekers that year that came ashore on North Keeling that had seventy people on board.

'Their boat actually sank,' she says, 'so they came ashore with nothing and we picked them up three days after they got there, which is good, because I am not sure how long the coconuts and whatever else they could find would have sustained them. Anyway, they had made little camps up and down the beach, and so while I was on North Keeling the last few days I was having to go through the tents and sort them out. I was picking them all up and that's when I thought, *Oh, this is a heavy tent.* I knew it was one of the Sri Lankan tents because they tried to hang them up with anything they could find, and they had used pink flagging tape to try and attach them to the trees. I looked inside and there was something heavy, it was hanging from the roof of the tent.

It was a little deity or something, some religious figure. Again, it just felt very personal.

'When we left, we had to burn almost everything as we did not know what had been contaminated. And some of the backpacks had only a toothbrush and a tube of toothpaste and a little deity, and I found it so confronting. Coming into contact with asylum seekers was another side of park management that I really never had any idea would be part of my work, so I felt really privileged that I had been able to be part of that and understand the issue from another side, rather than read about it in the media. It was firsthand and I felt really fortunate to be able to share that story for what it was. It was so unexpected, but it was very real.'

'Mum, have you seen my boardies?' Trish's eldest son asks, appearing in the doorway. Trish and I catch each other's eye, aware that, given Trish's large family, our small window of time for talking may soon come to a close.

'No, ask Dad, but I will be with you in a few minutes,' Trish answers.

'Okay,' he says, 'but I need them for school tomorrow, we are going to South End and Dad isn't sure where they are.'

'I'll help you after Reneé and I have finished. Can you close the door please?' Trish asks patiently, and her son leaves, closing the door quietly behind him.

'Ah, it's hard to believe you are going in a few days,' Trish says. 'We have just got used to having you around again.'

'I feel like when I get back home I will be able to pop over if I need a cup of flour or something, or to see if you guys want to go camping.'

'You know what one of the nicest things was about this trip to North Keeling?' Trish asks, going back to our former conversation.

'It was getting to take a couple of Home Islanders with us to talk about some of the issues we have up there. It was nice to be able to say, actually this is the reason it is locked up, this is the reason for the legislation, because look at it, if you guys came here whenever you wanted, it would look like Home Island does, there simply would not be any birds. Getting the Home Islanders to be able to see that was pretty good. I think it was an awakening for them, actually. They said, "Oh, this is what you do up here, yeah right, I think I get it", and they were looking at what Parks does in a different way. They obviously have a history of taking birds for food, and then when the federal legislation came in they were not allowed to do that anymore, and they still have that decision hanging over their heads. But talking to these fellas the last two days, they could see why we wanted to keep it like this, it is pretty special.'

'And what about you personally, Trish, you've really sunk your roots here, do you think you will always live on the Cocos Islands?' I ask.

'No, I don't think I will always live here,' she answers. Trish tells me that probably one of the biggest challenges for her is the 'isolation factor', the high cost of airfares making visiting the atoll prohibitive for many people, including family and close friends.

'That we have lost touch with a lot of very close family and friends over the last seven years has been really difficult. Every time I have people who are actually able to afford to visit and they leave, I think, I *don't understand why I live so far from everybody*. So the geographical location is probably one of the hardest things. None of your family seeing your kids grow up. Cutting yourself off from people you should be surrounded by, parents and siblings and grandparents, that sort of thing. Wanting people who really know you, who share your DNA.'

'Mum, Dad wants me to ask if you want lasagne or fish for tea,' one of the older boys calls, opening the door a fraction. Trish and I look at each other and laugh.

'Looks like you're off the hook,' I say, and I turn my recorder off. Out on the verandah, I turn to Trish to thank her and kiss her goodbye. By the time I have reached the bottom steps, I can hear someone is crying, see Tony has put down his phone and is quickly consoling, while their eldest son calls from the back of the house that he still hasn't found his board shorts.

24. Home Island (Pulu Selma) – Part I

It is just after sunrise when I get off the bus at Rumah Baru to catch the ferry across the lagoon on Tuesday morning. The strange sense of no-time returns as other familiar faces congregate at the end of the jetty, also heading to Home Island for work. The ferry service used to run from the northernmost end of West Island, but the old wooden jetty's exposure to incoming swells sweeping across the Indian Ocean caused the structure to become repeatedly damaged during storms. A decision was made to locate the new jetty further south within the shelter of the lagoon, and an impressive catamaran was bought to replace the old small ferry to move islanders more efficiently across the atoll. The stretch of lagoon that was chosen to house the large new jetty is the site of an important feeding ground for green turtles, who graze on the bay's seagrass beds. The area of Rumah Baru has been significantly affected by the construction of the new jetty as well as the turbulence created by the more powerful engine of the catamaran, turning the beach's clear waters a cloudy green. The sand that has become suspended in the sea water limits the sunlight reaching the seagrass beds, threatening the green turtle's vital source of food. Yet as I chat, I see their small heads repeatedly come up for air like bald jack-in-a-boxes, the dark almond shape of their watching eyes, until the ferry arrives and they disappear into the murky water.

From the ferry, more familiar faces disembark, the women a stream of bright colour in their ankle-length *baju kurungs* (literally, 'enclosed dresses'), as Home Islanders arrive to work or visit West Island.

'*Pagi*, Mak,' the islanders call, smiling briefly, moving quickly to make it to the bus that will take them to the small hub at the centre of West Island. Once on the ferry, I make my way to the top deck of the boat, looking down to where the turbines stir up more white sand. Turtles like large oblong platters dive down and away from the boat, then slowly come up again, raising their curious heads as the ferry speeds away. As we head out into the lagoon, the waters clear once more and I lean out over the metal railing to watch the intricate formations in the undulating terrain of coral that slip by. Two flying fish leap from the boat's wake, blue wings wide in the morning light.

As we head toward the centre of the lagoon, the great 'U' of the atoll wraps around me, a flat map where I am not looking down but across a large-scale work of cartography. I feel like I could lower a great finger from the sky and point, leave an arrow saying, 'I was here', as the large arc of Pulu Atas, South Island, and its many smaller siblings is revealed in hues of washed-out greys and blues. At the same time, Direction Island, or Pulu Tikus, comes into view to the north, defined from this angle by the thick coat of trees that runs the long, thin line of its spine. Soon after, the tiny speck of Pulu Beras, or Rice Island, becomes visible. Mainly referred to now as Prison Island, this lonely clump of trees clinging to a tiny dune at the edge of the outer reef is tenuous in the extreme. During the time of the settlement of the Cocos (Keeling) Islands, Pulu Beras was much more substantial; so substantial, in fact, that Alexander Hare (the atoll's original coloniser) moved his household here in order to contain and control not only his supplies of rice, but also his 'family' of around twelve women and thirty children. The women and children, purported by the Clunies-Rosses and others to have been used by Hare for prostitution, were confined to the first floor of Hare's dwelling, giving birth to the tiny island's contemporary name.

Soon Home Island comes into view, unfolding as a line of silhouettes as the ferry slows. As the catamaran glides into the jetty, the black shapes of palms and houses define themselves more sharply as we emerge though a thin screen of haze. At the dock, I look down on a neat line of motorbikes, quad bikes and golf carts parked in front of the jetty's railing. Home Island, being too small and too densely populated to allow for individual car ownership, relies on these vehicles as the island's main form of transport. This morning the bikes and buggies are parked so perfectly parallel and evenly spaced from one another that they look like part of a display. I descend down the stairs as the ferry is tied to the pier, the smell of diesel thick in the air, stepping out into sunlight on the jetty. As I walk down the streets of the kampong, islanders rake leaves into piles as thin plumes of smoke rise slowly in the tropical air. All along the swept paved streets, my nostrils fill with the scent of burning foliage. Images of my family's brief time of living in Indonesia flash into my mind, and I almost have to remind myself that I am not in Asia, but rather on the very fringe of Australia, in a tiny village that seems like a barely visible bridge between two seemingly disparate worlds.

When I was working on Home Island, it was fascinating hearing the Cocos Malay education assistants teaching the students about their own cultural traditions, and I once found myself going back home on the ferry to West Island smeared in turmeric paste after a lesson looking at traditional practices in local Cocos Malay weddings. On the islands' campuses, the legacy of the feudal regime appeared to be skirted around, and I wondered what it was like for Cocos Malay people to be working alongside the wife of the seventh-generation member of the Clunies-Ross family, a teacher employed at the Home Island school, what this meant for the Cocos Malay community's ability to honestly share their own history.

Reaching the edge of the kampong, I can make out the cluster of yellow-and-blue buildings surrounded by ovals and palm trees that form Home Island's primary school campus. I find the year three-to-six classroom where I am about to teach and unpack my things while I wait for the students to arrive. Spurred by the stimulus of returning to Home Island, I try to cast my mind back, attempt to recall how the relationship between the Clunies-Rosses and the Cocos Malay community was first communicated to me when I was a new arrival in 2012, and find I am left with a sense of overwhelming silence around the atoll's history. The spaces and omissions are a difficult thing to read, but thinking things through once more, I recognise that the silence was not only a result of the cultural diplomacy of the Cocos Malay community. There was a strong sense on West Island, in particular, that it was best to let difficult sleeping dogs lie, especially when members of the former family dynasty continued to live among you. I also distinctly remember critics of the Clunies-Ross legacy (who no longer lived on the atoll) being scathingly personally attacked by several long-standing members of the white community, including Johnny himself. If discussed at all, on West Island, the Clunies-Rosses were conveyed as imperfect but progressive for the time, with the Clunies-Ross family cast as caring colonialists who had the Cocos Malay people's best interests at heart.

'*Jalan, jalan!*'

My thoughts are interrupted by the staccato slap of feet on concrete and the sound of the education assistant's call for the students to walk as they reach the classroom's verandah, but the children ignore her instruction as they run happily back to class after the end of daily fitness. Waiting inside, I try to make out their conversations, enjoying the sounds of the familiar language I have come to love breezing lightly in through the louvred windows.

Taking out a Mary Oliver poem, I bookmark the page, spread out my lesson plan as the children come laughing and chatting through the door.

Despite the diverse range of ages in the class, the young students have surprised me with the originality of their work and the freshness of their images: blue shine in the fins of trevally, glow of sandbags in tropical sun, scent of burning leaves they too have noted and savoured as they ran along pale paved roads on the way to school. It is another three and a half hours until the return ferry, and I try to figure out what I could do in the time between now and then. I reach into my bag and pull out my hat to ward off the sun that has climbed high into the sky, walk across the volleyball field and turn back into the kampong, moving between stands of banana plants glowing greenly from the gardens of row upon row of fibro houses. The sound of laughter rises up from across the road from where a line of trestle tables covered with brightly coloured food has been placed in a concrete yard. The smell of sugar and spices wafts into the air and I wonder what the family in this home are celebrating.

Turning right, I come across a short street almost too tidy to be true. Bright floral curtains hang inside a window with a red sill; an immaculate blue retro motorbike leans against the wall by an open front door. I get out my camera, wondering at the ethics of photographing other people's homes without their consent, when I hear the sound of a golf cart coming toward me. Quickly putting my camera back in my bag, I try to look nonchalant, feeling white and conspicuous, standing randomly in the middle of an empty road. The bright green buggy slows down and I look up, and much to my surprise I see the driver is Nek Su.

I wave and Nek Su frowns at me curiously, so I take off my hat and see his brow unfurrow, full lips stretching into a broad smile.

'Mak!'

'Nek!'

'It's you!' Nek exclaims. 'Did you just walk past? I was sitting outside the house; did you see the one with the tables?'

'Yes, but I didn't see you, I didn't know you were back!' I reply. 'How funny! Nek, actually I was thinking ... I was wondering,' I begin, hoping this could be my window but not wanting to put him on the spot, 'seeing you are here, would you have time for a cup of tea? Could I ask you and Jeannette a few of the questions we talked about?'

'What, now?' Nek asks.

'Sure. Or another time if that's better ...'

Nek Su looks surprised, but then gestures toward the spare seat next to him and I jump in. Though clearly elderly, Nek Su's appearance is striking. Handsome and self-assured, body lean from his life of fishing, Nek's stature is upright and proud, eyes holding a compassionate and intelligent directness. He has the air of a leader, someone both wise and incredibly kind. I bounce beside him on the golf cart, feeling grateful that his world has come into mine.

A few metres down the road, we pull into his driveway. Under the shade of a large annexe is an extensive outdoor area paved with concrete and framed on all sides by fibro buildings. Parked at the back of the pad are a sizable white motorboat and two aluminium dinghies.

'These are my boats,' Nek tells me, not in the least bit trying to downplay his pride. His grin is so broad I can only mirror it, but not being a huge fan of motorboats myself, I am not quite sure what to say.

We head inside, where I can see Jeannette is preparing food in the kitchen.

'*Pagi,* Mak!' I wave, and she turns to see us coming through the back sliding door.

'Reneé!' Jeannette exclaims, surprised. She washes her hands, dries them on her apron and comes toward me. We kiss each other hello and walk back to the lounge to sit down. Nek Su and Jeannette's house is defined by a long hall that extends from the front door, opening to several rooms either side and a wide, open-plan kitchen and living area where we are standing. I notice that their home is imbued with what strikes me as a female touch: walls painted a pale blue with blue patterned throws over couches, blue framed artworks on the walls. There is a warmth to the space that makes me feel at home, light pouring into the open living area through gauzy lace-draped windows. On a pine shelf are framed photos of what appear to be Jeannette's grandchildren, and I wonder what price she pays being here, married to the man she loves, so far from her own children and the mainland she once called home.

'Jeannette, I was wondering if you and Nek had time to talk briefly with me while I am on Home Island. I would love to hear both of your perspectives on your life here.'

'Sure,' Jeannette answers, 'though there is a celebration this afternoon, but I am sure we can cover most things in the next hour or so.' Jeannette puts on the kettle and we settle into our places on the couch. I dig around in my bag to check my recorder is there and the pad with my questions.

There is a palpable tenderness between Nek and Jeannette as they sit next to each other on the couch. Ostensibly, they look like the most unlikely couple, Nek with his deeply coloured skin and full lips harking back to his Javanese heritage, and Jeannette, short and distinctively pale, suggesting an ancestry that is probably English or Scottish – yet as I see them together in their own home, they make complete sense. In front of me are two intelligent and capable people who fell in love twenty-five years ago when Nek Su took Jeannette out on his boat to teach her how to fish.

'Was she any good?' I ask Nek.

'Yes, because I taught her,' Nek says, face deadpan, playfulness flashing across his deeply set eyes. Jeannette's face, however, is lit with the memory. I laugh affectionately at her and she blushes and grins self-consciously, looks at the floor, a smile spread wide across her face.

Nek tells me he was born on Cocos in 1942 and that his family are spread between Cocos, and Katanning and Port Hedland in Western Australia. As we chat, he shares about the changes he has seen on the tiny atoll. As a man finely tuned to the tides and nuances of season, he is worried about the shifts he is observing in the weather. He tells me that even as late as 2000, he used to be able to read patterns in the behaviour of the wind, accurately predicting when there would be a spell of good weather. These days, he tells me, he cannot read what the weather is going to be like in the weeks ahead, cannot predict its pattern – everything seems to be changing. Nek tells me that though there have always been fluctuations in both the weather and the atoll's shape, these days the changes are much more dramatic and are happening faster.

'South Island and West Island are quite different now. At that time on South Island we sail to Pulu Kecil, Pulu Bulan, Pulu Maria and South End. That time we could sail from Pulu Kecil to South Island but now West Island, South End, it comes very close to Pulu Maria. You know the big cannon on Horsburgh Island?' he asks. 'Last time, we could not see that because of the land. Now it is on the water.'

I try to imagine the World War II cannon being set well back behind a large expanse of sand. The last time I visited Pulu Luar (or Horsburgh, as it is referred to on West Island) salt water was swirling around the rusted weapon's concrete foundations, working steadily at its steel, eroding the reinforced feet of this stark piece of military history, threatening to pull it face first into the sea.

Nek goes on to tell me that while he does worry about all the sudden changes, the atoll belongs to Allah, it is up to Allah whether things change quickly or whether they will start to slow and stabilise.

I ask Nek how often he is out on the sea. He tells me sometimes three times a week, sometimes every day. Nek explains he and Jeannette make fairly regular trips to the mainland as Jeannette, semi-retired, currently lives off nursing contract work. Even in Jurien Bay, a rural town on Western Australia's coast, after three or four weeks without his boat, Nek starts to feel imprisoned in that windy mainland town. When this happens, he imagines himself out on the water, visualises himself heading out into the lagoon, holds his memories of sitting in one of his quiver of boats surrounded by nothing but sea.

Nek goes on to tell me that when he was around ten years old there were many people living on Home Island. I later research the population statistics for the number of people living on the island in 1950. Records indicate around one thousand eight hundred people lived on Home Island, compared to approximately five hundred people today.

'That time if you go fishing in the early morning until the afternoon, you maybe just get ten or fifteen fish because there were too many people,' he tells me.

When Nek Su was around twelve, many people from Home Island were sent to Sabah in Borneo in an effort to depopulate the crowded atoll. After about ten years the fish started to return to the lagoon, and the atoll's population of turtles, once an important part of the Cocos Malay diet, also started to improve. Today there are so many turtles, Nek Su tells me, he has to be careful driving his motorboat; the lagoon is so abundant with their large bodies that it is far too easy to accidentally run into these creatures that share the atoll's waters.

The first time I met Nek Su was in December 2013, days before my family and I left the Cocos (Keeling) Islands. As a going-away present, Trish and Tony had bought us a voucher for a ride in a *jukong*, originally one of the main forms of transport on the atoll. Nek Su was our skipper, and also on board was a Cocos Malay friend's son, whom Nek was teaching to sail. Nek Su's reputation had preceded him, and I was so excited not only to ride in a *jukong*, but also to meet this legendary man I had heard so much about. The day was windy and Nek was quiet and focused as we headed off from Home Island. Trish and the boys sailed with Pak Yati alongside us. The two boats looked so beautiful with their white sails and varnished prows against the palm-lined beaches that it felt for a moment out in the middle of lagoon (away from the infrastructure of the atoll) like we were travelling alongside the original Cocos Islanders, transported into another time.

Nek Su was brought up learning how to set up and work the *jukong* rigging from a young age. Education was sporadic on Home Island. Nek Su remembers being taught Jawi (Arabic script that enabled the reading of the Koran) for a short time when he was around eight years old, after which he tells me he received no education at all. In the 1950s, Nek tells me, *jukongs* were still the main form of transport on Home Island and, as a capable and inquisitive twelve-year-old, Nek Su began to teach himself how to sail. Every week he would go out sailing alone, becoming more and more adept at his craft, his mind having the stimulus of the working of the boat, reading the water, its tides and the atoll's weather.

When I express my surprise at Nek's lack of education, he is silent for a moment, like he is turning something over in his mind.

'When I left Cocos in nineteen seventy-six, I have a friend who has passed away. He said the Cocos people cannot really tell their story because of no school. I worried about that.'

Nek's words trouble me. I had heard that the education provided to the Cocos Malay people during the reign of the Clunies-Rosses was not to Australian standards, but I presumed it had, for the most part, existed. I consider I had largely believed the rhetoric on West Island that the life the family dynasty afforded the Cocos Malay inhabitants was better than the islanders would have received in other parts of the world at that time. Perhaps this could be argued for the 1800s, but Nek is talking to me about recent history, about the 1950s. Australia accepted the Cocos (Keeling) Islands as a territory from the British in 1955, and though the islands were under the rule of the Clunies-Rosses, the idea that an incredibly capable person like Nek Su was not able to receive even the most basic education in our country is both shocking and disturbing.

On my return to the mainland, I turn my attention to researching the history of education of the Cocos Malay people on Home Island. Of all the ironies, it is *The Clunies-Ross Cocos Chronicle* itself that provides the most damning evidence of the negligence of even the most recent incarnations of the paternal regime. The *Chronicle* repeatedly documents the way in which great lengths were taken to ensure a very high standard of education was maintained for the children in the Clunies-Ross family, by either sending them away to boarding schools in Europe or through the provision of private tuition in the family home. In the 1940s, in the Clunies-Rosses' own words, fifteen-year-old John Cecil Clunies-Ross was studying 'all the science subjects: maths, additional maths, chemistry and physics, plus English, one modern language, French, one classical language, Latin, and an arts subject, English literature' while attending Exeter Grammar School in Devon. At the same time, a military administrator, Lieutenant-Colonel Jessamine, was sent to the Cocos (Keeling) Islands. Jessamine's role was to oversee the running of the atoll, as the British Government briefly assumed control of the islands as a strategic outpost during World War II. While noting the pride the Cocos Malay people took in both their homes and dress, he also noted the glaring absence of education for the indigenous people of the atoll:

> The very sad point is the whole population is illiterate. There are approximately 800 children on the island with no school. If ever such a decision occurred as to transfer the population elsewhere, they would be easy prey to all the unscrupulous. What is to become of them?

Yet despite these observations, *The Clunies-Ross Cocos Chronicle* seems to be attempting to portray the Clunies-Rosses as benevolent paternal carers of the Cocos Malay people. Christmas Island's District Officer, G.W. Webb, who was sent on an official visit to the islands in 1937, is quoted in the *Chronicle* as saying the Eastern Extension Telegraph staff (who worked on nearby Direction Island) had 'nothing but the highest praise for [John Clunies-Ross's] kindness and methods of dealing with the islanders. His heart and soul are in the place, and he regards them as his own children.'

The Clunies-Rosses' and Webb's shared paternalistic attitude toward the Cocos Malay community is extended to the men's attitude toward education. Webb describes the lack of schooling as 'rather an advantage in such a community on the present lines'.

This sentiment is echoed in the *Chronicle* in a special chapter on education by David Heath, a former teacher on the Cocos (Keeling) Islands in the 1970s. Heath, presumably under the direction of John Clunies-Ross who 'compiled' the *Chronicle,* writes: 'Traditionally education on Cocos was vocation orientated ... This form of practical education suited the island's needs.'

To whose 'advantage' was the 'lack of schooling' for the Cocos Malay population that Webb describes? Whose 'needs' did the 'practical education' serve?

Toward the end of my interview with Johnny Clunies-Ross, I had asked him if he wished his family did more to raise the standard of education for the Cocos Malay people, which I believed at the time to be simply below par. Johnny responded by saying that his father did a lot of reading on the 'need to educate the masses'. He told me that his father understood that if 'you educate your children, they will all leave home. The communities will die from the young people having a wider horizon ... what you need is an agricultural, agrarian economy to soak everyone up.'

Johnny's statement would seem to suggest that the Clunies-Rosses knew exactly what they were doing when they withheld education from the Cocos Malay people. While ensuring their own family were empowered by some of the most elite forms of education available at the time, the Clunies-Ross family deprived almost all of the Cocos Malay inhabitants of even the most basic forms of literacy and numeracy. In this way, the Clunies-Ross dynasty maintained their hegemony, their exclusive power over a strategic workforce, who were conveniently out of sight and out of mind of the international community.

However, occasional efforts were made by some members of the family's ruling patriarchs to introduce basic levels of education on Home Island. George Clunies-Ross educated a clerk with the aim of getting his employee to run a school on Home Island in 1891. Yet by 1898, for reasons that are unclear, this venture had failed, and no concerted efforts were made to improve the situation until more than half a century later. It was not until 1973 that a professional teacher (David Heath, author of the chapter on education in *The Clunies-Ross Cocos Chronicle*) was appointed from the mainland, but, even then, Heath's role was overseen by John Clunies-Ross, education was non-compulsory and the achievements of the students were well below Australian minimum standards. Heath notes that even these early and very basic efforts at education on Home Island were instrumental in the Cocos Malay community beginning to shift toward 'a less Clunies-Ross-reliant island governance'. It was not until 1980 that the Australian Government took on a direct role in the administration of education on the Cocos (Keeling) Islands, as well as enacting an ordinance that made education on the island compulsory, a move the *Chronicle* describes as 'unnecessary'.

I ask Jeannette about her life in the Indian Ocean Territories, how she found herself living in Australia's only Muslim-majority island on land two metres above the sea, almost exactly halfway between Australia and Sri Lanka. Jeannette tells me she first lived on the Cocos Islands as a nurse in 1980. She met her ex-husband, who was a government administrator at the time, on the atoll, and the couple returned to Perth to have a family. Jeannette then lived on Christmas Island with her young family from 1984 to 1987. Jeannette experienced Christmas Island as very isolating, as she found herself stuck at home with young children, trying to form networks with a transient white population that would repeatedly come and go. After three years, Jeannette's husband's contract on Christmas Island ended and they returned to Perth.

When back in Perth, Jeannette continued her nursing studies but also took on some units in Indonesian as she dreamed of returning to Cocos (Indonesian and Cocos Malay being very similar languages). Jeannette's language skills helped her secure a job on the atoll in 1991, where she was based on Home Island as a registered nurse.

'I loved living with the Cocos Malay community,' Jeannette tells me. 'I felt right at home there, I really loved it. I enjoy that sort of healthcare, mainly community health nursing. It involves a lot of health promotion and that sort of thing. We made cooking books with Nek Dila and we did cooking classes and I took exercise classes. It was such a big change, because even in nineteen ninety people didn't have access to things like paracetamol or cough mixture. Those medications were at the health centre, and if people were sick they had to come into the centre in order to get their medication. In fact, when I was there in nineteen eighty, people who were on antibiotics had to come into the healthcare centre four times a day to get their medication.'

'What was the logic?' I ask.

'Because the attitude was that the Cocos Malay people could not be trusted to take their own medication. There was no running water, no toilets ...'

'In nineteen eighty?' I ask, feeling I must have misunderstood.

'In nineteen eighty. There were no toilets or running water.'

'So people would go the toilet in the lagoon?' I venture, thinking, *surely not ...*

'Yes, in the lagoon.' Jeannette laughs. 'I remember walking along the front of the lagoon and waving to one of the healthcare workers, saying "Hi, Wak James!" because I didn't realise what he was doing.' The three of us begin to laugh, imagining the playing out of the scene. 'He was having a poo in the lagoon of course, and

I had no idea. Poor guy, there I was just standing in front of him waving!'

We laugh for some time at the image of Jeannette innocently confronting someone in such a private moment, when down the hall comes a slender woman in a black floral *baju kurung* carrying a plate of food boasting an array of bright greens, whites and pinks. Nek introduces his daughter-in-law. She greets me warmly and places the platter down in front of us: bright jelly cakes in rainbow colours, sticky rice wrapped in banana leaves and thick slices of what looks like vanilla cake. We thank her as she disappears, waving, back down the hall. I choose a parcel of sticky rice, telling Nek its texture looks a bit like squid. As I bite into it, thick palm sugar oozes into my mouth, its sweetness singing on my tongue.

Jeannette finishes her piece of vanilla cake and then begins picking the small crumbs from her lap as she continues.

'It's funny, you know, how things come back to you. When I was driving in Perth recently, I remembered a fellow who was working at the Quarantine Station in the nineteen eighties, who had helped bring in some cattle. He said to me, "Oh, they live such an idyllic life, the Cocos Malay people want for nothing." But at the time people had hookworm, there were no toilets, like I said, and no running water. We used to test the water out of the wells and it was almost pure *E. coli* that the people were drinking. There was so much rheumatic fever because the people didn't get proper healthcare, which then caused more illness as time went by. The Cocos Malay community had allergies and they were so anaemic that people didn't grow properly – the malnutrition affected people's growth.'

I sit on the couch across from Nek Su and Jeannette, trying to take in the information they are telling me. I trust Jeannette's observations as a medical practitioner, but I can also barely believe what I am hearing.

'The people from West Island weren't allowed to come to Home Island, only on very special occasions,' Jeannette continues.

'Why?' I ask.

'Because it was a closed sort of town, a closed community. People from Home Island weren't allowed to go to West Island.'

'So the government decided this?'

'No, the Clunies-Rosses,' Jeannette replies.

'That is why the Clunies-Rosses were stopped by the Australian Government in nineteen seventy-eight,' Nek Su adds.

'It was that sort of transitory time,' Jeannette continues. 'I was based on West Island in nineteen eighty and we used to go over, the doctor and the nurse and I used to go to Home Island twice a week.'

'So the Clunies-Rosses actively separated the communities?'

'Yes.'

Former Cocos Island resident and researcher Pauline Bunce writes: 'Up until the turn of the century, the inhabitants of Cocos rarely saw individuals from the outside world.' Bunce writes that in 1901 the Eastern Extension Telegraph Company was established and a relay station was built on Direction Island. George Clunies-Ross was wary of the effect that the new arrivals might have on his tightly controlled community, so he instructed all contact to Home Island to be through the Clunies-Ross home at Oceania House, while supervising all the visits the Cocos Malay people made to Direction Island. The controlling tendency of the Clunies-Rosses continued though successive generations, limiting the Cocos Malay community's freedom of movement and communication. This included controlling Home Islanders' access to Direction and West Islands, the breach of which meant risking fines and punishment through unpaid work, as well as ensuring that entry to Home Island by West Islanders and the outside world was allowed by invitation only.

In the early 1960s, the Clunies-Ross estate began doing contract work for the Australian Government on West Island. A supervisor for the Department of Housing and Construction, satisfied with the work done by the Cocos Malay employees, encouraged John Clunies-Ross to tender for government contracts on West Island. John Clunies-Ross followed his advice and won some lucrative contracts on both West and Direction Islands.

One of these contract workers was Nek Su. Nek Su tells me he was contracted as 'a jack of all trades' for a company known as GHD.

'Oh, I can do everything,' Nek tells me. 'I can do the plumbing, I can do the welding, drive all the vehicles for the company, bulldozer, front-end loader, grader, all the vehicles I can drive, whatever they let me do I can do it.'

Nek Su quickly ascertained that his access to West Island was an opportunity to have a voice in the wider world. Sick of his low wages and the layers of injustice he experienced on Home Island, he repeatedly used his work in the offices of West Island to form networks and report the conditions under which the Cocos Malay inhabitants were living to the Australian workers in the government and administrative offices on West Island.

Nek Su tells me that his wage of one hundred and fifty dollars was paid directly to the Clunies-Ross estate, and in turn the estate paid him ten and a half rupees a week. This amounted to about one dollar at the time, but the dollar was paid to him in the Clunies-Rosses' currency of plastic money (all other forms of currency were prohibited on Home Island), a currency he could only spend at the Clunies-Rosses' store.

'And this is why I am leaving Cocos,' Nek Su states matter-offactly. I watch Nek's face, holding its usual calm and openness, and wonder what this monumental decision must have been like for a man so intimately connected to the atoll. How must he have felt to be driven from a place he loved, to find himself stepping on a plane for the first time, then driving through a city, into a world of wide-open paddocks in the wheat and sheep town of Katanning in Western Australia's south?

Nek Su was able to leave the Cocos (Keeling) Islands despite the Clunies-Rosses' control over his wages, as the meat company that offered him a contract in Katanning loaned him the $760 in airfares so he could move his family of five to the mainland. Nek Su worked in Katanning for four years in the abattoir until someone discovered he was also a self-taught welder and offered him a job in Wagin, Western Australia. In the time during which Nek forged a new life on the mainland, the Cocos (Keeling) Islands were never far from his mind, and his homesickness for his island home never left him. Nek tells me that about one month into his time working in the abattoir, a senator came to Katanning to ask to meet with him. In the meeting the senator told Nek Su not to worry, that change was coming to Cocos and that he would soon be able to return home. Two years later, Nek Su was visited by two officials from Canberra. They personally informed Nek Su that he was safe to go back to Cocos, the Australian Government had purchased the atoll, and that it was stories like those he had shared with the West Island officials during his time as a contractor that had helped this monumental change to come about. In 1980 Nek Su left Wagin and returned to the Cocos (Keeling) Islands.

Jeannette and Nek Su have established a bed and breakfast from their house on Home Island, where they receive guests from all over the world, including researchers such as linguists and musicologists researching Cocos Malay culture. They have several investment properties in Perth and, of course, a selection of boats with which to enjoy their tropical lifestyle. I consider what a remarkable journey it has been for them both and how much has changed since the 1980s, when Jeannette had first arrived on the atoll.

'Do you think you will always live here?' I ask. Nek Su and Jeannette chat as Jeannette translates the question. I sit for a moment, trying to take in something of what I have heard.

'I think so,' Nek Su answers. 'I will stick to Cocos forever. I was born on Cocos, that is why I love Cocos. I like teaching the younger boys their culture at the school, teaching *jukong* rigging, sailing and Malay dancing. I am teaching the younger boys Scottish dancing because long ago the Clunies-Ross taught me when I was fourteen, fifteen years old. Oh, I was so many dancing, when I was about twenty-four or something like that. I can still do it, that's why I teach the younger boys.'

The respect the Cocos Malay boys, in particular, have for Nek Su is clearly evident in the brief amount of time I have spent on Home Island. It makes sense to me that he would want to pass his knowledge on, that he felt he had a strong role to play mentoring the next generation of Cocos Malay people as they make their way into adulthood in this unique, but also rapidly changing, culture. I wonder if Jeannette feels the same way.

'So Jeannette, you'll be staying too, then?' I ask, smiling.

'Yes,' she answers, 'I'll be here as long as he's here. And then, I don't know. I don't really think about it. I just take life as it comes, really. I am accepted here for who I am. I am a member of the shire council now; I can teach first aid and I am treasurer of the *jukong* club. My skills can be utilised. I understand the community and I know the people and how the community works, sort of. I am not sure if you think about this, but the deeper and deeper you get into a community, the more you realise what you don't understand. It all changes. I am accepted but then I am not accepted, but that's okay because I am different. I go and pray at the mosque, I fast, yet though we all pray together, I didn't grow up with the Cocos Malay community, Nek did. Nek Su grew up with every single one of them. But I believe the Cocos Malay people know and respect where I am coming from.'

'So as long as Nek's here, this is your home?' I ask.

'This is my home, yes.'

25. Home Island (Pulu Selma) – Part II

Leaving Jeannette and Nek Su's place, I am buoyed by the feeling of warmth and connection I have experienced in their company. There is so much to process from what they have shared. Making my way through the kampong, heading toward the shops, I glimpse the island's large figs leaning over the road, framing the ferry and the dazzling blues of the lagoon. The colour draws me, and instead of getting lunch as planned, I find myself walking along the foreshore, past the jetty and into the grounds of Oceania House. A lush hush falls over the day and a moist acidic smell of rotting leaves reminiscent of Christmas Island rises from under my feet. On my left are iron gates that have rusted into a gesture of invitation, permanently open. From the gates a high mossy brick wall marks the edge of what was the Clunies-Ross estate, from behind which rises a tower of tropical plants that screens the rest of my view. On my right the ocean is continually framed by large spreading trees, their mature branches forming canopies so wide that as I continue walking, I experience the sensation I am moving through a glowing tunnel of green and yellow leaves.

When I reach the former Clunies-Ross mansion, I can see there is no-one about, and all the windows and doors are closed. Assuming the current owners are not on the island, I make my way up to the impressive green-and-white two-storey residence. I consider the logistics of building such a palatial home: bricks imported by ship from Glasgow, gardens rich with soil carted nine hundred kilometres from Christmas Island, making all the abundance and beauty possible. I am both awed and disturbed imagining the former grandeur of Oceania House and its surrounds, made possible by the hard labour of the Cocos Malay people. Hard labour – I feel my breath draw in in a sharp gasp. *Surely not*, I think to myself as I hurriedly put my bag down on the ground and dig around to find my notebook, *surely not*. I look back through the notes I have made from *The Clunies-Ross Cocos Chronicle*, and it is then the penny drops: 'The Christmas Island Phosphate Company was incorporated in London on the 14th of January 1897 ... Murray and Ross sold to the company their lease for 500 paid-up shares each.'

George Clunies-Ross and Sir John Murray together discovered the rich deposits of phosphate on Christmas Island in February 1896. Clunies-Ross was a major shareholder in the company, as were many members of his extended family. These shares were not sold until 1949, after World War II. The Clunies-Ross family were not only incredibly wealthy from the exploitation of their Cocos Malay employees, but they also made enormous amounts of money from the Chinese indentured labour imported to Christmas Island. Together with Murray, the Clunies-Rosses were major investors in a mine that caused incredible suffering to a large number of Chinese workers over a period of forty-five years. Early labourers, some as young as thirteen, worked eleven-hour days, six days a week and eight hours on Sunday. Between October 1900 and December 1902 alone, 313 men working the mines had died. No wonder the Clunies-Rosses thought they treated the Cocos Malay community like their own children, when on a nearby island just out of sight, this same family showed indifference expressed in the extreme to the lives of Chinese labourers who, for all intents and purposes, were slaves.

I stand looking up at the sheer height and breadth of Oceania House. To the north and west wings of the house, verandahs shade wooden French windows and doors that must frame spectacular views of the sea. I try to take in all the disturbing pieces of the Clunies-Ross legacy that are coming together. The grounds around me are full of walls and shadows. There is no-one around, so I walk right up to the verandah and peer through the glass to get a view of the front rooms. A teak staircase spirals artfully through the house's full height in the entryway, and in what must be a study, a wood-panelled room holds spine upon spine of well-ordered books. I wonder if the texts originally belonged to the Clunies-Rosses. What did the family hold in their collection, and what could it tell us about the minds of the men who held on to power and privilege for so long in this very place?

Around the back, Oceania House continues to ramble on, even bigger than I initially perceived, having never before come so close to the building when visiting Home Island. Room has been added on to room, but the extensions appear more recent and, though large, lack the grandeur of the front facade. Weeds push up through concrete, paint wears from back walls, everything seems a little ramshackle and overgrown. On this side of the home are what seem like copra sheds, and I guess that the building beyond where I am standing was the estate's office that was converted into a classroom when John Clunies-Ross attempted to start a school in the grounds of Oceania House in 1967.

I wander through the garden's different walled sections, some brick, some limestone. Embedded in the walls are small arched alcoves; in the doorways, carved wooden lintels spiral gracefully in the corners above my head. Yellow blossoms cascade from high trees, bamboo forms its own small forest, frangipani flowers fragrance the air and, by a disused dovecote, giant palms fan themselves resplendently, netting tropical sun. It is beautiful here, but sad, a tired memory, haunted by suffering, a broken and exclusive dream that no longer has a place on this atoll. In the distance, framed by foliage, are the large monuments of the family's graves. I wonder if Johnny ever comes here anymore.

The call to prayer rises up from the mosque and, in that moment, something shifts, like time has been suspended. The universe pauses and I pause with it, an expansiveness drawing my eyes from the gardens up into the canopy and sky above – the day is stilled. Then the chant ends equally abruptly and I register I am completely surrounded by mosquitos. Moving quickly away from the swarming insects, I walk out through a crumbling section of the estate's walls, between large stacks of sandbags stored in the sun, to the kampong, where I can see the shops are closed as people have left to get to the mosque for afternoon prayers.

Looking at the buildings, I notice one neon sign in a door that flashes 'OPEN'. A small bell rings as I push on the door and step into the fibro building, filled wall to wall with bright packaging: lollies, long-life milk, oceanic wall hangings, sports shirts and women's blouses, children's toys, fishing supplies and umbrellas. In the middle of this abundant display I am surprised to see my friend Ossie – a fit, amiable and entrepreneurial Home Islander in his early forties I first met through the cultural tours he ran on Home Island when I first arrived in 2012.

'Hey, Mak Greta!' Ossie says, looking surprised. 'What are you doing here?'

'Ossie,' I reply, 'so good to see you!'

We hug and talk about our families, give updates on our partners and children, Ossie telling me that he and his family are thinking about moving back to Perth. We discuss the pros and cons, the weight of the decision, as customers come in and out of the door.

I tell Ossie about my research as well as my conversation with Jeannette and Nek Su and ask if he would like to be involved. He is interested in what I am doing but hesitant to agree after also witnessing the misrepresentation of islander views in the SBS documentary on education on the Cocos Islands. As we chat, it feels so easy to be with him, and I enjoy the relief of familiarity after spending so much time out of my comfort zone on my trip, the wonderful ordinariness to be spending time with someone I knew as a friend.

'*Salaam*,' a man calls as he enters abruptly through the door.

'*Salaam*,' Ossie replies, and they chat in Cocos Malay as the man tries to decide what flavour of cool drink he is going to buy and, smiling at me, seems to be asking in a friendly fashion who I am.

The man waves, leaves. A radio speaks to itself in Malay in the background. Ossie turns it down and, looking a little nervous, says it is okay, he would like to help me, that if I would like to ask him some questions it would be okay. Coming from the larger world of Malaysia, living in a tight community has not always been easy for Ossie, so I can understand why this is not an easy decision for him. However, what I understand of Ossie's story is intriguing to me, his family part of the large group of Cocos Islanders that moved to Sabah in the late 1940s and early 1950s when Home Island's population was at its peak. What is it like to be a Malay-born Australian and Cocos Islander? Where, for Ossie, is home?

Ossie tells me his father was born on the Cocos (Keeling) Islands, but he left for Tawau (now Sabah) in the north of Borneo after World War II. The second war had a huge impact on the Cocos (Keeling) Islands. At its peak, there were eight thousand three hundred military personnel on the atoll, and a large amount of clearing took place as coconuts were removed for the construction of a new runway on West Island. The new arrivals dramatically altered the economy: much of the copra harvesting gave way to a bartering economy, leaving the plantations largely neglected. The sudden end of the war left the local economy in ruins. The Clunies-Rosses had been living abroad during the period of conflict and, on their return, decided that the best solution was to push the islanders toward emigration.

Tawau was seen by the Clunies-Rosses (and the islands' British administrators in Singapore) as a suitable solution to Home Island's unemployment and overpopulation issues. A development company was seeking to restore an abandoned Japanese estate in the area and needed recruits to work on its palm oil plantation. The Clunies-Rosses allowed the Cocos Malay community to be deliberately deceived into thinking Tawau was just like Cocos, and large numbers of people were shipped off the atoll, starting with one hundred and eighty emigrants in 1949. As the Cocos Malay migrants were 'deck passengers', many Cocos Islanders became seriously ill or died on the voyage to Borneo from diseases such as pneumonia. The separation of the close community was incredibly traumatic, the effects of the fragmentation of this isolated population continuing to be felt today. The offer was a one-way ticket, and when the Cocos Malay people arrived at their new home, they were shocked to find they had been misled. The plantation was far from the ocean, the climate was dramatically different, as it was hotter and characterised by wet and dry monsoons. The working conditions were hard and many of the Cocos Malay migrants died from malaria and other diseases that their bodies had not previously encountered. Some of the Cocos emigrants even went mad, and one woman is known to have committed suicide.

Ossie was born in Sabah and lived there until he was fourteen years old. He says he had a happy childhood in a small community but Cocos was always in his family's consciousness. In particular,

Ossie recalls the stories of how wonderful fishing was on the atoll, but among these stories were also those of mistreatment of the Cocos Malay people and the hard living and working conditions people experienced there. When his father heard the news that the Australian Government had taken control of the Cocos (Keeling) Islands, Ossie's father knew that life on Cocos was going to improve, so he applied to immigrate back to the place of this birth. In 1989 Ossie's father was finally successful and the family returned to the Cocos (Keeling) Islands.

'When we were in Sabah,' Ossie tells me, 'the only language we were speaking in Malaysia was Malay, so even though there was an English subject to study, we turned a blind eye to it. Then when I arrived, I realised how important English was because by then there was a proper school because the island had been taken over by the Australian Government. So then I am thinking, *oh no*; you know, I was fourteen and I could not go to primary school because I was too old, but then I could not go to high school because I could not speak the language. So I had to make a drastic decision, what was I going to do?'

Ultimately Ossie made the difficult decision to leave Cocos and move to Perth, where he was able to stay with family. Though only fourteen, Ossie managed to enrol in an adult English class at an adult migrant centre. Though unqualified, through sheer initiative and hard work Ossie eventually secured a job as a fitter and turner. He stayed at the job for several years, supporting his mother back in Malaysia until he was able to bring her to Australia.

'In the back of my mind, I always wanted to live on the mainland,' Ossie tells me. 'As much as Cocos is a lovely place to stay, you do feel a sense of freedom, if you like, on the mainland ...'

'Is it claustrophobic here sometimes?'

'Yes and no,' Ossie replies. 'It is because you are living in such a small community, you constantly need to keep your eyes open all the time. What I mean by that is that there are things you can and can't do. There are always people that are going to judge you, what you do, and there are always people who are going to think that what you do is wrong. You can never please people. But if you were on the mainland, for example, it is a bigger world out there, you can mind your own business.'

'You are more anonymous.'

'Exactly. You could go down the beach in your bikini, if you like, and no-one is going to question why you do that. You could have five jobs and no-one cares. Unfortunately, here if you do that, people think you are a bit different. So there are challenges living in a small community because everyone expects you to blend in and do the same thing over and over again. If you experience the outside world and then come and live here, it is a bit hard because you have to try and adapt to the way people live on Home Island.'

I think of Ossie and his work in the shop on Home Island, and his role when I first met him as a tour guide, charismatic and articulate in his second language, explaining the Cocos Malay culture to visiting tourists. During the time that I lived on Cocos, Ossie was also collaborating with Tony on West Island to produce a line of local gourmet foods. I wonder what pressures are placed on Ossie to go with the flow of the way things are on Home Island, a world where there is no place for 'tall poppies', where I once met a woman who had arrived from a nearby Asian country and who, after ten years, was only just beginning to feel let in.

The conservative culture of the Cocos Malay community stems from the social microcosm that Home Island represents. The tiny landmass, approximately two metres above sea level, maintains its cohesive community through an emphasis on social harmony, a world where direct confrontations are rare. Social life revolves around family groups, children are a pinnacle of personal achievement and social standing, and individual ambition appears to be treated with a degree of suspicion, almost a betrayal of the emphasis on the collective.

I experienced Cocos Malay culture as so peaceful and unified when I lived on the atoll that it is interesting to consider Ossie's experiences. While Home Island life is incredibly stable and the culture strong, I can see how, for some who have had different experiences or hold different priorities, this larger social cohesion can come at a cost.

'And that is always why it is in the back of my mind that, for me personally anyway, I always wanted to move back to Australia,' Ossie says. I think of the delicate dance he must do to try to meet the needs of his family, the wishes of his beautiful Cocos Malay wife and his twin high school-aged children immersed in their life on Home Island.

I ask Ossie if he thinks of himself as predominantly a Cocos Islander, an Australian or a Malaysian. Ossie tells me when he is in Perth, he thinks of himself as an Australian, and when he is on the Cocos (Keeling) Islands he thinks of himself as Cocos Malay Islander. For him, his experience of self is largely in response to the part of his identity that is being reinforced by the culture around him. He tells me his father always reminded him to say he was Australian or Cocos Malay, never to say he was Malaysian. This confused Ossie, and he wondered where his father was coming from. Later Ossie understood there were two reasons behind his father's position: one was that in a post–September 11 environment, Ossie's father felt there would be less prejudice extended to him as a Muslim man if he emphasised his Australian heritage. The second reason was Ossie's father was born on

Cocos and circumstances beyond his control had forced him to leave, a decision that resulted in his family becoming Malaysian citizens. His father had worked hard for the family to return to the place where he was born. Ossie's father believed, as Cocos is part of Australia and his father's descendants were the original inhabitants of the Cocos (Keeling) Islands, that he was essentially a unique indigenous Australian, indigenous to this isolated part of the nation. He wanted Ossie to own this distinctive heritage.

Young children spill into the shop dressed in their yellow-and-blue school uniforms. They smile shyly, buy juices and lollies and leave as a small group, chatting quietly as they climb into the back of their parents' golf buggies.

'I don't know if you have heard the story about Johnny's mother who passed away,' Ossie says. 'Johnny's mum, Daphne, passed away in Perth but her ashes are here. Not many people know the story or, if they do, they don't really understand it. I remember about ten years ago Johnny's father and mum always wanted to retire here, they were hoping to die here, but there is no place for them, nowhere for them to stay. You have probably heard the story about how some people liked them and some people hated them because of what they did with the coconut planation and the issue of money. In the back of their minds they keep that knowledge there, that people hated them more than liked them, that is how it was planted in their mind, not necessarily how we feel. They thought we hated them, but the good thing about us is we forgive and forget. This is how Cocos Islanders are now. You could treat us bad, Reneé, but three or four months down the track, we would say, "Hi Reneé, how's it going?" and we would forget all about what had happened.

'John Clunies-Ross's wife thought we hated their guts, so that is why it took her a long time to come back here. But when they came back and people heard they were coming, she was wondering, *How on earth are we going to be treated?* She probably thought they were going to be booed or we would throw eggs, but to her surprise, when she arrived, we treated her and John like a king and queen, like how we treated them when they were the king and queen on the island back then. She could not believe it. All the mums came and the people with the drums, all sitting there welcoming them. Now it could be a story that is made up, or it could be true, but what I heard on the grapevine is that when she came here she was healthy, and when she went back, she became sick. When Daphne went back to the mainland she could not move on or leave her past behind. She could not believe how she was welcomed after what she had done to us. I heard she felt so sad, she died of a broken heart.

'My dad always reminds me that whether people think that what the Clunies-Rosses did was good or not, at the end of the day, look how we ended up, look how things turned out for us. Yes, my great-great-grandfather had a hard life, but their sacrifices led us to where we are, we have a good life. My ancestors were originally from Indonesia, and if my ancestors never came here and my father and I were born in Indonesia, things could be very different, they could be worse. The Cocos people made good of the situation for themselves. It is a sensitive topic to talk about because you are always going to have people with a different view about the Clunies-Rosses' role here, but my dad always said the Clunies-Rosses should be awarded a medal. I asked, "Why is that, Dad?" And he'd tell me it is because, like I said, how things have turned out in the end.'

Ossie's story has had me intrigued, has drawn me in so much that I have lost track of the time. The arrival of the school children must have given my subconscious a subtle clue, because suddenly I realise it is after two-thirty and the ferry is about to go.

'Oh no, Ossie, I am going to miss the ferry!' I exclaim.

Ossie looks at his watch. 'Quick, you better go!'

'I'm so sorry,' I say. 'This has been so helpful, I really appreciate your time.'

'No worries,' he says, 'but really, you better run ...'

'I know,' I say, and I wave, sprinting out the door, relieved to see they have not untied the ferry or the ramp to get on board, so I might still make it in time. As my bag bounces against my back, running into the glare of the afternoon sun, I wonder at this strange, shifting and unpredictable place that continually reinvents itself, a cartographer's nemesis, a castaway's dream. Just when I think I understand how things work on this horseshoe of sand in the middle of the ocean, something always moves, a new layer is uncovered, causing me to reassess what I thought I had learned, start my mapping all over again.

26. Direction Island (Pulu Tikus)

Two days after my trip to Home Island, I find myself wandering along the palm-lined foreshore near West Island's main jetty at Rumah Baru. Here the trunks of palms are so closely packed together that they seem like a crowd of curved brown bodies swaying to an inaudiable song. Further along the shore, large figs rest their gnarled and woody elbows in the water. Their stillness and beauty fills me with a gentle sadness, knowing that soon it will be time, once again, to leave this luminous world of blues and greens.

My time with Ossie and Nek Su has drawn me in deeper, like my ear is resting against the atoll's beating heart. The islands are steeped in story, and what has been silenced rises, knows itself, and demands to be understood as history. I can almost see their words settling between the grains, trying to find their new shape, water eroding and building, shrouding and exposing.

I sit, held for a moment in the arms of a fig, mind settling, feet cooling in the shallows. Continuing, I step into sun, walking toward a small sandy point, when the events of a remarkable morning come back to me.

When my family and I lived here in 2013, my husband and I had been walking along this stretch of sand, looking for our tent after a camping trip that went dramatically wrong. The dinghy that we had been towing behind our catamaran, filled with our camping supplies, had tipped in high winds on our way to South Island, spilling all of our carefully packed possessions into the sea. The next day, much to our surprise, our prediction of currents was right, and we found our tent tangled in the roots of these very trees. We continued walking, wondering what else we might reclaim, when we were met by the most shocking and remarkable sight.

There on the beach past the figs, washed up by the morning tide, was the enormous form of a tiger shark, around three metres long. Our hearts skipped a beat, our base brains shouting that we should be extremely careful and very afraid. Slowly we circled her form, quiet and in awe, checking that the enormous creature was indeed dead. Then, gaining confidence, we approached her streamlined design, admiring the beautiful pattern of her denticles, the sea floor's shadows echoed in the nuance of her tigery stripes. I pored over her face, surprised by the amber colour of her iris, lit bright by the day's full sun. It was as I gazed at her streamlined snout that I suddenly saw it, felt my body jolt again. On the underside of her jaws, the most sensitive part of a tiger shark's form, pushed into the softness of her skin, was the incision of a blade repeatedly driven in.

This time around I don't push past the figs. I am at Rumah Baru to catch the ferry and it will soon depart. I glance back once more, almost seeing the shark's monstrous shape, then quickly make my way back to the jetty. Once it departs, the ferry first heads out to Home Island then makes its way back to markers in the reef that show the channel out to Direction Island. Here white sand reflects the light back though liquid in perhaps the most iridescent of blues of anywhere on atoll. Dolphins rush in from both sides and begin to race the ferry, zooming in and out of its wake, then after a while seem to tire of the game and speed away. I am photographing the markers in front of a large blue boat in the atoll's entry, when through my viewfinder I recognise the vessel I am looking at.

Framed in my lens is the same turnback boat I witnessed at the end of my time on Christmas Island. The large Border Force ship has been parked between West and Horsburgh Islands for most the time I have been on the atoll but I had not realised, as it was so far in the distance, it was not clear to the naked eye. I curse its presence under my breath and put my camera away, yet happily this very stretch of the journey is also marked by a far more positive experience of those who preside over Australia's borders.

In 2013, on a Saturday morning as my husband and I took the same boat ride to Direction Island, I was amazed to discover the ferry was approaching a cluster of bright Sri Lankan fishing boats moored in the centre of the lagoon. As we got closer, it became clear there were Customs officials working on the decks, their inflatable Zodiac tied to the side. As the ferry came closer still, the passengers on board and I began to comprehend the colourful vessels had asylum seekers on board. I held my breath, as this was a time when there were growing tensions over the new arrivals, and it felt like a litmus test as to how the community and a handful of tourists were going to respond. I ran up to the top deck and raised my hand in a long slow wave at the same time as some of the men on the boat, all donning bright orange life jackets, also began to wave at the people on the ferry. There was a pause, then a collective shift as people began to understand what was happening, and people on the ferry raised their hands high and waved in return. A Customs official on the top deck smiled and waved at us too. The asylum seekers on the fishing boats laughed and waved their arms higher again, and it felt like lightness, I felt like dancing. In that moment, our small gestures felt like the most hopeful thing in the world.

On Direction Island, the only boats arriving these days are yachts, and there is an influx of them: red yachts, white yachts, yellow and blue yachts, moored in the tranquil waters of the bay. The yachties' dinghies hum to and from the shore, washing hangs in the sun from the boats' metal rails. The ferry pulls in and we all spill out, quickly marking out spots in the shade in between the busy scuttling of hermit crabs. After all the intensity of the interviews, this time of silence and relative solitude is exactly what I need. I spread out my towel and start to read my book in the shade.

After a while I walk along the shore, the scene pristine in the extreme. I strip down to my bathers and sink into the balmy water, watching the boats' bright colours against the blue of sea and sky. As I swim further out, I hear my name called, and recognise the person sitting in the immaculate white motorboat anchored off the island's shore is my old neighbour, Di. I swim over, climb in and we chat for a while, enjoying the warm tendrils of sun on our backs. As I am about to go, Di asks if I want to swim out to the Cabbage Patch. I have heard of this dive spot, know this beautiful coral mound is quite a bit further out, but I am really quite scared of the atoll's abundance of sharks.

'We can swim out with The Rip,' Di says, 'and Ian can bring the boat round and pick us up so we don't have to swim back.'

I am frightened by the idea, but agree. Thinking again of the strange mass on my shoulder, I feel spurred to take greater risks. Di and I walk down the long stretch of sand to the reef, palm fronds gently shifting in the midday sun along the bright white of the shore. Ahead of us we can see the gap in the reef where the swift waters of The Rip run through, behind which the surviving stand of trees on Prison Island cling to remnants of the island's dune.

We pull on masks and flippers that Di had stored in the boat and push out across The Rip's aptly named strong current, kicking hard to make it across the deep channel to the slower waters on the other side. Once across, I cling to a rocky knoll on the other side to stop myself getting swept along as I catch my breath. The water's current means I don't need to move in order to make my way along the reef so, as I duck back under the surface, I find I effortlessly glide, the sea's bright menagerie unfolding before me. There are some fish here than I can name, but so many more that I do not recognise. I let my body descend down the ledge of reef, where angelfish and neons come in and out of swaying soft corals. Moving unhurriedly over the sandy channel between the reef's cliffs, I can see leatherjackets, rock cod, tusk fish, parrot fish and wrasse, as well as strange silver fish watching me in slow-moving schools. Thin striped fish gather under plates of coral as if waiting under a wide, textured umbrella. There are unicorn fish with their outrageous horns, shy blue trevally with their iridescent designs and, curiously, dark sharks sleeping on the ocean floor with their heads tucked out of sight under a lip of reef. As the channel widens and slows, a barracuda flashes silver in sun, its mouth crowded with row upon row of thin blades.

Di is already well ahead of me, but as I turn to kick away from the sandy shallows and head out to the lagoon, something catches my eye. I move slowly forward and then realise what I am seeing is a hawksbill, a critically endangered sea turtle, bending its head toward something that has captured its attention on the sea floor. The small turtle sees me, but when I stop moving it decides I am not a threat and continues to forage with its pointed beak in the sand. I stay, hovering like that for some time, watching the turtle feed, utterly enchanted, until I feel a whack on my back and wonder why Di, even in jest, would slap me so hard. I turn around and there is no-one, nothing, there. I am unnerved, and despite the beautiful sight of the hawksbill, I look around quickly to see if I can find Di. My heart is beating hard in my chest, but now I doubt myself. After all, I saw nothing, perhaps I imagined the sensation and nothing actually happened.

Soon a large coral knoll comes into view and over its shape I can see Di swimming. I kick toward her, feeling a little less brave and very relieved to have her company. Over the knoll a huge array of coral grows, and amid the coral more fish hide and feed among its colour and texture. As we move along a series of other outcrops, a large blacktip reef shark glides slowly toward us. I stare at it, which causes the shark to warily watch me as we pass each other, and I kick myself, understanding my fear of reef sharks is irrational and only makes the sleek creatures more edgy.

As the reef formation comes into view, I can see how the Cabbage Patch earned its name. Over a large round piece of reef, around ten metres wide, is a proliferation of distinctive yellow coral that arranges itself in much the same way a cabbage forms, as a series of wide, flat and interlocking leaves. We hover over the shape of the outcrop, taking in its colour, yellow striking against the water's azure blues, a cloud of fish rising, hovering like hundreds of equally yellow insects echoing the underwater bloom.

Out in the blue water, just beyond where Di and I swim, friends had taken me out for a dive from their boat when I first arrived on the atoll. As we headed into the blue, several dolphins had come to play in the boat's wake, and our friend had started to play with them, turning his boat in tight circles, doing doughnuts, churning up wake, until more and more dolphins came to join the fray. After a while, our friend cut the engine and we all quickly put on our flippers and masks, easing ourselves into the warm water. Instead of being frightened, the dolphins seemed to think our entry into their world was an event. Six or seven bottlenoses raced in, circling us, zooming off and coming back, swimming playfully underneath us or gliding past at face height, looking curiously into our eyes.

We swam away from the boat, and the dolphins sped around us, clicking and calling, coming so close I could see the sucker fish riding on their bellies, the damage and scarring to one large dolphin's dorsal fin. The light traced white, laced patterns on the greys of their skin, and all around us the water resonated with a luminous sapphire hue. In a moment I could barely believe to be true, a mother dolphin swam toward me with her calf. They came so close I could have reached out and touched them, like she was showing me, showing off her young.

Then, as though wanting to continue the spirit of the initial game of chasing the boat, one young dolphin began swimming up to the surface of the water, leaping out and then turning, speeding straight down, picking up a hapless sea cucumber lying on the ocean floor, throwing it high and spinning into blue light, and catching it again in its snout. There was no doubt in my mind that these wild creatures had come simply to meet us, they wanted an event, they wanted to play. They checked us out, tried to start a new game, but we were such slow-moving creatures in their world that I suspect we may have been a bit of a disappointment. Still, the dolphins seemed curious and hopeful. When we finally appeared to lose our novelty and the avenues of exchange became exhausted, the dolphins slowly turned and quietly went on their way.

After Ian picks Di and me up in the boat, Ian drops me back on Direction Island. It is nearly time for the return ferry to arrive. I quickly gather my things and walk out to the jetty. If you miss your ride home from Direction Island there is no way back to West Island other than an incredibly long swim past the tiger sharks, and no mobile reception with which to hatch a Plan B. I drink in my last view of the island from the elevated perspective of the two-storey ferry, gazing down over the aqua curve of clear water, the lush crowns of palms swaying in the wind.

Heading back to West Island, after a day of sun and salt, I long for the solidity of land, look forward to being inside, to a hot shower and the shelter of four walls. Nevertheless, on the afternoon ride home, I remain on the top deck, watching the northern islets slip away. The sky has turned cloudy, washing the sea with grey, light breaking through gouache clouds in smatters of silver. The turnback boat anchored further out has also lost its colour, turning into a suggestion on the horizon, a distant shadowy blur. It is up here on this deck, salt-caked and spent, I realise with sudden certainty I want to go home. Though I am grateful to be in this extraordinary place, I miss my family and I want to be with them, I miss the warm tone of my husband's voice, the lightness and wit of my daughter. I want to be able to be anonymous again. I want to see a band in a pub. I want gallery openings, good coffee and writing groups. I want to go back to a place that is not this shifting, restless surface, I long to return to a life not so deeply steeped in sea.

27. North Point

On my second-last morning I sit on the strip of white sand at the water's edge near my old home by the sea. Around my feet, red and tawny hermit crabs navigate their small Sahara, bodies busy with the endless business of finding food. The tide is going out and I imagine it being drawn on great strings of the moon. For a moment, the world is quiet. The wind dances like a small child around my ears, and the waves say *hush, hush.* Like so many times before on this tenuous sandbar, I feel hushed and small, the world has reminded me it is big, so big. Grey cloud settles in the stratosphere.

Though my overwhelming experience was a life lived in peace in this place, not all my days were balmed by the islands' beauty. After months of sun and the hammer of trade winds, some days I resented the sea intensely – like a dazzling, demanding lover, it was always in my eyes, filling my ears, leaving its trace on my skin. One evening, when we were quite new on the atoll and I was still reeling from the death of my father, Pete and Emma invited us around to dinner. It had been a warm reprieve, this growing sense of friendship after all the challenges of moving and mourning. After our meal we sat and watched surf movies together, chatting and drinking wine when, without warning, the police appeared at the door. They called my husband aside, talking in subdued voices, standing in shadow on the driveway. They had come tell us that my husband's forty-six-year-old brother had experienced a heart attack. Two hours before, Ash's brother had fallen in a friend's bathroom and died.

Grief gave way to anger. I resented the world, I resented the atoll, the sea, the islands' innate transience, a world in flux. I needed to control my life. I needed to stop losing the people I loved, I needed to protect my husband and defend my daughter from having to experience any more suffering. But everything around me said *relent*. The swell worked at me all night. The elemental powers that whirled around me told me that my wiII meant nothing; on its scale my actions were barely perceptible. Out on the horizon, people were drowning; I had found their bags, their life jackets and shoes. I raged and I fought and stayed angry as if this somehow made me strong. Then one afternoon, as I sat watching the tide moving steadily away as I do now, crabs eating at the body of a small shark, the tideline scattered with pieces of broken boat and children's sneakers, something in me gave way. In that moment, I understood and accepted my insignificance, accepted everything over which I did not, and never had, control: the slow, cruel death of my father, the mortality of the people that I loved, the incredible suffering that continued to play out even on this atoll's shores, a world that would not stop moving and changing. For a moment I was utterly bereft. Then, unexpectedly, I found myself imbued with lightness and peace. In my new humility, I found I could let the whole shifting and fluvial world in. I was broken, finally broken wide open.

For my last two nights I have moved into Trish and Tony's house, where one of her boys has generously given up his room. It feels good to end my journey here in this hub that for two years was my stand-in family; Trish often felt like a sister to me. The four boys seem to enjoy the novelty of my presence – I am an extra pair of hands, two extra ears. The boys and I play dinosaurs in the lounge room, I run and supervise baths, chop tomatoes in a small team as we all help with dinner. As we are eating our meal on my first night staying in their home, Tony's phone bings at the end of the table.

'Ah, well, you'd be interested in this, Reneé,' Tony says, reading the screen. 'It's Ossie wanting to get through to Johnny. There is a Cocos Islander from Sabah who lived here fifty-three years ago wanting to get his birth certificate from Johnny Clunies-Ross.'

'What?' I reply. 'Surely not? Surely the Clunies-Rosses do not still have their birth certificates?'

'Apparently so,' Tony says, as he messages the request to Johnny, and indeed Johnny messages back that he has the birth certificate and will leave the Cocos Malay man a copy, in keeping with tradition, for an exchange of food.

Finally, my last night in the Indian Ocean Territories comes around. Trish has organised a going-away picnic dinner for me at the beach. We grab our things and jump in the car, all squeezing into the 4WD. Soon we arrive at North Point. Tony parks the car and we walk through the tunnel of palms that frames the bright spit of sand, behind which the lagoon's waters jostle, swirling and foaming, tide pushing against the swell as makes its way back out to sea. I sit with a group of friends both old and new, filled with a sense of their love and acceptance both of me and of what it is that I am needing to do out here on the islands. I have experienced nothing but generosity and goodwill on Cocos, and I feel so grateful, so held, and incredibly thankful to simply be alive.

The light starts to fade on our little gathering and we begin to gather our things. Tony puts out the fire and the clouds transform the light into a monochrome painting of blue–grey sky. A military plane arcs around the edge of the atoll and comes in to land.

Once back at Trish and Tony's, Trish and I lie on her son's

bed, talking. We laugh about the last time we were together out at North Point, staying well after sunset by the light of the fire. As we had been chatting, we had noticed a Border Force boat going back and forth in the dark outside the reef in front of us. Then, as if from nowhere, three Border Force officers stepped out of the bushes surrounding our small group, large flashlights in their hands shining in directly into our eyes. The officers seemed embarrassed when they realised it was only our two white families having a picnic together by the sea. Perhaps they were confused as they could not make out the colour of our skin through the lenses of their infrared binoculars, or perhaps it was the Sri Lankan mat we were sitting on that threw them, a mat Trish had found the day she discovered the messages left by Tamil asylum seekers on North Keeling.

28. Heading Home

On my final morning in the Indian Ocean Territories, the day is quiet and still. As I pack my last things, I have the house to myself, Trish has left for work, the older boys for school, and Tony and their youngest son have gone to work at The Farm. To be alone in this final moment feels so right. When I finally set off for the short walk to the airport, the small wheels of my suitcase cause my bag to rattle madly as I drag it over the bitumen. Out on the reef, I watch for the last time as the turtles' heads come up to the surface to breathe between sets, comical, like a child's game. Soon I arrive at the airport's foyer and stand in the short queue waiting to check in, looking at the Cocos Malay people milling under a large tree as they wait on West Island for someone either arriving or leaving. Further up the line I see an arm wave to me over the other passengers' heads, and recognise that the tall person looking smart in a blue-checked shirt, is in fact Nek Su.

'It's okay, Mak,' he says. 'I have told them you are here. I have moved your seat; you are sitting next to me.'

I laugh, taken aback that it is even possible to check someone else in and move their seat on a major airline without their consent, but then I am flattered that Nek felt comfortable and wanted to do so. It seems such a fitting way to end my journey.

Soon the plane's engines roar, and the outrageous blues of the atoll vanish like a brilliant dream behind us as we are surrounded by a vista of endless sea. It is a bonus having Nek's company for the flight to Christmas Island. Nek tells me he is heading to the hospital on Christmas Island as he is having trouble with his heart. I quietly hope that he will be okay. It is comfortable between us. We talk about island weddings and trips to Perth, then somehow get onto the subject of the challenges of living on an atoll with so many sharks.

'I find it amazing, considering how many sharks there are in the lagoon, that no-one on the atoll has ever been attacked,' I say.

'That is why I got that one,' Nek tells me, 'that long pole with a knife. If I see that tiger shark, I just get him. It's best just to get him, then, that way, not so many sharks.'

'What, you stab them?' I ask, unable to hide my shock. 'Even if they aren't worrying you?'

'Yes, when I am fishing, I sneak up, that tiger does not even know I am coming.'

As Nek talks, it dawns on me that it is quite possible that the person who killed the exquisite creature I found washed up near Rumah Baru several years ago was Nek Su. I know I will have to find it in myself sometime to let this go, but for now I smile at the irony that this gorgeous gentleman I have come to adore killed a creature that had inspired in me a sense of wonder and awe. It seems, even at this distant point, the atoll is still teaching me, keeping me supple.

Outside my window, the Indian Ocean continues to spread itself like a richly dyed cloth over the earth's curved surface. Small tufts of cloud are mirrored as shadows. The clouds begin to gather and become thicker the closer we get to Christmas Island, until we are eventually completely swallowed by a sea of white light. Emerging out the other side, we sit above the dense canopy of green interrupted only by the red wounds of phosphate mines, then suddenly we are bouncing along the tarmac, plane brakes screeching and wing shields roaring as we grind to an abrupt halt.

As we walk across the tarmac, people press their faces up against the fencing, looking for loved ones. Immediately inside the glass door of the airport reception, Border Force tape divides us into those staying and those moving on. Nek and I say farewell, warmly shaking hands, and as he passes me again on the other side of the tape, he gently squeezes my arm. I savour the moment, the easy affection between two new friends, as we walk toward our separate doors.

When it is time for the plane to leave once more, rain begins to pour and we are handed colourful golf umbrellas to make our way across the tarmac. Once all passengers are finally seated and the cabin doors locked, the plane taxies slowly to the edge of the runway, where it turns around, humming and vibrating. Sound bursts from the propellers and the aircraft accelerates rapidly, pushing up into sky, until golden bosuns are shining below, disappearing as the clouds close their curtain once more. Heading home. The thought is like the memory of sunlight, of something luminous and warm. Every cell in my body wills me on my way. I sit in silence as, in my own company, I am starting to process that I am also flying into a future I am unsure of. I don't yet know that my diagnosis will be all clear – the strange shape into which the moles have grown is simply the 'trauma' of a scrape. Receiving this news will be an incredible moment in which I feel I am gifted back my life on my return. Yet I wonder if it is this very uncertainty that has made my experiences on the islands so raw, so rich. I also don't know that my poetry book will be published and go on to win a major award, which will allow me the incredible opportunity to tell the story of my young students on Christmas Island. Through social media, their lived realities will go on to reach thousands of people all over Australia – for a moment the compelling fact of each child's precious life will transcend the silence of detention.

In the aisle seat, the fit-looking passenger next to me stands up to pull his phone from his backpack in the overhead lockers, snapping me out of my thoughts. When he sits down I introduce myself, and the man tells me his name is James and that he works for Border Force on the ship that patrols the water around the islands. James tells me he works three weeks on and one week off and is heading back to Perth while he is on leave. Though I concentrate on making my face look neutral, my mind starts to whir. I can't quite believe my good fortune. I wait for James to put his seatbelt on and settle back in his seat. I glance casually at my phone and then out the window. I have a million questions for the man strapped into the seat next to me, and all either one of us has for the next three hours is time.

But for now, I look out of the plane window at the vast ocean to see Christmas Island disappearing completely from view. Both my fellow passenger's vocation and my own path here have been moulded by forces so much bigger than either of us. As we hurtle toward our respective futures, there seems a tenderness to this truth, a view so different to distinctions between me and others I have sometimes held so tightly. This time around in the Indian Ocean Territories, I have finally not only understood the entanglement of my life with the lives of others, but also embraced that interdependence, held it like a fine cloth to the light to see its golden thread woven through everything.

Epilogue: The Archipelago of Us

I returned to Fremantle from the Indian Ocean Territories with a suitcase full of stories. They whisper from my digital recorder, sit as stacks of words in fat files, slip under my skin; each person's pared-back truth a shimmering thing; precious, tenuous and ever-shifting. These stories give me hope. In these stories I find generosity, openness, fluidity and possibility, courage, honesty and acceptance. In many of the encounters with people who shared their lives with me in the Indian Ocean Territories, I see a country I can believe in, an expression of the best notions of our nation – an idea of Australia that can both embrace and define, as well as invite.

These stories have gifted me a map, a winding way back to the country that I loved, undone and reinvented. But can these stories give me back my belief in 'Fair Go' Australia, a place where each person's inherent worth is upheld? I think back to the beginning of the time when this belief had been so deeply unsettled, to the playful students I met in the tiny community outside of Fitzroy Crossing. I think about the children's hunger, their classmate on suicide watch whose brother had hanged himself only days before, this story part of a far bigger narrative about our country's brutal frontier history, as well as our ongoing failure to 'Close the Gap' in the life expectancy and standard of living for the First Australians. I consider the lack of wage parity for Asian Australians on Christmas Island mining phosphate for Australian farmers, the apartheid system that Pete had to endure in that same community even into the late 1970s, the consequences of the White Australia policy for him and so many other non-white citizens on both Christmas Island as well as the mainland, the legislative sanctioning of prejudice in the hearts and minds of the Australian populace.

I turn over the stories of the lives that found their way into mine in this excised world: the children locked in detention without so much as a playground, their slow forgetting of how to laugh and play. I think of Zainal's heartbreak, the seeming failure of our Navy to protect those aboard the *Janga*, the exclusion of families from the memorial for those who suffered such violent deaths, even when the memorial service was about their own loved ones. I think of Massom, hand held to the flow of the waterfall, those same hands later lifting cleaning fluids to his lips as he was robbed of his hope by a cruel regime of incarceration and punishment for those who fled to our country seeking safety. And I think of Nek Su, his courage and overcoming of his severely limiting circumstances, our country's failure to ensure his education, health and basic freedoms. I consider the excision of the entire Indian Ocean region to avoid our obligations under the 1951 Refugee Convention, the way we have both legally and emotionally cut ourselves off from our places that unsettle us, even when these places are at our country's centre, even if it has meant cutting ourselves off from our nation's heart.

Even in their diversity, these stories point to the common conclusion that our present hostilities at the border are not an aberration. I can now see no time since that fateful day in 1770, when Captain Cook placed one well-heeled foot upon this continent's shore, when Australia (as it came to be called) was truly egalitarian. I can't find my way back to my 'Fair Go' nation because that nation never existed. 'Fair Go' Australia is a myth.

So what does it mean when our imaginations fail us, if narratives intended to nurture a nation – a 'Fair Go', an 'island home' – reveal their shadows of denial, hostility, exclusivity and even violence? What then? I believe the answer lies in the image of two thousand Canberrans defiantly displaying 353 poles – courageously taking the weight of each lost life, in the quiet actions of those Christmas Islanders inscribing again and again names of those lost at the border on coral pebbles in black pen. Perhaps it is in learning to see and remember, even when the remembering is difficult, to listen and be attentive, not only to each other but to Country itself, that real change can come about.

And how can we imagine our country? If we are not 'Island Australia', then who are we? Asking myself this question feels like opening a door in a windowless room, a rush of new air spilling into every corner. Many islanders in the Caribbean see not only terrestrial spaces as home, but also the watery world of outer islands, atolls, reefs and the shifting sea between. According to this view, Australia simply cannot be reduced to 'Island Australia', but is something far more complex, nuanced and changeable. I like to imagine the 'Archipelago of Us' – in such a conception there is still a place you can name in which to belong, yet this very definition allows porosity, flexibility, fluidity and multiplicity.

I believe these stories shared on the margins of our nation are asking us as Australians to take courageous responsibility. Can we as a country be courageous enough to stretch our definition of 'Australian' to become more supple, more bountiful and open? Can white Australians collectively show a willingness to finally turn and fully face the violence with which the nation was forged? If as citizens could find this less fearful version of who we are as people, as a society, perhaps the ideal of a 'Fair Go' Australia could finally guide us – perhaps it is precisely what we need.

Notes

Christmas Island

Paley quote sourced from Dee, J. (et al.) (1992).

2. Trees Honour the Company They Keep

'Incarceration rates for Aboriginal children' sourced from Owen (2016), p. 455.

Reference to guano mining in the Kimberley and violence as 'the exception rather than the norm' in Owen (2016), pp. 6, 9.

The phrase the 'violent logic of the border' is a quote from Perera (2009), p. 102.

The reference to 'twenty-seven different tribal groups representing between ten thousand to thirty thousand people (a quarter of the total number of Aboriginal people in Western Australia) were reduced to "approximately" five thousand in less than two decades' from Owen (2016), pp. 5, 6.

'Between 1918 and 1945, Japan purchased around seventy-five to eighty percent of Christmas Island's phosphate' sourced from Hunt (2011) p. 167.

World War II facts drawn from ibid pp. 117, 187, 189, 196, 197, 198.

Census information drawn from Australian Bureau of Statistics (2017).

The reference to the 'hundred and twenty Chinese men' landing in 1899 from the provinces of 'Kwangtung (Guangdong), Kwangsi (Guangxi) and Fukien (Fujian), as well as Hainan', sourced from Hunt (2011) p. 1.

Translation of Coolies memorial as cited in Bartleson (2008), p. 50.

Information about Gordon Bennett's history and legacy sourced from Kelley, M. (et al.) (1999).

Plaque quote sourced from Kile (2013).

The metaphoric role of birds 'bridging the deceased ... back to their homeland' is drawn from Bartleson (2008), p. 27.

Facts about the Christmas Island frigatebird sourced from *Islander Explorer Holidays* (2008), p. 11 and Gray (1995), p. 97.

The reference to the dragon that swam from China to live above The Grotto from Tierney (2007), p. 101.

3. Our Tenuous Place

Early images of Christmas Island sourced from Neale (1988) and Hunt (2011).

The Christmas Island boat tragedy cited as 'the worst disaster in more than a century in Australia's maritime history' sourced from Doherty (2016).

5. Remembering

Roles of the British-appointed District Officer sourced from Tierney (2007), p. 27.

SIEV X memorial information from SIEV X Memorial Project (2007).

7. At the Bottom of Our History is Race

References to the *Border Force Act* from 'What are the secrecy provisions,' (2016) and *Australian Border Force Act (2015).*

Reference to the White Australia policy as being one of the 'founding pieces of legislation introduced to the newly formed parliament on 23 December 1901' from National Museum of Australia (n.d.).

Reference to Australia as a 'working man's paradise' sourced from ibid.

8. A Door in My Ribs

Names of asylum seekers who drowned aboard the SIEV X sourced from Mahood (2002).

9. Hand Held to the Flow

Facts on land crabs from Department of Infrastructure, Transport, Cities and Regional Development (2014).

The statistic of twelve attempted suicides a day in Christmas Island's Immigration Detention Centre sourced from Iggulden (2011).

13. Leaving Space

Information on the landslides and 'Edinburgh settlement' (including the reference to amahs teaching white children Malay) sourced from Hunt (2011), pp. 116, 155.

14. Walking Backwards Toward Light

Nauru Files sourced from Farrell, P. (et al.) (2016).

Forgotten Children report from Australian Human Rights Commission (2014).

References to the 'Thonglines' project from Bannister (2011).

15. An Island of Hungry Ghosts

Information on the Festival of the Hungry Ghost sourced from the chapter, 'Pudu: The Hungry Ghost Festival' in Tan (2018), pp. 83–95.

Quote from *Island of the Hungry Ghosts* sourced from Brady (2019).

18. Between Islands

Line from song 'I Am Australian' from Newton and Woodley (1987).

Warren Snowden quote from Christmas Island Shire (2011), p. 6.

Quote from Zainal's speech from Joint Select Committee in the Christmas Island Tragedy, Shire of Christmas Island (2011), p. 7.

Quote from the Department of Immigration and Citizenship records sourced from ibid, p. 3.

Doka's term 'disenfranchised grief' sourced from Yalom, 2010.

'Residents on the island who witnessed the incident tried to save us throwing life jackets and ropes. And so did the Navy and Police.' Quote from translated letter, unnamed asylum seeker, Shire of Christmas Island (2011), p. 3.

Quotes from survivors of the Christmas Island boat tragedy from 'Christmas Island survivor slams rescue operation' (2011) and Briskman, L. and Dimasi, M. (2016), p 257.

Ramin's quote from Shire of Christmas Island (2011), p. 7.

For class action reference see 'Christmas Island survivor slams rescue operation' (2011).

Quote from NSW Supreme Court Summary sourced from Bellew J. (n.d.).

'Wishful sinking' is a phrase first coined by Ghassan Nakhoul, but has since been adopted by Perera, Bui and others (see 'Every Boat is the First Boat'). 'Wishful sinking' refers to the way in which asylum-seeker drownings have taken on a more sinister role in formal and informal policies of nation states, such as deaths at sea being used as a form of deterrence.

Text *Dark Victory* referring to Marr, D. and Wilkinson, M. (2003).

Interview between Biddulph and Doogue from Australian Broadcasting Corporation interview (2011).

Evidence of 2013 drowning and bodies left in water from Jabour, B. (2013).

Excision legislation sourced from Commonwealth of Australia (2001).

Information on the implications of excision for asylum seekers from Crawshaw (2008).

The reference to 'White colonial paranoia' and the idea of 'changing back' from Hage (2003), pp. 4, 48, 65.

The reference to Howard giving orders 'for Australian troops to join America in the war in Iraq and Afghanistan' from National Museum of Australia (n.d.).

John Howard's quote 'we will decide who comes into this country and the circumstances in which they come' from Department of Prime Minister and Cabinet (2001).

Cocos (Keeling) Islands

Quote from de Certeau (1988), p. 129.

19. West Island (Pulu Panjang)

Poem 'Pinggiran' from Pettitt-Schipp (2014), p. 224.

Text *The Clunies-Ross Cocos Chronicle* references Clunies-Ross (2009).

Reference to 'the original John Clunies-Ross was born in 1786 on the Shetland Islands' from Clunies-Ross (2009), p. 10.

The 'labour force of illegally kept slaves predominantly from Malaysia, but also Indonesia, China, Papua, Africa and India' sourced from Bunce (1988), pp. 36–43.

The history of the relationship between Hare and Clunies-Ross sourced from ibid, pp. 13–28.

20. The End of the Line

The reference to every Cocos Malay woman being required to serve an 'apprenticeship' in the Clunies-Ross household sourced from Clunies-Ross (2009), p. 64.

21. Quarantine

Information on 'Fast Tracking' asylum seeker claims sourced from Asylum Seeker Resource Centre (2014).

22. South Island (Pulu Atas)

Reference 'once the Earth had enormous tides surging hundreds of metres' from Carson (1968), pp. 10, 11.

23. North Keeling (Pulu Keeling)

Information on biodiversity on North Keeling sourced from Department of Environment and Energy (n.d.).

24. Home Island (Pulu Selma) – Part I

History of Prison Island from Clunies-Ross (2009), p. 27.

Statistics of Home Island population from Bunce (1988), p. 136 and Wynne (2019).

Quote re John Cecil Clunies-Ross studying 'all the science subjects: maths, additional maths, chemistry and physics, plus English, one modern language, French, one classical language, Latin, and an arts subject, English literature' sourced from Clunies-Ross (2009), p. 132.

'The very sad point is the whole population is illiterate ...' sourced from ibid, p. 132.

The Eastern Extension Telegraph staff who had 'nothing but the highest praise for [John Clunies-Ross]' sourced from ibid, p. 118.

Webb describing the lack of schooling as 'rather an advantage in such a community on the present lines' sourced from ibid, p. 119.

Heath quote 'Traditionally education on Cocos was vocation orientated ... This form of practical education suited the island's needs.' from ibid, p. 235.

Heath's statement that very basic efforts at education on Home Island were instrumental in the Cocos Malay community beginning to shift toward 'a less Clunes-Ross-reliant island governance' from ibid, p. 239.

The Australian Government's enactment of an ordinance that made education on the island compulsory described by Clunies-Ross as 'unnecessary' in ibid, p. 241.

'Up until the turn of the century, the inhabitants of Cocos rarely saw individuals from the outside world' and reference to supervision of all the visits by the Cocos Malay inhabitants to Direction Island in Bunce (1988), p. 53.

This included control of Home Islanders' access to Direction and West Islands, as well as ensuring that entry to Home Island by the outside world was allowed by invitation only in ibid, p. 61.

John Clunies-Ross's lucrative contracts on both West and Direction Islands sourced from ibid, p. 61 and Clunies-Ross (2009), p. 175.

25. Home Island (Pulu Selma) – Part II

'The Christmas Island Phosphate Company was incorporated in London on the 14th of January 1897 ...' and the reference to George Clunies-Ross and Sir John Murray together discovering the rich deposits of phosphate on Christmas Island in February 1896 sourced from ibid, p. 79.

The reference to shares not being sold until 1949 from ibid, p. 150.

The reference to labourers as young as thirteen, working eleven-hour days, six days a week and eight hours on Sunday, as well as the 313 men working the mines that died sourced from Hunt (2011), pp. 13, 28, 30.

The Estate office that was converted into a classroom in the grounds of Oceania House when Clunies-Ross started at school sourced from Clunies-Ross (2009), p. 236.

This impact of World War II on the Cocos (Keeling) Islands, including the 'eight thousand three hundred military personnel on the atoll' and the push toward emigration from Bunce (1988), pp. 56–59.

The deception of the Cocos Malay community about Tawau sourced from Clunies-Ross (2009), p. 152.

Information about numbers of people who were shipped off the atoll, the death of 'deck passengers' on the voyage and suicide sourced from Bunce (1988), p. 59.

The reference to the Cocos Malay community as a conservative microcosm sourced from ibid, p. 99.

References

AIATSIS (3 July 2020). AIATSIS Map of Indigenous Australia. aiatsis.gov.au/explore/articles/aiatsis-map-indigenous-australia.

Anim-Addo, A. (2011, January 6). Book Review: 'Routes and roots: navigating Caribbean and Pacific Island literatures' by E.M. Deloughrey, *Cultural Geographies*. 18 (1): 137, journals.sagepub.com/doi/10.1177/1474474010180010906.

Asylum Seeker Resource Centre (2014, July). 'The Fast Track Process', asrc.org.au/wp-content/uploads/2014/07/Fast-Track-Process_July-2014.pdf.

Austin, C. and Fozdar, F. (2018). 'Framing asylum seekers: the uses of national and cosmopolitan identity frames in arguments about asylum seekers', *Identities*, 25:3, 245–265. doi: 10.1080/1070289X.2016.1214134.

Australian Border Force Act, 2015. (2015), abc.net.au/mediawatch/transcripts/1524_act.pdf.

Australian Broadcasting Corporation (22 October 2011). 'Questions still abound ten years after the sinking of SIEV X', abc.net.au/radionational/programs/saturdayextra/questions-still-abound-ten-years-after-the-sinking/3595014.

Australian Bureau of Statistics (23 October 2017). 'Quick Stats', quickstats.censusdata.abs.gov.au/census_services/getproduct/census /2016/quickstat/SSC90001.

Australian Human Rights Commission (12 February 2015). *The Forgotten Children: National Inquiry into Children in Immigration Detention (2014)*, humanrights.gov.au/our-work/asylum-seekers-and-refugees/publications/forgotten-children-national-inquiry-children.

Bannister. B. (5 July 2011). 'Christmas Island "Thonglines" lets you walk in their shoes', abc.net.au/local/photos/2011/07/05/3261737.htm?site=perth&xml=3261737-mediarss.

Barlow, K. (16 May 2013).' Parliament excises mainland from migration zone', [Press release], abc.net.au/news/2013-05-16/parliament-excises-mainland-from-migration-zone/4693940.

Bartleson, H. (2008). *Golden Leaves: An introduction to the Chinese cemeteries of Christmas Island.* Springwood: Boobook Editions.

Benitez Rojo, A. (1985). 'The repeating island', *New England Review and Bread Loaf Quarterly*, *7*(4), 430–452, jstor.org/stable/40375647.

Bellew J. (2017). *Ibrahimi and ors. v Commonwealth of Australia [2017]* NSWSC 1051, caselaw.nsw.gov.au/decision/598be9abe4b058596cba92ea.

Biewen, J. (1 March 2017). Episode 32: 'How race was made: seeing white, Part 2'. [Audio podcast], sceneonradio.org/episode-32-how-race-was-made-seeing-white-part-2.

Bird Rose, D. (2013). 'Slowly – writing into the anthropocene', *Text Journal*, 20, textjournal.com.au/speciss/issue20/Rose.pdf.

Brady, G., Wadough, A. (et al) (Producers), Brady, G. (Writer/Director). (2019). *Island of the Hungry Ghosts* [Documentary]. Germany: Chromosom Film.

Brinkoff, T. (2013). Christmas Island (Territory), citypopulation.de/php/australia-admin.

Briskman, L. and Dimasi, M. (2016). 'Re-living Janga: Survivor Narratives', *Migration by Boat*, New York, Berghahn Books.

Bui, M., Perera, S., Pugliese, J., Qwaider A. and Singh, C. (2020). 'Every boat is the first boat', *Deathscapes: Mapping race and violence in settler states*, deathscapes.org/case-studies/every-boat-is-the-first-boat.

Bunce, P. (1988). *The Cocos (Keeling) Islands: Australian atolls in the Indian Ocean.* Queensland: The Jacaranda Press.

Carson, R.L. (1968). *The Sea.* London: MacGibbon and Kee.

Chandler, R. (2004). Book review of *The Labour of Loss: Mourning, memory and wartime bereavement in Australia*, in *Grief Matters*, 7 (1): 18.

Christmas Island Shire. (11 March 2011). 'Memorial service for the December 15th tragedy', *The Islander*, p. 478.

'Christmas Island survivor slams rescue operation' (27 July 2011), abc.net.au/news/2011-07-27/christmas-island-shipwreck-survivor-slams-rescue/2812682.

Clunies-Ross, J.C. (2009). *The Clunies-Ross Cocos Chronicle*. Western Australia: John C. Clunies-Ross.

Commonwealth Attorney-General's Department. (2009). 'Climate change risk assessment for the Australian Indian Ocean Territories', regional.gov.au/territories/publications/files/Final+Report+CKI+and+CC.pdf.

Commonwealth of Australia (2001). *Migration Amendment (Excision from Migration Zone) Bill 2001*, legislation.gov.au/Details/C2004A00887.

Crawshaw, D. (21 February 2008) 'Govt denies backflip in island excision', *Sydney Morning Herald*, smh.com.au/national/govt-denies-backflip-on-island-excision-20080221-1tmq.html.

de Certeau, M. (1988). *The Practice of Everyday Life, Volume 1*, (translated by Steven Rendell). Berkley: University of California Press.

Dee, J., Jones, B. and MacFarquhar, L. (1992). 'Grace Paley, the art of fiction 131', *Paris Review*, 124, theparisreview.org/interviews/2028/grace-paley-the-art-of-fiction-no-131-grace-paley.

Department of Environment and Energy. (N.d.). 'Welcome to Pulu Keeling National Park', environment.gov.au/topics/national-parks/pulu-keeling-national-park.

Department of Prime Minister and Cabinet. (2 November 2001). Transcript of the Prime Minister the John Howard MP Address at the launch of a 'Stronger Tasmania Policy – Launceston, Tasmania', pmtranscripts.pmc.gov.au/release/transcript-12332.

Department of Immigration and Citizenship. (2012). 'Fact Sheet 81 – Australia's excised offshore places', immi.gov.au/media/fact-sheets/81excised-offshore.htm.

Department of Immigration and Citizenship (DIAC)'s Response to questions taken on notice – 27 May 2011. From House of Representatives (2011) Joint Select Committee on the Christmas Island Tragedy, pp. 1–3.

Department of Immigration and Citizenship (DIAC) Submission. In House of Representatives (2011) Joint Select Committee on the Christmas Island Tragedy (DIAC and Shire of Christmas Island Submissions), google.com.au/search?hl=en&source=hp&q=DIAC+submission+to+the+Joint+Select+Committee+Christmas+Island+Tragedy&sei=NJrRT4DNL-mM2gWEopHKBQ&gbv=2.

Department of Infrastructure, Transport, Cities and Regional Development (22 August 2014). 'Christmas Island environment and heritage', regional.gov.au/territories/Christmas/enviro_herritage.aspx.

Deloughrey, E. (2011). 'Island writing, creole cultures', *Cambridge History of Postcolonial Literature*, Ed. Quayson, A., pp. 802–832, english.ucla.edu/faculty/deloughrey/DeLoughrey_Island%20Writing,%2 0Creole%20 Cultures_Cambridge%20Postcolonial%202011.pdf.

Doherty, B. (27 September 2016). '"Too dangerous" to attempt rescue in Christmas Island boat tragedy, court told', *The Guardian*, theguardian.com/australia-news/2016/sep/27/too-dangerous-to-attempt-rescue-in-christmas-island-boat-tragedy-court-told.

Drew. K. (15 December 2010). 'Refugee boat sinks near Australia', *New York Times*, nytimes.com/2010/12/16/world/asia/16australia.html.

Farrell, P., Evershed, N. and Davidson, H. (10 August 2016). 'The Nauru Files: cache of 2000 leaked reports reveal scale of abuse of children in Australian offshore detention', *The Guardian*, theguardian.com/australia-news/2016/aug/10/the-nauru-files-2000-leaked-reports-reveal-scale-of-abuse-of-children-in-australian-offshore-detention.

Flanagan, R. (17 December 2010). 'Boat tragedy: how Australian's became complicit in the horror of Christmas Island', theguardian.com/commentisfree/2010/dec/16/christmas-island-tragedy-australian-humanity.

Franke, A and Weizman, E. (2003). The geography of extraterritoriality', slought.org/files/downloads/events/SF_1351-Franke.pdf.

Gibson, R. (2002). *Seven Versions of an Australian Badland.* St Lucia: University of Queensland Press.

Gillard announces Malaysia solution. (7 May 2011). *The Age*, theage.com.au/national/gillard-announces-malaysian-solution-20110507-1ed0h.html.

Gómez-Barris, M. and Joseph, M. (18 August 2019). 'Introduction: coloniality and islands', *Shima* 13(2), shimajournal.org/issues/v13n2/03.-Gomez-Barris-and-Joseph-Introduction-Shima-v13n2.pdf.

Gornick, V. (2002). *The Situation and the Story.* New York: Farrar, Straus and Giroux.

Gray, H.S. (Revised by Clark, R.). (1995). *Christmas Island Naturally* (2nd ed.). Perth: Christmas Island Natural History Association.

Grehan. H. and Scheer. (2016). *Stories of Love and Death.* Sydney: NewSouth Publishing.

Hage, G. (2003) *Against a Paranoid Nationalism: Searching for hope in a shrinking society.* Annandale: Pluto Press.

Hall, B. (20 April 2013). 'Asylum seekers denied legal rights: advocates', smh.com.au/national/asylum-seekers-denied-legal-rights-advocates-20130419-2i5pc.html.

Hau'ofa, E. (2009). '*Our sea of islands*', *A New Oceania: Rediscovering our sea of islands,* savageminds.org/wp-content/image-upload/our-sea-of-islands-epeli-hauofa.pdf.

Haebich, A. (1992) *For Their Own Good.* Nedlands: University of Western Australia Press.

Healy, C and Tumarkin, M (2011). 'Special issue: social memory and historical justice', *Journal of Social History*, 44(4): 1007–1018. doi:10.1353/jsh.2011.0040.

Hunt, J. (2011) *Suffering through Strength: The men who made Christmas Island.* ACT: Blue Star Print.

Hutton, M. (17 October 2011). 'SIEV X: 10 years on the questions remain', abc.net.au/news/2011-10-17/hutton-sievx-ten-years-on-the-questions-remain/3574870.

Iggulden, T. (11 August 2011). 'Report scathing of detention centre conditions', abc.net.au/news/2011-08-11/comcare-report-scathing-of-detention-centre-conditions/2835820.

Immigration Museum. (n.d.). 'Post visit activities and resources', museumvictoria.com.au/pages/2352/refugees-post-visit-resources.pdf.

Island Explorer Holidays (2008). *Christmas and Cocos Keeling Islands Birding Guide.* Inglewood, Australia: Author.

Jabour, B. (10 June 2013). 'Bodies of drowned asylum seekers to be left in water by authorities', *The Guardian*, guardian.co.uk/world/2013/jun/10/asylum-seekers-bodies-christmas-island.

John George Clunies-Ross (2016, August). [Facebook page]. facebook.com/john.g.cluniesross.

Karp, P. (28 January 2018). 'What happened to a Fair Go? Liberals' propaganda arm silent since August', *The Guardian*, theguardian.com/australia-news/2018/jan/28/what-happened-to-the-fair-go-liberals-propaganda-arm-silent-since-august.

Kelley, M. (Director), & Kelley, S., & Du Cane, P. (Producers). (1999). *Big Brother of Christmas Island* [video file]. Australia. National Film and Sound Archive. Retrieved from Alexander Street database.

Kerr, T. and Cox, S. (2016). 'Media, machines and might: reproducing Western Australia's violent state of aboriginal protection', *Somatechnics* 6(1). Edinburgh University Press, 89–95, doi: 10.3366/soma.2016.0176.

Kile, M. (20 October 2013). 'Christmas Island's other industry', quadrant.org.au/opinion/qed/2013/10/christmas-islands-industry.

Larsson, M. (2009). 'A disenfranchised grief: post-war death and memorialisation in Australia after the First World War', *Australian Historical Studies*, 40:1, 79–95, dx.doi.org/10.1080/10314610802663035.

'Lifejackets should have prompted search'. (28 May 2013) heraldsun.com.au/news/breaking-news/lifejackets-should-have-prompted-search/story-fni0xqi4-1226652318143.

Loewenstein, A. (2013). 'Profits of doom extract: politicised, privatised and silenced by bureaucracy', antonyloewenstein.com/2013/08/12/profits-of-doom-extract-politicised-privatised-and-silenced-by-bureaucracy.

Lowy Institute (Producer). (9 May 2014). 'The future of border protection – Scott Morrison MP' [Audio Podcast], lowyinstitute.org/news-and-media/multimedia/audio/podcast-future-border-protection-scott-morrison-mp.

Mahood, H. (15 November 2002). 'List of Families on SIEV X', sievx.com/dbs/SIEVX.

Malouf, D. (2014). *A First Place*. North Sydney: Knopf.

Manne, R. (March 2013). 'Australia's shipwrecked refugee policy', themonthly.com.au/australia-s-shipwrecked-refugee-policy-tragedy-errors-guest-7637.

Marr, D. and Wilkinson, M. (2003). *Dark Victory*. New South Wales: Allen & Unwin.

McMahon, E. (2013). 'Reading the planetary archipelago of the Torres Strait', *Island Studies Journal*, 8(1), 55–66, islandstudies.ca/sites/islandstudies.ca/files/ISJ-8-1-2013-McMahon.pdf.

Monash University (n.d.). Australian border deaths database, monash.edu/arts/border-crossing-observatory/research-agenda/australian-border-deaths-database.

Monument Australia. (2014, November 24). 'SIEV 221 Memorial', monumentaustralia.org.au/themes/disaster/maritime/display/103936-siev-221-memorial.

Moreton-Robinson, A. (2015). *The White Possessive: Property, power and Indigenous sovereignty.* Minneapolis, University of Minnesota Press.

Mountz, A. (2011). 'The enforcement archipelago: detention, haunting, and asylum on islands', doi.org.dbgw.lis.curtin.edu.au/10.1016/j.polgeo.2011.01.005.

National Archives of Australia. (2013). 'The Cocos (Keeling) Islands – Fact sheet 103', naa.gov.au/collection/fact-sheets/fs103.aspx.

National Museum of Australia. (n.d.). Defining moments: 'Tampa Affair', nma.gov.au/defining-moments/resources/tampa-affair.

National Museum of Australia. (n.d.). Defining moments: 'White Australia policy', nma.gov.au/defining-moments/resources/white-australia-policy.

Neale, M. (1988). *We Were the Christmas Islanders.* ACT: Bruce Neale.

Newton, D. and Woodley, B. (1987). 'I am Australian'. [Song], alldownunder.com/australian-music-songs/i-am-australian.htm.

O'Sullivan, M. (2011). 'Malaysia solution: High Court ruling explained',
theconversation.com/malaysia-solution-high-court-ruling-explained-3154.

Owen, C. (2016) *Every Mother's Son is Guilty: Policing in the Kimberley Frontier of Western Australia 1882–1905.* Nedlands: UWA Publishing.

Pascoe, B. (2014) *Dark Emu.* Broome: Magabala Books.

Perera, S (2002) 'What is a camp?' borderlands.net.au/vol1no1_2002/perera_camp.html.

Perera, S. (2009) *Australia and the Insular Imagination.* New York: Palgrave Macmillan.

Perpitch, N. and Barrass (et al.) (Updated 2012, July 19). '50 Feared dead in Christmas Island boat crash', *The Australian*, theaustralian.com.au/news/dozens-feared-dead-in-christmas-island-asylum-seeker-boat-crash/news-story/102bf9d6c576edec6d7395c885074020.

Perth Festival. (1 February 2018). 'An interview with William Yang', 2018. perthfestival.com.au/an-interview-with-william-yang.

Pettitt-Schipp, R. (November 2014). 'Pinggiran', fashiondocbox.com/Body_Art/71975645-Westerly59-2-the-best-in-writing-from-the-west.html.

Pettitt-Schipp, R. (2018). *The Sky Runs Right Through Us.* Crawley, UWA Publishing.

Pinkerton, P. (2011). 'Resisting memory: the politics of memorialisation in post-conflict Northern Ireland', *The British Journal of Politics and International Relations,* 14, 131-152. doi:10.1111/j.1467-856X.2011.00458.x.

Pipher (2013). *The Green Boat: Reviving ourselves in our capsized culture.* New York: Riverhead Books.

Poetry Foundation (2019'). 'Kamau Brathwaite', poetryfoundation.org/poets/kamau-brathwaite.

Pugliese, J. (2009). 'Crisis heterotopias and border zones of the dead', *Continuum Journal of Media and Cultural Studies,* 23:5, 663–679.

'Queensland Government to pay $190 million settlement over unpaid wages' (9 July 2019), abc.net.au/news/2019-07-09/hans-pearson-class-action-settled-qld-government/11292886.

Robertson, R. and Pettitt-Schipp, R. (et al), (2017). 'An Ambiguous Genre', *Text Special Issue 44.* textjournal.com.au/speciss/issue44/Robertson_et_al.pdf.

Rose, J. (2011). *The Jacqueline Rose Reader.* United States of America: Duke University Press.

Rothberg, M. (2019). *The Implicated Subject: Beyond victims and perpetrators.* California: Stanford University Press.

Schipp, R. (2013). 'The poetics and politics of identity in the Indian Ocean Territories'. Unpublished manuscript, School of Media, Culture and Creative Arts, Curtin University, Western Australia.

'Search and rescue operation focused on finding survivors', (2013, June 9), theaustralian.com.au/news/navy-searching-off-christmas-island-for-sinking-asylum-seeker-boat/story-e6frg6n6-1226660532791.

Shire of Christmas Island. (2011). 'Memorial Service SIEV 221' [pamphlet]. Christmas Island.

Shire of Christmas Island Submission from House of Representatives (2011)

Joint Select Committee on the Christmas Island Tragedy, pp. 1–10, google.com.au/search?hl=en&source=hp&q=joint+select+committee+shire+of+christmas+island+submission&sei=4ZTRT-XvJMK-2gXewJmoDw&gbv=2.

SIEV X Memorial Project. (2007). SIEV X Memorial, Western Park, Yarralumla [Image]. sievxmemorial.com/thememorial.html.

Smith, H., & Dean, R.T. (2009). 'Introduction: practice-led research, research led practice – towards the iterative cyclic web', in H. Smith and R.T. Dean (Eds). *Practice-led research, Research-led Practice.* Edinburgh: Edinburgh University Press.

Smith, I.C. 'His Silent Summer', *Island Magazine* (2010, Spring): 36–37.

Strakosch, E. (2007). 'Abstraction and figuration in monuments and counter-monuments', Crotty, Martin (Ed.) *When Soldiers Return: November 2007 Conference Proceedings*. Brisbane University of Queensland, pp. 270–276.

Tan, C.B. (2018). *Chinese Religion in Malaysia*. Leiden: Brill.

Tierney, B. and Tierney, S. (2007). 'The Essential Christmas Island Travel Guide. Christmas Island'. Christmas Island Tourism Association.

'UN slams Australia's "excision" rules for asylum-seekers'. (23 May 2013). theaustralian.com.au/national-affairs/immigration/un-slams-australias-excision-rules-for-asylum-seekers/story-fn9hm1gu-1226648882920.

'What are the secrecy provisions of the Border Force Act?' (27 July 2016), *ABC News*, abc.net.au/news/2016-07-27/what-are-the-secrecy-provisions-of-the-border-force-act/7663608.

Winton, T. (2015). *Island Home.* Australia: Hamish Hamilton.

Wright, S. (2011). 'Grief, stolen children and SIEV 221'. *Overland Literary Journal*, overland.org.au/blogs/cruel-miracles/2011/04/grief-stolen-children-and-siev-221.

Wynne (6 April 2019). 'When there was trouble in paradise', abc.net.au/news/2019-04-06/cocos-islands-marks-anniversary-of-self-determination-vote/10967630.

Yalom, V. (2010). 'Kenneth Doka on Grief Counselling and Psychotherapy', psychotherapy.net/interview/grief-counseling-doka.

Zubryski, T. (2011). (Producer, Writer, Director). 2011. *The Hungry Tide.* Australia, Tom Zubrycki.

Author Note

This manuscript was originally written as a doctoral thesis. In its initial conception, the work was intended to be a reflection on five different places (including Christmas Island, the Cocos (Keeling) Islands and Fitzroy Crossing) and how each of these distinctive spaces affected my sense of self as an individual and an Australian. However, the second I set foot back in the Indian Ocean Territories, I knew I would not be writing about anywhere else – the islands and I had unfinished business.

As a result of the impact of my return, the focus and nature of my research changed. I began to recognise the narrative was an unfolding journey, not something I could necessarily control or understand from the outset, this shift representing an enormous leap and a lesson in trust. As a result, I decided to invite the reader to come with me on a shared voyage of discovery. In this process, I consciously took on the role of a reliable narrator, someone who was attempting to be completely honest and transparent with herself and the reader in a kind of pact, an intimacy, forged to gain the reader's trust. To write lucidly and honestly into the familiar is by no means straightforward. At times the level of authenticity, of honesty, required in the process of clarifying the affective elements of my journey on the page was intensely confronting. This unpacking often demanded I inhabit the depths of my own and others' vulnerability, sometimes unearthing and exposing successive acts of violence done in my country's name.

There were days when this voyage of discovery allowed me to

feel so expansive that the world outside my window glowed with wonder. On other days the writing became so confronting I simply could not keep going. On these days I would leave my desk in order to remember the sensation of sun on my skin, or drive into the small country town where I live just to witness the ordinary and small acts of kindness people extend to each other every day – a waiter smiling as he hands a customer a cappuccino, a woman patting a dog in a park. Yet despite the sometimes harrowing nature of the research, my need to understand and bear witness was so compelling that I would ultimately find a way to return to the work. This story sat in my body like a living thing willing to be born, each time drawing me back to my desk.

During my return to the Indian Ocean Territories in 2016, the unique cultures of Christmas Island and the Cocos (Keeling) Islands created some distinctive challenges as I went about interview process. My first challenge was not being sure what it was, precisely, that I wanted to know (therefore making it difficult for me to articulate to the people I planned to interview on the islands what I wanted from them). My second challenge was that my past experiences in the Indian Ocean Territories had taught me that islanders are wary of mainlanders interviewing them. This was largely due to the damage done by media on both Christmas Island and the Cocos (Keeling) Islands, many articles written about the islands involving perceived breaches of trust, or an active misrepresentation of complex situations.

Almost all of the interviews were organised while in the Indian Ocean Territories, and many came about in the organic way in which they are described within this narrative. This approach was in keeping with the way things tended to naturally evolve on the islands. I knew some interviewees would have reservations about being interviewed, especially on sensitive topics such as the treatment of asylum seekers. Interviewees such as the witness of the boat tragedy in the chapter 'Between Islands' chose to remain anonymous because of the perceived potential for controversy in response to the stories she shared. Similarly, the character of 'Tom' was constructed, and identifying details from the speaker's recount removed, to protect the identity of the person who shared their experiences of the boat tragedy in the chapter 'A Door in My Ribs'. 'Tom's' story was not told in an interview context but resulted from an informal conversation that took place by chance. The chapter was written from notes taken on the island and recollections made once back on the mainland. During my return to the islands I allowed myself to be guided by the themes and issues raised by my interviewees, as well as my increasing understanding of the territory's history.

Each interviewee was given a copy of their transcript with the opportunity during a four-week period to correct any errors or remove anything that they wished to retract from the record. Only minor alterations were requested by one participant. All interviewees had a strong command of English except for Nek Su, who was happy for his partner, Jeannette, to translate for him.

Despite this transparent process, questions remain as to whether the contents of this creative work will make it difficult for me to return to the islands again. This has been a challenging and recent realisation, as the outcomes of my research, particularly around the history of the Clunies-Ross dynasty, surprised me. Sharing the stories unearthed in this work feels so important that the risk of being judged, even despised, for the difficult truths that have been exposed, seems worthwhile. However, the potential of my research to cause hurt and anger in a community in which I felt welcomed and accepted remains deeply confronting. It is difficult to weigh this cost against the potential benefit of publication, which I would argue is the work's ability to challenge readers to reflect more critically about Australian national identity.

The process of writing *The Archipelago of Us* was in itself a lesson in interdependence! This book would not have been possible without the support of so many fine people. I would like to thank all of my interviewees: Gordon Thompson, Jo Doble, Pete Ch'ng, Leon Mills, Stephanie Ong, Zainal Majid, Nek Su, Jeannette Young, Catalina Capstan, Norhapida Pirus, Pamela Jones, Johnny Clunies-Ross, Osman Macrae, Trish Flores, as well as those interviewees who do not wish to be named. The generous and deeply honest way with which you shared your lives with me led this tale to be a rich tapestry of our shared humanity. Thank you also to all the Christmas and Cocos Islanders who extended so much kindness to me on my return and assisted with my research. I would like to thank my PhD and Honours supervisors, Rachel Robertson, Thor Kerr and Suvendrini Perera: your support has been invaluable. In addition, Suvendrini's writing about the Indian Ocean Territories has given me a clear lens with which to make sense of my complex experiences in the Indian Ocean Territories, to which I am greatly indebted. I am also indebted to the work of historian Chris Owen, and his unflinching documentation of the Frontier Wars in the Kimberley Region. I would also like to acknowledge the contribution of an Australian Government Research Training Program Scholarship in supporting this research.

My sincere thanks also go to Vivienne Robertson, Ruth Halbert, Kate Noske, Rosemary Sayer, Pia Smith, Nora Paley, Michelle Dimasi, Rachel Hanson, Baden Offord, Marilyn Metta, John Ryan, Amanda Curtin, David Carlin, Gillian Whitlock, Nicole Setton, Jennifer Kornberger, Annamaria Weldon, Liana Christenson, Coral Carter, Amanda Joy, the Denmark community,

Ashley Schipp, Greta Schipp and my family for their support at different times on this journey. I would also like to acknowledge the Noongar, Gooniyandi and Bunuba people, whose stories and strength helped spur this work. I also pay my respects to the Menang/Merningar and Pibulmun people on whose land this work was written.

To the asylum seekers who shared their lives with me over my three years on the islands, thank you for your generosity, courage, warmth and humour, and for helping me to understand my incredible good fortune. And lastly, I would like to thank Georgia Richter, my publisher and editor at Fremantle Press, who has been on this journey with me, however directly or indirectly since 2011. I always knew you were the right editor for this work, and I am grateful that a story so precious to me was in your steady and capable hands. Thank you for your sharp mind and deep compassion. I hope your world continues to come into mine for many years to come.

ALSO AVAILABLE

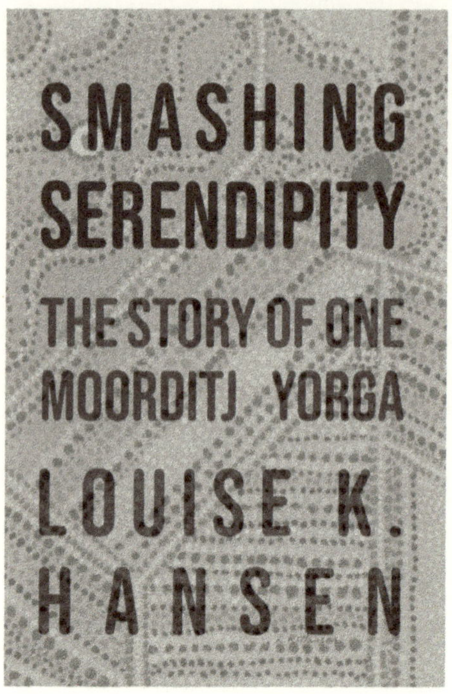

Life is tough for the Connell family, growing up in a small town where racist attitudes, discrimination and violence against Aboriginal people are commonplace. Lavinia is lucky: her parents ensure her family stays together while other cousins and friends are removed from the state. But violence and adversity occur over and over, even while young Lavinia also excels at sport and at school – drawing on her own inner strength and a physical resourcefulness. In time, Lavinia will find herself a homeless young widow, stripped of hope when her own four children are taken away. But she has a way of righting herself, using education and determination to bring her small family back together, and finding love when she least expects it.

ALSO AVAILABLE

Josie de Bray was a brothel madam who owned most of Roe Street, Perth from WWI up to the 1940s. This immensely readable social history uses the life of Josie de Bray as conduit into the lives of her friends and competitors – the many of the women who paraded in their petticoats on the verandas of Roe Street, and who were kept from the public view and were secret keepers themselves in the seamier side of town.

First published 2023 by
FREMANTLE PRESS

Fremantle Press Inc. trading as Fremantle Press
PO Box 158, North Fremantle, Western Australia, 6159
fremantlepress.com.au

Cover images: 'Cocos and Keeling Islands Last Paradise Drone Shot Yacht Club', JustAbove, shutterstock.com
Designed by Carolyn Brown, Tendeersigh.com.au
Printed and bound in Australia by Griffin Press

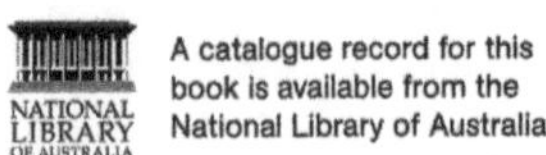

A catalogue record for this book is available from the National Library of Australia

ISBN 9781760992224 (paperback)
ISBN 9781760992231 (ebook)

Fremantle Press is supported by the State Government through the Department of Local Government, Sport and Cultural Industries.

Fremantle Press respectfully acknowledges the Wadjak people of the Noongar nation as the traditional owners and custodians of the land where we work in Walyalap.